In Prayer with Mary Mother of Jesus

Jean Lafrance

Translated by
Florestine Audette, R.J.M.

Éditions Paulines

Originally published as

En prière avec Marie, Mère de Jésus

by Jean Lafrance, Paris, France.

Phototypesetting: *Les Éditions Paulines*

Cover: *Antoine Pépin*

Imprimatur: Msgr Jean-Marie Fortier
            Archbishop of Sherbrooke
            January 25, 1988

ISBN 2-89039-183-3

Legal deposit — 3rd quarter 1988
Bibliothèque nationale du Québec
National Library of Canada

© 1988 Les Éditions Paulines
        250, boul. St-François Nord
        Sherbrooke, QC, J1E 2B9

Preface

IN PRAYER WITH MARY
THE MOTHER OF JESUS
(Ac 1:14)

As I begin to write this book, I would like to bring to mind an experience which many of us have already had or will have after reading about it in these pages. Time and again, I have heard of it from the lips of those who try to enter into contemplative prayer. They come to prayer and attempt, more or less happily, to seek contact with God, that is, to let themselves be hypnotized by the eye of the Father who sees in the innermost part of our self, for prayer begins from the moment one is aware that God does not cease watching us, says Saint Teresa of Avila.

There are few people who are able to affirm, with Ignatius of Loyola, that they "experience devotion as soon as they set about to pray". At this time, rather the intelligence and the imagination are the ones in action if not the commotion of ideas or distractions. However, there exists a shortcut friends of the Blessed Virgin are familiar with: it is the humble recitation of the rosary, of the *Memorare* or of any vocal prayer addressed to Mary at the beginning of the hour of prayer. Without being aware of it, they fall into prayer as one falls asleep, unable to watch for or to note the moment when sleep comes upon them or the instant when the fire of prayer lights up in them. They recognize it by a certain sweetness which permeates their heart and spreads throughout their body. The Holy Spirit has shifted them beyond fourth speed and prayer is set in motion in their heart without their being aware that it has done so.

I will not explain this fact for the moment — I shall have to come back to this later for we are touching here one of the basic laws governing a life of prayer — but we must recognize that we have here an intervention of Mary's prayer which has obtained for us the gift of prayer. For prayer, before being a work to accomplish, is first a grace to be welcomed and received. Let us rather say that, in a Christian context, every prayer and, ultimately, every contemplative prayer finds its norm, source and model in the prayer of Christ, of the Holy Spirit, of the Church and of the Blessed Virgin.

It is not so much a matter of "structuring" one's prayer as it is to enter into someone else's prayer or, taking up again the words of Paul and altering them somewhat, of making up in our body what has still to be undergone by Christ in his prayer for his Body which is the Church (Col 1:24). Actually, any Christian who prays today becomes a part of the prayer of the Church, which is nothing else but the prayer of the Holy Spirit, to continue and prolong the prayer of Christ. Without the Christian's knowing it and without his being aware of it most of the time, the Holy Spirit arouses the prayer of Christ in his heart and he pursues the dialogue of Jesus with his Father on the subject of men. In this sense, if it is possible here for us to contemplate Mary's prayer, it is because it is all related to Christ's prayer. This relation of faith is what unites Mary to Christ and gives her prayer all its worth and its power.

1. The Church hangs on the prayer of Christ

One of the greatest graces a man may receive in his Christian life is to experience what Paul describes in his epistle to the Galatians: "I have been crucified with Christ, so that it is no longer I who live, but it is Christ who lives in me. This life that I live now, I live by faith in the Son of God, who loved me and gave his life for me" (Ga 2:19-20). There comes a time when the Christian is so united to Christ that he feels and experiences, often in an inchoative way, that his life on earth is crossed, penetrated and possessed by the life of the Risen Christ. It is in this vital and sudden awareness that many saints have experienced the prayer of Christ within themselves. At a given moment, at the time when they least expected it, they received a communication of the prayer of Jesus so that they could actually apply to themselves the words of Paul, while altering them somewhat: "It is no longer I who pray, but it is Christ who prays in me".

This experience, which may seem extraordinary to us, is but the emergence, at the level of a clear conscience, of a reality which inhabits the heart of any person living in a state of grace, since he is united to and identified with Christ, dead and risen. Only, he bears this prayer within himself like a treasure hidden in a vessel of clay and, most of the time, he has neither a conducting nerve nor an antenna which would allow him to feel it. He has already come forth a big step if he believes that this prayer dwells in him, even if he has no immediate experience of it for the time being.

I believe that the same may be said about the Church. She must not try to produce or arouse prayer, but she must discover it at the very heart of her mystery. "At the heart of the Church, ..., I shall be Love", said Thérèse of Lisieux; she could have said in the same way: "At the heart of the Church, I shall be prayer". This is equivalent to saying that the Church is all inhabited by the prayer of Christ.

In her pilgrimage on earth, the Church is hanging on the prayer of Christ which inhabits and enlivens her. The author of the Letter to the Hebrews says that Christ is always living, always in the act of interceding on our behalf: "It follows, then, that his power to save is utterly certain, since he lives for ever to intercede for all who come to God through him" (Heb 7:25). Here we mean the prayer of the Lord of glory who is seated at the right hand of the Father with his glorious Body. Thus, we are secured in faith by the fact that a man of our human race, who is at the same time the Word of God, the second person of the Blessed Trinity, has introduced supplication at the heart of the Three. It is no more a question here of the humble entreaty of Christ in the days of his life on earth (Heb 5:7), of his prayer in his human countenance as *Homo viator*, of which we never lose sight, for he initiates us to our faith and leads it to perfection (Heb 12:2), but it is a question here of his prayer in heaven in his role as "comprehensor". The intercession of Christ in glory is the action of someone fully authorized and accredited (Heb 3:2), interceding with the One who holds power in favor of the people he has taken under his care. No one is better placed to intercede with God than the glorified Christ, for he has been enthroned forever at the right hand of God: "Jesus Christ died for us, — and moreover he rose from the dead, and there at God's right hand he stands and pleads for us" (Rm 8:34).

In Jesus, prayer and mission are totally identical and culminate in the mystery of the Cross of glory. For Him, "to adore in spirit and in truth" is to consecrate himself to the good will of the Father; it is a submissive existence, surrendered in the Holy Spirit to the eternal will of the Father and thus to the triune will. His adoration of the Father in the Spirit cannot be dissociated from the perpetually renewed "yes" to his accepted mission: they are united together in this eucharistic attitude in which Jesus allows himself, in thanksgiving, to be surrendered to the world by the Father. One then understands that the Church must make of the daily celebration of the Eucharist the summit and the source of her prayer. Thus, our desire to pray is always taken again "into" and "by" the prayer of Jesus who gives it its worth and power as he incorporates it into the universal prayer of the Church. This is also a source of joy and peace, for we are assured in faith that our poor prayer, absorbed into that of Christ, is agreeable to the Father.

2. Mary, model of the Church in prayer

We cannot speak about the prayer of Mary in the Church without placing it within the prayer of the only Mediator and Intercessor between God and men, that is, Christ. All those who are united to Christ by the bond of faith and love are associated to this intercession of Christ who prays for us in heaven, at the right hand of the Father. There exists then a communion among those who belong to Christ: whether they dwell on earth or, exiled from their body, they have made their home with the Lord (cf. 2 Co 5:8; also Mk 12:27).

Thus the intercession of the saints on our behalf exists in a way similar to the prayer which the faithful make for one another. Within this Church of heaven and earth, we understand the eminent place which belongs to Mary, the Mother of God. It is precisely her relationship with Christ, whose Mother she is and in whom she believed, that confers upon her an unparalleled role of a christological order in the communion of Saints. In the form of a prayer of praise and thanksgiving, the preface of the Virgin Mary, Mother of the Church, asserts this clearly:

"By receiving your Word in an immaculate heart, she became worthy of bringing forth your Son from her virgin womb. By giving birth to her Creator, she

9

prepared the beginnings of the Church. By accepting, at the foot of the Cross, the last will of love from her Son, she received as sons all men whom the death of Christ allowed to be born again to divine life."

In the same way that we keep our eyes fixed on the prayer of Christ during the course of his pilgrimage on earth to interiorize it and make it our own, so do we keep in our heart under our scrutiny the words and events in the life of Mary (cf. Lk 2:19 and 2:51) which thus become the source and model of our prayer. As we were saying, those who receive on earth the grace to experience the prayer of Christ, because they form only one being with Him, discover within themselves the same feelings which Jesus had for his Father, in prayer: a total trust in the Master of the Impossible and a tender surrender into his hands.

The same thing happens when Mary shares her prayer with those who claim her intercession: she allows them to experience something of the power of her prayer and faith and, at the same time, she teaches them to say: "Let it be done to me according to your word". This is what Paul defines as "the obedience of faith" (Rm 1:5 and 16:26). There is, nevertheless, a most original characteristic in Mary's faith; it is that she invites the disciples to believe in the person of Christ in whom are manifested the works of the Father. This is very clear in Mary's intervention at Cana: "His mother said to the servants, 'Do whatever he tells you'" (Jn 2:5).

But today, Mary's prayer for us must be considered in the actual context of all the Church in heaven, described in Revelation, which the Church on earth wishes to join through her communal and personal prayer: "Each (of the twenty-four elders) was holding a harp and a golden bowl full of incense made of the prayers of the saints" (Rv 5:8). "Another angel, who had a golden censer, came and stood at the altar. A large quantity of incense was given to him to offer with the prayers of all the saints

on the golden altar that stands in front of the throne"
(Rv 8:3) The preface of Mary, the Mother of the Church,
lays emphasis on her role in the prayer of the Church
in heaven: "Having been taken up into the Glory of
heaven, she accompanies and protects the Church with
her motherly love in its journey towards the homeland
in heaven until the day of the glorious coming of the
Lord."

3. Mary joins her supplication to that of the disciples

Between the all-powerful prayer of Mary in the Glory
of heaven and the humble prayer "in the days of her
flesh", there is an event which sets her well between the
two groups and which shows the tension between the
prayer of the actual Church, poor and imperfect, and the
prayer of the heavenly Church, radiant with Glory and
sure of the final victory of Christ: it is the presence of
Mary in prayer with the disciples in the Upper Room:
"All these joined in continuous prayer, together with
several women, including Mary the Mother of Jesus, and
with his brothers" (Ac 1:14).

In a certain sense, Mary is already in Glory, since the
risen Christ makes her share the power of his Glory, to
the point that Bossuet wondered how Mary could have
managed to live on earth after the resurrection of Jesus
while bearing such a burden of Glory! The presence of
Mary, screened from Glory, was absolutely necessary in
the Upper Room, for she was the only one, after Christ,
to have believed and hoped against all hope (Rm 4:18),
as if she could see the Invisible (Heb 11:27). Through her
faith and trust, she truly attracted the Holy Spirit, as
a parabolic mirror focuses the rays of the sun, and
ignited the fire of the Pentecost: "When the apostles were
waiting for the Spirit who had been promised to them,
she joined her supplication to that of the disciples, thus

11

becoming the model of the Church in prayer" (Preface ibid.).

It is her absolute and daring faith, her indefectible assurance (the parrhesia of which Paul speaks in 1 Th 2:2 and Ac 28:31) in the power of the Holy Spirit that makes Mary the Master of prayer for the disciples in the Upper Room. She teaches them, first by her very assiduity, to implore, to remain in the city and to persevere in prayer. The disciples are still under the shock of the departure of Jesus; they do not know very well anymore if they have faith, but Jesus has promised them that even though he has left through the front door, he will return by the back door: "And now I am sending down to you what the Father has promised. Stay in the city then, until you are clothed with the power from on high" (Lk 24:49).

On two different occasions in the Acts (1:4 and 8), Luke insists on the advice of Jesus which orders his disciples to remain in the city so that they may be invested with the power of the Holy Spirit. Mary well knows that the sending forth of the Holy Spirit by the Father, in the name of Jesus, is a gratuitous move on the part of God and that no one may be worthy of it, but she also knows that the Gift of the Spirit is not something given arbitrarily. To receive this gift, one must not only believe in it, but must ask for it, seek it and knock: "If you then, who are evil, know how to give good things to your children, how much more will the heavenly Father give the Holy Spirit to those who ask him" (Lk 11:13).

As Mary is aware of the lack of faith of the apostles, she acts as Christ does; she prays that their faith may not fail (Lk 22:32), but, at the same time, she tells them, as she does each time she appears on earth: "Pray, pray, that my Son may allow himself to be touched" (Words spoken by the Blessed Virgin at Pellevoisin). She knows that in order to touch the heart of the Father and to bring about the effusion of the Spirit, there must be an unfathomable depth of distress and, therefore, of supplication. But there is in Mary a trait of meekness and gentleness in her entreaty that makes her delicate and yielding. Too often, our prayer of entreaty is tense, bitter and uneasy because we do not sufficiently believe that God wishes to answer our prayer, even with our little faith: "I tell you therefore: everything you ask and pray for, believe that you have it already, and it will be yours" (Mk 11:24).

That is why the Fathers gave Mary the beautiful title of "the Almighty supplicant". She is all powerful on the heart of God, for she has found the key to permanent supplication, the key we have lost with the breach caused by original sin. Our first parents were always on their knees in prayer before God for they lived familiarly with him. At the same time, Mary implores because she is almighty and she knows that the least of her wishes will be answered even before she has formulated it. Mary's prayer is like the play of an artist: hardly has he touched the manuals of the organ that he releases most powerful resonances in the vault of the cathedral.

To understand the power of Mary's prayer, one must have already experienced it a little. The tragedy is that those who speak or write on this subject cannot describe this power: they can suggest images, words, or pour forth lyrical outbursts, but when all has been said they are unable to convey this experience. We cannot describe the geography of a country to a stranger. What must we do then to make prayer become our land?

There is the risk that all that has been said here may remain an abstract idea if we are not visited, one day or the other, by the power of the Holy Spirit who can make us experience the prayer of Christ or that of Mary. The *Veni, Sancte Spiritus* expresses that: "Come, Holy Spirit, and pour forth from heaven, a ray of your light from the Blessed Trinity". If a ray of light came forth from the heart of the Trinity and managed to touch us, our human heart would dissolve quickly and prayer would flow like living water.

13

When Jesus speaks of his Father who will send forth the Holy Spirit in his name — when he thus calls to mind the mystery of the Blessed Trinity — we must keep our eyes constantly fixed on Mary and the disciples in prayer in the Upper Room, for that is what prayer is all about. It is a ground swell welling from the heart of the Three, which throws Mary Magdalen down in tears at the feet of Christ, draws a cry of supplication from the heart of the penitent thief on Calvary and makes the Centurion exclaim: "Truly, this man was the Son of God!" Once we have been swept away by this white whirlwind, we will no more ask how to pray but instead, what we must do to stop praying.

4. "This is the man who loves his brothers and prays much for his people" (2 M 15:14)

"Israel, I shall leave but a humble and lowly people among you whose refuge will be the name of the Lord" (Zp 3:12). Thus when Yahweh looks upon his people, he perceives it first as humble, poor and pleading. Israel is a nation which prays because it has no other refuge but the name of its God. But at the heart of this nation, God raises men and also women (Esther) to whom he entrusts the mission of interceding for his people: Abraham implores the heavens that Sodom and Gomorrah may be saved (Gn 18:16); Moses raises his arms to heaven that his people may be granted victory over the Amalekites (Ex 17:12); of Jeremiah, it is said: "This is God's prophet Jeremiah, who loves his brothers and prays much for the people and all the Holy City" (2 M 15:14). We must not forget Elijah of whom Saint James will say: "The heartfelt prayer of a good man works very powerfully" (Jm 5:16). Psalm 99 admirably summarizes this mission of pray-ers of the Bible: "Moses, Aaron among his priests, and Samuel his votary, all invoked the Lord: and he answered them in the pillar of cloud" (Ps 99: 6-7).

In his turn, Jesus will be the new Moses and the new Elijah; he will also be Job who takes upon himself the cry springing from the anguish of men and bears it before his Father, for he took upon his shoulders the burden of our suffering and of sin. He will entrust the Church and, more specifically, his Mother with the mission of prolonging his prayer to the Father in the Holy Spirit: thus, the event of the Upper Room remains also the sign of the perennial character of this prayer at the heart of the Church and of the world. This is the very significance of the departure of a multitude of Christians for the desert when the persecutions came to an end.

Still today in the Church, men and women receive the vocation and the mission to remain in the city (Ac 1:4), and to dwell in the Upper Room of the Cenacle (Ac 1:13), to be solely devoted to prayer with Mary, Mother of Jesus, and with his brothers; they are waiting for the Promise of the Father and they beg him, in the name of Jesus, to send them the power of the Holy Spirit which will make them his witnesses unto the ends of the earth (Ac 1:7-8).

This life consecrated to prayer is neither an evasion nor a retreat from the world, but a true battle, the kind which Paul speaks of in relation to Epaphras: "This servant of Christ Jesus never stops battling for you in prayer in order that you stand firm, perfect, in total agreement with the will of God" (Col 4:12). This was first the battle of Christ who "during his life on earth, offered up prayers and supplications with loud cries and tears, to the one who had the power to save him out of death, and he submitted so humbly that his prayer was heard" (Heb 5:7). For Christ, the abysmal point of the struggle at the depths of his distress, which is also ours, was the Agony at Gethsemane: "Abba! Father! Everything is possible for you. Take this cup away from me. But let it be as you, not I, would have it" (Mk 14:36); this is a cry of supplication, of surrender, of fidelity and of obedience unto death, of true prayer during which Jesus gives up his last breath and yields himself up to the Love of the Father.

At the source and in the image of the prayer of Jesus, all prayer — and especially the prayer of those who have consecrated all their life to intercession — will be, at the same time, one of supplication and surrender, of death and birth. Intercession is not to be understood as a way of "informing" God about our needs. No prayer may be held as such in the eyes of God whose knowledge is infinite, who wishes to give us everything, first and foremost, the Holy Spirit, the Gift in the highest sense of the word. We must, therefore, deepen our heart by the prayer of entreaty, open it to the will of God and to the love of the Father for us and for others.

To understand the full sense of entreaty, we must focus our eyes on the Community of the Acts, in prayer (Ac 4:23-31). It is not so much a matter of praying for ourselves or for particular intentions, nor even to be freed from battle or from enemies, but within the context of the persecution of the Church, we ask God to be attentive to the threat of our persecutors and to grant the apostles the courage to speak the Word with complete assurance (parrhesia): "Stretch out your hand to heal and to work miracles and marvels through the name of your holy servant Jesus. At the end of their prayer, the house where they assembled rocked; they were all filled with the Holy Spirit and began to proclaim the word of God with confidence" (Ac 4:31). It is always when the Church is persecuted that prayer becomes insistent and pleading, for we may then look only to God for the strength to hold on: "All the time Peter was in prison, the Church prayed to God for him unceasingly" (Ac 12:5).

Still today, those who dedicate their life to the prayer of supplication ask that signs and healings be worked in hearts and bodies in order that the power of the Holy Spirit in action in the name of the Risen Lord may be recognized. The apostles are men like other men (Ac

14:15) called to conversion; they must not be considered
as if it "were by their own power or holiness" (Ac 3:12)
that they perform miracles, but uniquely because they
are filled with the Holy Spirit: "It was by the name of
Jesus Christ the Nazarene, the one you crucified, whom
God raised from the dead. It is thanks to him that this
man is able to stand... here in your presence today...
There is no salvation in anyone else, for there is no other
name in the world given to men by which we are to be
saved" (Ac 4:8-12).

In short, the ultimate goal of the prayer of entreaty
is to ask the Father, by the power of the name of the
Risen Jesus (Jn 16:23), for the effusion of the Spirit of
Pentecost on the Church and on the world: "Father, in
the name of Jesus, give us your Spirit". Those whom
the Lord calls in this way to a continual prayer of
supplication base their life on these words of Jesus:
"So I say to you: Ask, and it will be given to you; knock
and it will be opened to you; search and you will find"
(Lk 11:9). They have no other refuge or recourse but the
invocation of the Name.

5. "Keep your vigils in an untiring intercession" (Ep 6:18)

Such a vocation to prayer is a pure gift of the grace
of the Father of all light from whom comes everything
that is perfect (Jm 1:17). To receive this grace, we must
have experienced (or at least have had the feeling thereof)
that, cut off from Christ, we can do nothing (Jn 15:5), and
that without the power of the Holy Spirit, there is
nothing in us that is not perverted, as is expressed in the
Veni, Sancte Spiritus. Only the humble, the poor, the
modest, the wounded, the merciful, and those who weep
may hear this call and make of their life a permanent
and continual prayer. This must really be a gift to them;
the same may be said about them as what Christ says
about those who remain celibate for the sake of the

17

Kingdom: "Let him, who can, understand" (Mt 19:21). But man may ask for this grace and cooperate with it, for the only way to receive a free gift is to beg for it: "God gives the gift of prayer to the one who prays", says Saint John Climacus. In this area, we must not try to be understood or to please men, but God alone. It is a question of vocation; Christ could say to us as he did to Saint Peter who was casting an envious look on the contemplative vocation of John: "If I want him to stay behind till I come, what does it matter to you? You, follow me (Jn 21:22).

All those who have received this vocation will realize they have it from an inner evidence that the Holy Spirit will generate in their heart: they will feel the fire of continual prayer burn in them and they will truly understand these words of Jesus: "Until now you have not asked for anything in my name. Ask and you will receive, and so your joy will be complete" (Jn 16:24). Whatever may be the prayers they have already said, the desolation they have known in the course of which cries and groanings may have been wrung from their heart, they will be convinced that they have not yet begun to pray. All this is nothing compared to what God expects of them and wishes to give them as prayer of entreaty. God would spare them certain trials, battles or temptations or deliver them from these, but he cannot do so for this is the only means for him to draw a cry of plea from their heart, on the condition that they do not resist him too much. One word always recurs in the memory of their heart: "When the Son of Man comes again, will he find any faith on earth?" (Lk 18:8).

Finally, this vocation to continual prayer will assume all its dimensions when it is ratified by the Church and by the bishop who will be able to say to us as Saint Paul did to the Christians in Ephesus: "May the Spirit lead you in prayer. Pray all the time, asking for what you need, on every possible occasion. Keep your vigils in an untiring intercession for all the saints. Pray for me that God may put his word on my lips, that I may courageously make known the mystery of the gospel of which I am an ambassador in chains; pray that in proclaiming it I may speak as boldly as I ought to" (Ep 6: 18-20).

As he recalled on Radio Notre-Dame, on January 4th, 1984, the portrait of Saint Geneviève who, in Paris, lived the recluse life of consecrated virgins, in fasting, prayer and silence, Cardinal Lustiger said that if we wandered in Paris in order to look for its unknown social strata, as in a spectral analysis, we would discover the hidden dimension of prayer flowing like a torrent of living waters of supplication, never exhausted and never interrupted, and this right in the city of Paris. There are places where men and women devote their time to prayer, some for a rather short time, some for life. It is a hidden pool where the Christian conscience of the Parisians draws its substance from the intercession of the poor and the humble for the salvation of men and for the Glory of God.

A contemplative, he yet added, is one who has given his life to prayer, not from a natural attraction to this style of life or to silence. Contemplative life is something else: it means to be called by God to devote all of one's strength to prayer as a priority, not to a prayer for oneself, nor because prayer is agreeable, but to a prayer of intercession for the Church. In such a life, all activities are structured around prayer: work is accomplished with prayer in view; whether we eat or rest, all is done so that ordinary life may become prayer. And these men do not, in their mind or in their heart, go over lists of names and intentions for which they would pray, but they are part of the ecclesial Body and, as they pray, they integrate prayer into the Church.

Thus we could draw a map of Paris with little flames showing the places where a man or a woman, a group or a community are praying, interceding and asking God for forgiveness for so many sins, rejection and oblivion, are imploring for so much misery and folly, asking that God may grant courage and strength to his children whom he loves, begging that forgiveness may be stronger than hatred and praying God to enlighten those who are harassed by doubts and who are weakening. It is in the heart of these spiritual realities that the true stakes of life are played. The real dimension of History is spiritual and those who have the greatest impact on History are those who worship and pray.

Finally, he was outlining a map of Paris pointing to the various places where the life of man is staged: schools, offices, banks, churches, labor union activities, transportation centers and places of pleasure. There is also, as he was explaining, another map which rejoices the heart of God and my heart as a bishop: it is the one made by those who keep vigil during the night and who pray with their brothers and sisters for their brothers and sisters; in the silence and the poverty of their heart, they intercede for all men. Finally, the Cardinal did not hesitate to say that this unceasing prayer is a task to which we are all called; as disciples of Christ, we are called to keep vigil for the entire Church.

Chapter I

MARY... PONDERED THESE THINGS
IN HER HEART
(Lk 2:19)

It is a great favor to understand that we receive everything in prayer: what we must think, read, write or hush up. When we have a task to do, we must do it in prayer. Occasionally, we should speak, write, or enlighten someone, but we can find nothing, we can do nothing: I shall pray, then I shall act and I shall manage. It stands to reason that, when we undertake the task of writing on the prayer of Mary, we must do it in prayer; that is where we find inspiration.

1. I prayed and I was given understanding

This is the reason why, as I begin this work, I wish to invoke the Virgin Mary, so that she may give me some insight into the mystery of her relationship with God and, therefore, into her prayer. Mary had an interior life, an intimate life which may be qualified as secret: "My heart has its secret, my soul has its mystery", says the poet. What characterizes Mary's secret, like the secret of any man, is that no one may unlock it unless the door is opened. We can be forced to tell material things or to relate events which concern us. No one can oblige us to reveal the innermost part of our heart, if our personal freedom refuses to do so.

This is the tragedy of totalitarian systems where the innermost secret of the other is forced into the open by torture or violent means. But in a life of normal relationships, it takes much time, friendliness and trust before a man shares his secret with another, whether it concerns his image of glamour or of woe. The further I move into the knowledge of the other, the more I find that he is mystery and that there is a part of his being which he cannot and must not reveal. We especially must not seek to break through this mystery; that is the worst of the sins against chastity, for to covet the soul of others is yet more serious than to covet their bodies, the discretion of the body being but a reflection of that of the heart and of the soul.

However, it is absolutely normal that two friends share their secret, which is often their reason for existing. Love and friendship aspire to knowledge. The same may be said of the secret of the Blessed Virgin: if we truly love Mary, we naturally hope to see and know her secret of her mystery, which amounts to the same thing. The secret of an individual is often the secret of his prayer: let us examine more closely the approach to this mystery.

We can study Christ and the Blessed Virgin as closely as we wish; if they do not want to tell us what they have in their heart, we shall never know. This does not depend on our own spiritual inadequacy but on a decision freely taken by the other who will or will not admit us into his intimacy. Whatever our insight may be as we meditate on the prayer of Mary, if she does not open the door to her mystery, we shall remain at the threshold without knowing anything more of it.

It is not by dint of ascesis and natural contemplation that we will ever manage to penetrate into God or Mary: "We teach the wisdom of God, mysterious and hidden, that God predestined to be for our glory before the ages began,,, the things that no eye has seen and no ear has heard, things beyond the mind of man, all that God has prepared for those who love him" (1 Co 2:7-9).

If Mary is a person, however much we strive to know her through natural contemplation, she remains free to reveal or not her mystery. This is what the philosopher Gabriel Marcel expresses in these terse words: "Knowledge of the other is a perpetual invocation". If this is so for all humans, all the more so is it for Christ and also for Mary. Any progress we make into the knowledge of God and of his mystery is a gift from the Father who draws us to Jesus or to Mary: it is a free initiative on the part of God who opens his secret to us. He reveals himself to whomever he wishes (Mt 11:25-27).

This doctrine on the knowledge of the mystery of the person does not stem only from sane philosophy, it is also part of the tradition of all spirituality. Saint Louis Mary Grignion of Montfort wrote a small book entitled: *The Secret of Mary* and he speaks of it at length in his other works. To convince ourselves of this, we only have to read paragraphs II, 248 and 264 of the *True Devotion to Mary*.

It is a secret, he writes, for the place and the function of Mary in God's plan of salvation are not yet understood enough nor sufficiently translated into the reality of Christian life. This secret must be entrusted only to men of prayer, who live the mystery of the Cross, in a word, to true apostles. He adds that a particular grace of God is necessary to "understand and savor" this secret and that before "going on in an eager and natural wish to know the truth", we must pray much, not only by external deeds, but with a spiritual attitude of the heart, an attitude of longing and prayer. Similarly, he also adds, "you will thank God every day of your life for the grace he gave you in revealing to you a secret which you did not deserve to know".[1]

1. From *Œuvres complètes de saint Louis-Marie Grignion de Montfort,* Seuil, 1966, pp. 442-443, par. 1 and 2.

This is to say that to know the mystery of Christ, we must be on our knees in supplication; in other words, we must invoke. The same may be said for the mystery of Mary, whom we must never separate from Jesus, and for her obedience to the Father. Thus, when his mother and his brothers wish to see him, Jesus immediately answers: "My mother and my brothers are those who hear the word of God and put it into practice" (Lk 8:21). To know the Blessed Virgin, we must keep vigil in prayer at her door and tell her: "Make me know your secret, reveal your prayer to me!" When liturgy makes us celebrate a feast of Mary, it often gives us a text from the Book of Wisdom which speaks of prayer and supplication: "And so I prayed, and understanding was given me; I entreated, and the Spirit of Wisdom came to me" (Ws 7:7).

If we must entreat to write about the Blessed Virgin, the reader must also pray to have the spiritual understanding of what he is reading, for this mystery is hidden from the wise and the intelligent, but it is revealed to the humble, to those who do not pretend to know everything. A poor woman who recites her rosary every day knows much more about the prayer of Mary than a learned theologian who does not pray. She is certainly not able to express her knowledge clearly, but when she hears her parish priest speak about the Blessed Virgin, she feels a mysterious world stirring within herself which places her in a direct relationship with Mary, and she understands the power of her prayer. She does not perceive Mary as one who gives graces but as the one who prays God for men.

2. Mary holds her secret

This is what must have been going on for the Blessed Virgin if we believe Luke's account. On two occasions, he asserts that Mary kept within her heart the secret of her relationship with God concerning the fact of the birth of Jesus. First, when the astonished shepherds report what they have seen: "As for Mary, she treasured all these things and pondered them in her heart" (Lk 2:19). Then, when Jesus speaks in the Temple for the first time: "His mother stored up all these things in her heart" (Lk 2:51).

In Biblical language, the expression "to ponder in one's heart" is a formula of the apocalyptical type. We find it in the story of Joseph whose father Jacob keeps the dream in his mind (Gn 37:11). This is still clearer in Daniel 7:28: "I, Daniel, was greatly disturbed in mind, and I grew pale; but I kept these things to myself". In the two cases, the depositary of the revelation keeps it in the memory of his heart for the days to come until it is time to reveal it.

We have there a most precious clue which may give us an insight into the prayer of Mary, from the day she received the visit of the angel at the Annunciation until the day she feels she should speak, for these times are fulfilled. Without any doubt, Luke wants to note here the prayerful meditation of Mary on these facts whose significance will be manifested only in the paschal revelation.

From the moment a man really begins to pray in earnest, he has only one wish: to know how to proceed and, like the disciples, he says to Jesus: "Lord, teach me how to pray" (Lk 11:1). I think we react the same way when it concerns the prayer of Mary. When we hear words like those of Luke, where it is said that Mary meditated and prayed in her heart, we experience the irresistible longing to know more and to question Mary about her prayer. But on this subject, the gospel is very discreet and, apart from a few words at the Annunciation, in the Magnificat, at Cana or in the Upper Room, it leaves us resting on our wish. The gospel is happy to assert the fact without being explicit on the how.

Now is the time to apply the reflection of Saint Ignatius of Loyola when he recalls the apparition of the Risen Christ to his mother: it is enough to have some intelligence to understand, in other words, to be a spiritual man who knows the thought of the Lord, since he has received the Holy Spirit who probes unto the depths of God (1 Co 2:10-16). Here is what Ignatius says on the subject: "He appeared to the Virgin Mary. Undoubtedly, the Holy Scriptures do not mention this but they lead us to understand this by saying that he appeared to so many others. For the Holy Scriptures suppose that we have some understanding, since it is written: 'Are you also without any understanding?' "[2].

So, during Jesus' life on earth, Mary's prayer is just about unknown to us and we can only scrutinize, in the light of the Spirit, the few words the Gospel has left us on this subject. There is nevertheless one passage to which we shall come back later and which must hold all our attention: "She pondered in her heart". This is where we must have the intelligence, according to Saint Ignatius, to understand that Mary's silence in prayer was more eloquent than all her words. From all appearances, she must surely have prayed as did all the Jewish women of her day, with the words of the psalms and the prayers of blessing and thanksgiving of the Synagogue. Interiorly, we could say of her prayer what Thérèse of Lisieux says about her own: "I was doing contemplative prayer without knowing it and God was teaching me in secret"[3]. The prayer of Mary was like an iceberg whose hidden and sunken parts were without proportion compared to the visible surface.

Mary is a simple woman who prays and believes; she is absolutely unaware that she is the chosen one of the Lord, the one upon whom the eyes of the Father have rested in order to associate her with his plan. Thus she

2. Translated from *Exercices,* n. 299.
3. Translated from *Manuscrit A,* 33v.

prays but she is not conscious of her prayer as Father Georges explains: "Mary is a mystic who does not know how to express her experience". She does not know this oblique look by which we can observe ourselves and note the character we are playing, especially in prayer. She is centered on God and not on herself. Cassian was already saying in his time that "prayer is pure when the monk is no longer conscious that he is praying". He prays as he breathes without being aware of doing so, or rather, his prayer has slipped into his breath and has become permanent like his very breathing. When a man is totally immersed in prayer, he cannot speak or write anything about it anymore.

And so, it appears normal that Mary keep her secret which is not really hers, to begin with, but God's: the decisions are up to him. Before Joseph, who has doubts, she will be silent and will leave it up to God to shed light and to defend her cause. We sense here the atmosphere of silence which clothed the secret of Mary: "The Blessed Virgin did well to keep everything to herself, said Thérèse of Lisieux; one cannot begrudge me for wanting to do the same." Basically, Mary always lived under the eyes of the Father who sees into the secret; she knew she was loved by him like a precious pearl and she revealed herself to others only in the measure that he demanded of her. As Jesus recommends to those who pray, she avoided making an exhibition of herself to men who derive their glory from each other. God alone must rejoice in her beauty; that is why he clothes her in silence in the eyes of men and in her own eyes. With Mary, the spirit of silence was a safeguard for her prayer.

So is it said in the Canticle: "You are the loveliest of women if you do not know yourself" (Sg 1:8). This is why Mary is hidden, even from her own eyes, because she is the Blessed Virgin, the Spouse of the Holy Spirit: she must belong to him alone. The bridal union of Mary with the Holy Spirit is celebrated in the depths of her heart, where the Father is forever embracing the Son in the love of the Spirit. In this sense, Mary's virginity is bound to her humility: she lives in a total oblivion of herself and sees herself uniquely in the eyes of the Father; her sole wish is to live united to the Word: "The Word, Son of God, dwells, in essence and by his presence, in the company of the Father and of the Holy Spirit in the very essence of the soul and he is hidden there... Whoever hopes to find a hidden object must go down to the depths where it is hidden and, when he has found it, he also will be hidden... Since the Beloved after whom you sigh dwells hidden in your bosom, be diligent in order that you remain well hidden with him, and in your very bosom, you will feel him and you will embrace him with love".[4]

In the first pages of his *True Devotion to Mary*, Saint Louis Mary Grignion of Montfort very strongly insists on this aspect of the life of Mary: "Mary was hidden during her life; this is the reason why she is called Alma Mater, the hidden and secret Mother, by the Holy Spirit and the Church. Her humility was so profound that she had no more powerful and more constant attraction on earth than to hide herself from herself and from all other beings, to be known of God alone".[5]

The effusion of the Spirit will have to come down on Pentecost in order that Mary evoke the virginal conception of Jesus. There is a relationship between the birth of Christ in his mother's womb and the birth of the Church, two events which are the work of the Holy Spirit. It is when the apostles will have received the Holy Spirit that Mary will speak of the virginal conception of Jesus and reveal that he is born of the Spirit. Thus Jesus gives the Spirit since he himself is the fruit of the Spirit in his human nature. This is the reason why Mary kept all these

---

4. Translated from St. John of the Cross, *Cantique*, St. I, n. 6, 9, 10.

5. *Op. cit.*, p. 488, par. 2.

events in the silence of her heart, storing them for the days to come.

Mary owed this openness of heart to those who had become her children; she had to tell them, especially to John and Luke, how God had acted towards her. Since Jesus had shared everything about the secrets of the Father with the apostles, his friends, Mary spoke to these who were her sons. There was nothing spectacular in the words of Mary except the mystery within her of the espousal of God with humankind.

3. Mary prays in the silence of her heart

One must not chatter too much about the prayer of the one who did not speak and of whom very little is known. But Luke tells us enough to make us suspect something beyond the words, the silent prayer of the Virgin whom we call blessed. On two different occasions, which we have already mentioned, he notes: "As for Mary, she treasured all these things and pondered them in her heart" (Lk 2:19 and 51). We have seen what the expression "to meditate in one's heart" means at the exegetic level. Let us now examine its meaning in Mary's life of faith, that is, in her prayer. When we speak of Mary, we must never leave the realm of reality; we could say about a book on the prayer of Mary what Thérèse of Lisieux said about a sermon on the Blessed Virgin:

"In order that a sermon on the Blessed Virgin may please me and do me some good, I must see her in real life, not in a hypothetical one; and I am certain that her life in reality must have been all simple. We show her as an unapproachable person; we should see her as one capable of being imitated, we should bring out her virtues, say that she lived in faith as we do, offer proofs of that from the gospel where we read: 'They did not understand what he was saying to them'. And this other verse, no less mysterious: 'His parents marvelled at what was being said of him'. This admiration supposes a certain astonishment, don't you think, my little Mother?"[6].

"To meditate in one's heart", "not to understand", "to be in astonishment and admiration"... are so many expressions which refer to the profound attitude of the heart of the Blessed Virgin, an attitude of silence, of interrogation and why not of adoration as well? To say that the Blessed Virgin prayed in the silence of her heart is not to assert "an unlikely fact unknown to us", to use another expression of Thérèse of Lisieux,[7] since Luke expresses this clearly in his gospel. He must have learned this from the mouth of John or even perhaps from watching Mary pray. We know that John took her with him, but we do not know where John went. Tradition mentions Ephesus; this is very likely. Mary would have followed him. It matters little where she lived. What interests us here is her silence and the silence which surrounds her. Mary remains silent in prayer as she was during the early childhood of Jesus, as she had been before the Annunciation.

All those who have contemplated the Blessed Virgin to enter into the mystery of her prayer — I am thinking here particularly of Bérulle — have been impressed by her silence and become aware that all true prayer finds its perfection and is fulfilled in a prayer of pure silence. Those who come to the school of the Blessed Virgin to learn how to pray are led, one day or the other, to this silence of attentive listening, sight and adoration. Silence is the movement of every being reaching out to the other; it is the contemplation of his Face or the listening to his word.

This is the reason why all silence is relative to the word brought forth from the lips and from the face of

6. Translated from *Derniers entretiens*, DDB-Cerf, 1971, Annexes, pp. 310-312.

7. *Derniers entretiens*, p. 330.

another. Mary's silence is more profound than any other silence of man, for it is relative to the very Word of God, the eternal Word of the Father, brought forth from the Face of the Most High. To greet this Word, it was necessary for Mary to be in a silence devoid of any thought, wish, and image. Mary made silence of herself, or rather the Father, in a certain way, put her in silence so that she might receive his Word in all its reality.

When God sees that a man has immersed himself in a true silence, in the measure of his strength, then he raises him to another level of silence, his own. We can hardly suspect what this "divinum silentium" is, the silence where the Father engenders his Word, his Logos, without any sound of words. He expresses himself totally in his Word, "the radiant light of God's glory and the perfect expression of his nature" (Heb 1:3). As Saint John of the Cross explains: "The Father said but one word, namely, his Son, and in an eternal silence he is always saying it; the soul must also hear it in silence".[8] It is in this triune silence that Mary was placed to receive in the depth of her being the incarnation of the Word. God alone can say "himself" in one only Word which, at the same time, is his Son. Man must speak many words in his attempt to explain his nature and he never manages to do so. This is the reason why God must put him in the silence of the Blessed Virgin, so he may greet the Word and discover again his true being in him.

Mary keeps silent to listen to the Word of God speaking to her through the Scriptures or to listen to the people who come to her: Gabriel, Elizabeth, the shepherds, Simeon, Anna. She also listens to the events which involve her to discover their meaning. A golden thread links all the moments of her life which she integrates into "the hidden plan which God has so kindly made from the beginning" (Ep 1:9). She never interposes between

8. Translated from *Les Œuvres spirituelles*, P. Lucien-Marie de Saint Joseph, DDB, Maxime 164, ed. 1947, p. 1714.

herself and God or between reality and her imaginary fantasies; she is divested of power in order to be totally attentive to the mystery of God. Little by little, not knowing where this was to lead her, she developed the habit of living in silence until the day God put her in a yet more profound silence before sending her the angel bearing the message of the Incarnation.

Mary so listened to the word of God, that one day she was able to conceive the Word of God. Silence had so deepened her body, her heart, her spirit and all her being, that she had become pure capacity to give a body to the Word of God. This is the reason why she said only one word: "*Yes*, let it be done to me according to your Word". In her "Fiat" and by it, acting in conjunction with God, Mary conceived a child who is the Word, in substance, of the Father and the total expression of her nature as woman. In the silence of the Trinity, of the entire creation and of humankind, which was somewhat centered in her, Mary became the Mother of the Eternal Word.

When she received the Word of God in her womb, Mary acknowledged another silence: a silence of attention to the mystery which was coming to be within her. One can really say that she gave body to the Word of God; the Father fashions in her womb the only offering agreeable to him, the one which someday will become the unique intercessor before the Father; prayer-made-man grows in Mary, the Temple of God and a true house of prayer. In the epistle to the Hebrews, we hear the Son of God, Christ, say to his Father: "You, who wanted no sacrifice or oblation, prepared a body for me" (Heb 10:4). It is through Mary that the Father prepared this body. While Mary was silent before the mystery of the Son taking flesh in her, the Father was also silent. The silence of the whole Trinity is reflected in Mary as the shadow of the Most High is cast upon her before she gives birth to the Son who is bringing salvation to the world.

All those who, by consecrating their life to intercession, are called to become "houses of prayer", must love to contemplate this silence of Mary, who was attentive to the birth of the Word within her. By their baptism, they have also become "Temples of the Spirit" and "Abodes of the Trinity", and prayer dwells in them without their knowing it. Mary will teach them how to weave bonds of filial love with the Father, of attentive listening to the Word and of total consecration to the action of the Spirit. We shall see later how Mary's prayer was triune, but it was good to see even now how her silence prepared her to receive this prayer of the Three in her.

How can this attitude of silence of the Blessed Virgin in prayer be lived in a concrete manner? Going back to what we have said on the word in relation to silence, let us say that, for us as well, the meditation of the Word of God must take us somewhere beyond the Word. Each time we get in touch with the Word of God, we must convince ourselves that these "words" of God take us into a mysterious zone of hidden silence where the true Word resounds, the Logos which does not spend itself in any human word. When the Fathers commented on the Word of God, they always declared that the best of what they were saying was, in fact, what they were not saying and could not say because God is unknowable and unutterable. And this is why they were saying such "interesting" things about God!

This is very important to those who practise the Jesus prayer or the prayer of the rosary, for there is the risk of falling into what Christ condemns when he says: "In your prayers do not babble as the pagans do, for they think that by using many words they will make themselves heard" (Mt 6:7). All spiritual masters have warned their disciples against this mechanical type of prayer which is not an aim in itself, but a simple and practical means of opening out into the silence of the prayer from the heart. When this prayer of the Holy Spirit erupts in our heart, we must enter into it in silence. The same relationship exists between the word and silence as between the Word and the Holy Spirit.

Liturgy itself culminates in the double aspects of silent contemplation: that of the child (in-fans: without word) of Bethlehem who does not speak and that of the Crucified Christ who is also silent ("Jesus autem tacebat"). On this matter, Saint Paul speaks of the "verbum Crucis", that is, the "language of the Cross" (1 Co 1:18). What interests the Church is God who opens his heart in the silent language of the Cross. It is the ultimate confidence that God shares with us. The contemplation of the Church, inseparable from the contemplation of Mary, moves from one silence to the other: from the silence of the child Jesus to the silence of Jesus crucified, far beyond his last cry (Mk 15:37). There is the privileged word which Mary and the Church contemplate assiduously. At the Nativity, Mary contemplates the Word who, for our sake, lowered himself to the point of being unable to say anything. At the foot of the Cross, she gazes with love upon the Word who accepted to be put to silence by men. Between these two silences, there will be the words of Jesus in his public life, but these direct us and make us flow into the contemplation of Jesus on the Cross.

For this reason, we must listen to the silence of the child Jesus and to the silence of the crucified Jesus. God is discreet and the folly of his love which he wishes men to understand cannot be expressed. Thus says the author of the Letter to the Hebrews: "In times past, God spoke in fragmentary and varied ways to our fathers through the prophets; but in our own time, the last days, he has spoken to us through his Son, the Son he has appointed to inherit everything and through whom he made everything there is" (Heb 1:1-2). God, as it were, searched for words to express the unutterable, so he spoke it in the silence of the child Jesus and of the crucified Jesus. Saint Bridget of Sweden would say: "If preachers knew what the love of God is, they would be reduced to silence and would be unable to speak of it anymore".

Thus the silences of Christ are more eloquent than his words, but we need his words to come out into silence. This is the reason why Mary meditated these words in her heart, to become the first to adore the child Jesus. The angel had spoken to her at the Annunciation as did the angels on the night of Christmas, but this was to direct her to the silence of Jesus at Christmas and on Calvary, where the cradle becomes a tomb. We must also note that the resurrected Jesus speaks very little: he shows himself as in a theophany. Thus the paradox of the Incarnation is that the Word of God made himself silence. The folly of God who allows himself to be crucified is already present in the folly of God who takes flesh.

To understand these concepts which are very difficult to express in human words, we must go through the Blessed Virgin: she begets the author of life in silence, who assumes the nature of a child to become the crucified Word. This is the mystery of the God, poor and helpless in face of the hardness of the heart of man. This is why Jesus wishes to present himself to us in the vulnerable weakness of a child. Mary must wrap us in the silence of prayer to teach us to let ourselves be touched by the "sight" (Ga 3:1) of her Son on the Cross. As long as our heart remains untouched and unperturbed, nothing will be accomplished. Gently, Mary must wrap us in the silence of her prayer to lead us to the true conversion of the heart.

Chapter II

PRAYING WITH MARY
AT THE ANNUNCIATION

I. GOD'S "PRAYER" TO MARY

There is no question here of writing a biography of Mary, but of journeying with her through the various stages of her life, of which we have accounts in the Gospel, to discover how she prays, that is, how she responds to an initiative of God with regards to herself. In fact, man is not the one who prays God, it is God who prays man to willingly receive him. If the title had not appeared so shocking, we would have readily written: "God's prayer to Mary at the Annunciation".

"If man must pray God, it is because God first prays man. 'God was the first to love us' (1 Jn 4:10); he was the first to tell us his wish and to address us a prayer: what I am offering to you — Myself — will you accept it? When man answers God's prayer, he attains the highest level of existence".[1]

If we examine closely the account of the Annunciation in Saint Luke, we see God coming to meet Mary and, like

---

1. Translated from François Varillon, *La souffrance de Dieu*, Centurion, 1975, p. 66.

a lightning stoke, springing from the depths of her being;
she beholds herself as "full of grace", "beloved of God".
She believes it on the word of the angel and, immediately,
this becomes an experience; Mary sees, knows and loves
herself "totally beloved of God".

It is in this experience of love that we can speak of
a "prayer" of God to Mary. She had to know herself as
the "Beloved of God" so she might hear the prayer of
God who asks her: "Will you be the mother of my Son?"
The only language which is suitable for love, says Jean
Lacroix, is that of prayer. God does not "will", he
"prays".[2] We have mentioned previously that God is
helpless and gives up his power: he makes himself the
mendicant of Love who knocks at the door of our heart.
In fear and in hope, he addresses a prayer to Mary: "Will
you?". We shall understand later in what sense we speak
here of "prayer" of God to Mary. In the following
chapter, we will then be able to speak of Mary's prayer
to God, that is, of her response. But let us keep this in
mind for our own life of prayer: as long as we have not
heard in the silence of the heart the "prayer" of God in
the groanings of the Spirit within us, we will not know
how to pray.

1. You are the Beloved of God

In the same way that to understand the events in
Jesus' life on earth, we must read them in the light of
Easter, for it is through the preaching of the Risen Christ
that we call to mind his words and actions in the course
of his pilgrimage on earth, so Mary's words and actions
in the Infancy Narratives and in the course of Jesus'
public life become foundation-events in the paschal
mystery. As the exegetes say: it is in the posthumous

---

2. Translated from Jean Lacroix, *Le désir et les désirs,*
PUF, 1975, p. 145.

survival of a famous man that we begin to question ourselves about his birth and the facts of his life. Thus, the apostles experience the Lordship of Christ when they have a close experience of the power of his resurrection. In the effusion of the Spirit, they discover the true personality of Jesus and, like the centurion, they can say: "Indeed, this man was the Son of God" (Mt 27:54).

Very naturally then, they come back to the events of his life on earth and they question the Blessed Virgin to know how he was born, how he lived and what he said. Mary could not have given an account of the virginal conception of Jesus if the apostles had not lived Easter.[3] Now they are ready to hear what the Blessed Virgin will tell them about her Son; furthermore, they hang on Mary's words for they do not wish to lose anything which concerns Jesus. We must always keep in mind this innermost depth of the paschal mystery when we meditate on the words of the angel and Mary's response at the Annunciation. For this is here very much a question of Mary's prayer, since she will lift the veil a little to reveal her dialogue and her relationship with God.

Therefore, we can act like Saint Luke, that is, question the eyewitnesses, the ministers of the Word, and "carefully gather information about everything from the beginning" (Lk 1:1-3). Saint Luke really wants to do the work of a historian and write a gospel based upon tradition. His purpose is clear: in setting the Blessed Virgin in her historical, geographical, personal and social context, he wants to show that God always chooses concrete and situated people to entrust them with a mission. The Bible and the gospel do not report ideas about God, but show us men and women, sinners or saints — it matters little — whom God meets and whose

---

3. Translated from the TOB. It offers an annotation on this subject: "The virginal conception is the sign of this unique and mysterious filiation" (Note "u", p. 191).

life is completely disrupted as a result. All of them could say with Aragon. "What would I be if you had not come to meet me?" All of Mary's prayer will originate in this initiative on the part of God and it is there that it will draw its sustenance in all the stages of her existence.

Thus God dispatches Gabriel — the one who is commissioned to transmit his messages to men — to tell Mary: "Rejoice! You so highly favored of God! The Lord is with you" (Lk 1:28). Let us set aside for the moment the "Rejoice" to which we shall come back later, and contemplate the words: "You so highly favored of God", often translated by "full of grace". Very clearly, this does not refer to the reality we hold in the expression "sanctifying grace"; this concept is strictly unknown in the Old Testament.

In the Bible, the meaning of grace is "favor". Thus Moses will say: "If indeed I have won your favor" (Ex 33:13). To avoid prolonging this any further, let us say that it is a concept very close to "mercy" and "tenderness". The angel will take up again later, almost word for word, the words of Moses and apply them to Mary: "Mary, do not be afraid for you have won God's Favor" (Lk 1:30).

God looks upon Mary with a love so intense that he clothes her with his own mercy to make her "full of grace". She becomes "favored" by God; the word which would best convey the meaning in the Bible is that of "Beloved". This expression will become, after The Song of Songs and psalm 44, the very name of the People. God has centered in Mary all the love which he has showered upon the People and then upon the Church. Mary simply lives her faith and prays naturally: she has no idea that God has cast his eyes upon her to make her become the Mother of his Son. The angel must tell her that she is the "Beloved" of God, so that she may experience this fact in her heart. That word is her new name, her vocation: through it, Mary learns that she is the unique one, the elect, the "Beloved".

Mary is surprised to find out that the eyes of God have rested upon her. She knows that others before her have already stood in favor with God: Abraham, Moses, David, but she is surprised to have found favor in this absolutely unique way. To whom has God ever said: "You are the Beloved"? Mary is the only person in the world to whom God has spoken that way. We can understand that she would be surprised and perturbed to behold herself without sin and loved by God in a very particular way. In her simplicity, poverty, and humility, Mary did not know that she was at the center of history: "All generations will call me blessed" (Lk 1:48). If we wish to have the least insight into the prayer of adoration and thanksgiving of Mary in the Magnificat, we must stop here and pray ourselves to understand what was going on at that moment in Mary's heart.

Until then, Mary had to turn her eyes towards God to pray. Then, suddenly, she sees the eyes of God turned upon her, with an intensity of love and tenderness that we can hardly imagine. For her, it was no more a matter of loving God, but of being humble and poor enough to accept this "white tornado", a hurricane of love. She really needed the childhood spirit to take refuge in the cleft of the rock so as not to die. So says Teresa of Avila while speaking of contemplative prayer; she did not need to think of God nor to discuss about his love, she saw it: "I do not ask you at this time to focus your thought on him, nor to elaborate numerous arguments or high and learned considerations. I am asking you but one thing: to look upon him... For he, your Spouse, never loses sight of you".[4]

Teresa again explains that to do contemplative prayer "is to entertain an exchange of affection, often dealing on a one-to-one basis with the One who, we know, loves

---

4. Translated from *Chemin de la perfection*, ch. 26, *Œuvres complètes*, pp. 452-453.

us".[5] With regard to Mary, I dare use a simpler definition: "It is the meeting of eyes which consume each other
in love". I was recently told the story of a young man
in a train who was fascinated by a glance which overwhelmed him; on the spot, he left everything, annulled
his commitments and went to live with this person. Until
then, as Father Molinié would say, he knew love at the
normal temperature of thirty-seven degrees, but there
he suddently discovers it at forty degrees.

This is what happens when a man undergoes conversion: he passes straight off from thirty-seven to forty
degrees. We then understand the Father speaking of this
subject as a "prayer of fire"! By the way, this man can
experience a certain pride as opposed to those who do
not know such an intensity. At this temperature, he can
have the illusion of loving God with a feverish fire. But
the day he truly meets Jesus Christ and discovers within
himself the burning Bush, he will understand that,
between forty degrees and the temperature of Jesus
Christ, there is the abyss of the Infinite which will heal
him of all forms of pride.

At the Annunciation, Mary discovered with amazement that she was loved infinitely by the God of the
burning Bush. She already had some notion of love since
Luke tells us that she "was betrothed to a man named
Joseph, of the House of David" (Lk 1:27). But in asserting
that she was his "Beloved", God raised this human love
to such an incandescence that it revealed the Infinite to
her. In our lives the first revelation of the Infinite often
comes through human love or friendship, but Christ is
always the one who gives us the Infinite through this
broken mirror of love or friendship. Human love which
reveals God to us is not necessarily the one we are living
but it is the one we are not living and which leaves in
us an emptiness, a void, because the place has already
been taken by God. Instead of playing this love with a

5. Translated from *Autobiographie*, ch. 8, p. 56.

41

creature, we play it with God to gain time. It is in this discovery of the infinite Love of God that we must seek the unique motivation of consecrated virginity and, especially not, in our poor desire to love God above everything.

When a man is seized by the infinite love of God, he also needs to take refuge in humility and the childhood spirit. He understands that it is awesome to yearn for the fire of the burning Bush and he learns to seek the cooling shade. There he discovers the humility of the Blessed Virgin, the secret of meekness, of poverty and of the childhood spirit. If the first conversion was to discover the infinite Love of God, the second conversion will be to go through the narrow door of humility, for it is dangerous to let oneself be touched by the fire of the burning Bush if one is not clothed in a fireproof garment. To enter into God, we must carry within our-selves — allow me the expression — "a refrigeration circuit" of meekness, of humility, of security and also of delight. Having wished for the fire of God, we develop a thirst for the living waters. Then is the time when we aspire to penetrate into the deep silence of Mary, a silence made especially of meekness and humility.

The second conversion in spiritual life is always marked by the discovery of Mary and of the Church who gives orders for security. It is then a great grace to hunger and thirst for the silence of the Blessed Virgin which gives us this security more than does the thirst for fire. I have often asked myself why the Blessed Virgin has so little place in the life of many Christians; it is simply because they have not discovered the fire of love of the burning Bush which dwells in Jesus Christ. We cannot speak of the Blessed Virgin to someone who does not thirst for Christ, otherwise this becomes insipid, a refrigeration unit without fire... that is what the Blessed Virgin means to many Christians!

2. Rejoice, o Mary

Thus Mary discovers and understands, at the word of the angel, that God loves her with an infinite love which numbers each of her hair and watches over each moment of her life. Not that she began to be loved by God at that moment: it was always like this. But then, she has understood it from experience and that shows up in her conscious prayer. The salutation which the angel addresses to her is not a trivial greeting, it is the declaration of the Good News of salvation which fills her heart with joy (Lk 1:14). In order to understand the prayer of Mary, we must go down to the sources of this joy. For her, as for Christ, we must exult with joy in the Holy Spirit to praise the Father (Lk 10:21 and 1:47). Here again, we must pray to understand and to "feel" that this joy is the very joy of God, not only a human joy and happiness such as we may experience in the best moments of our life, but the joy of God, the one that is refracted in the heart of Christ when he speaks of his joy (Jn 16:22) and of his peace (Jn 14:27). We would know nothing of this joy if the only Son who is in the Father's bosom had not revealed it to us.

One must go yet further in the exploration of this joy felt by Jesus and experienced by Mary at the Annunciation. Jesus speaks of it on two occasions in the parables about Mercy: "I tell you, there will be more rejoicing in heaven over one repentant sinner than over ninety-nine virtuous men who have no need of repentance" (Lk 15:7 and 10). This is the kind of joy that made Mary's heart exult at the Annunciation and in the Magnificat: not the complacency of the man who believes or knows he is just but the joy of the forgiven sinner, a source of joy even for God. In the infinite and merciful love which God has for her, Mary understands infinitely better than all of us how much God has forgiven her even above all the sinners that we are. He preserved her from sin by a grace coming already from the death of his Son (prayer for the feast of the Immaculate Conception). She discovers that to have been preserved from sin is for her the summit of forgiveness.

At the very time when all human beings know that they are sinners because they discover sin in their daily experience, Mary finds that she is without sin. As Father Raguin says, "She awakens to her reality in the utmost depth of her being, an awakening to the depth of her relationship with God... Mary did not come forth from the purity of her original nature... Adam and Eve having yielded to the enticements of the devil did come out of the purity of their original nature. Mary, on the contrary, never comes out of it, she was never seduced neither by the devil, nor by the world, nor by herself. This is what we mean when we proclaim her the "immaculate". The how of this grace escapes us, but we believe in it".[6]

I believe that Mary truly understood that when she was at the foot of the Cross with Saint John and Mary Magdalen. The latter was weeping because the cruelty of her sin had misunderstood and wounded the infinite love of Christ. Mary was weeping at the sight of her Son, the most beautiful of all the children of men and the fruit of her flesh, agonizing in the throes of death and, in a certain manner, she was dying with him. In his hymn of the Virgin at the foot of the Cross, Romanos the Mélode expressed well this suffering of the Mother of God. Her words and her feelings are similar to ours. How can we manage to understand and express more tender and more grief-stricken feelings and, for all that, have a concept of them and express them in a supreme peace, a purity of which we have no experience, and blend them to the most certain intuitions of divine realities? In turns, the poet makes Mary and Jesus speak:

---

6. Translated from *Le Livre de Marie*, Suppl. to « Vie Chrétienne », n. 259, pp. 6-7.

Come everyone, let us celebrate him,
He who for us was crucified.
On the gallows, Mary saw him bound:
"You well can, she told him,
Be crucified and suffer:
You nevertheless remain
My Son and my God."

Thus it was that Mary, heavy with grief,
Crushed with pain, groaned and wept.
Then her Son, turning towards her, said this:
"Mother, why do you weep?
Why like the other women
Are you so distracted with grief?
How can Adam be saved
Unless I suffer, unless I die?
How will they be called to life,
Those who are withheld in hell,
If of the tomb I do not make my home?
And this is why, you know, I am nailed to the cross,
And that I die.
Why then are you weeping, Mother?
Rather say in your tears:
It is from love that he dies,
My Son and my God.

Then banish, Mother, banish this grief;
It is not right that you lament,
You who were named "Full of grace".
That name, do not tarnish its honor, with your sighs,
Do not like the foolish, O Virgin most wise!
You dwell in the center of my abode;
Do not, as if you were without,
Allow your soul to collapse.
Those in your house,
Like your servants, call them;
They will all rush to You, O Holy One,

As soon as you ask:
Where is he, my Son and my God?"[7]

But Mary was also weeping out of gratitude, for she understood from what abysmal depths she had been drawn when the Father had loved her to the point of preserving her from sin. Thérèse of Lisieux would say: "God has forgiven me much more than he did for sinners..., since he preserved me," which is the ultimate of healing. We must often linger on this suffering of Christ and of Mary on Calvary, for sin has so obscured our sight and hardened our heart that we have become unable to understand this suffering due to the coarseness of our nature.

It becomes clear to us then why Mary bathed in the peace and joy of the Holy Spirit, beyond suffering. The greater the joy of God in her heart, the more this joy was restrained and oppressed, not by her sins, but by the cruelty of our own and those of the world: this is what our brothers of the East term "the sorrowful joy" of Easter. Mary suffered all the more as she rejoiced in being loved and protected by God. Those who experience that are crucified by joy and glorified by the Cross.

Saints suffer and die of joy or, as people said in the days of Thérèse of Lisieux, "they die of love". Joy is bound in their heart by sin in the same way that the torrents of merciful Love are confined in the heart of the Blessed Trinity. That is why saints offer themselves to this Love in order that they and, through them, the world may be invaded by it. We can understand then that the joy of God may coexist in the heart of man along with great suffering. It is the "suffering" of God in face of the hardening of man's heart. A friend was telling me one day: "We are cruel because we weep for ourselves while

7. Translated from *Les plus beaux textes de la Vierge Marie*, presented by Father Régamey, La Colombe ed., 1942, pp. 74 and 76 st. I, V, VI.

God weeps for our sin", Origen expressed that in a magnificent way: "God, he says, suffered a passion of love".[8]

3. The joy of trust

One must go as far as that to understand the "Rejoice" of Mary at the Annunciation and the very nature of her profound joy whose root is the Love of Mercy. All those who practise the Jesus prayer experience the joy of being sinners and yet being loved by God to that degree. Joy is perhaps the only sign showing that we can become involved in this type of prayer; otherwise we remain centered on ourselves as sinners. In prayer, we must not be afraid to ask God to make us experience this joy of Mary by dropping in our heart "a few drops" of this happiness of heaven. We must not only believe in this truth, but seek to know it by a direct experience, for that is one of the realities which can best introduce us to the contemplative prayer of union.

This is the joy experienced by the Father of the prodigal son when he sees his son return and embraces him in his arms. Teresa of Avila says the following about this prayer: "That Father greets us like the prodigal son, he consoles us in our trials and he must nourish us for he is forcibly kinder than all the fathers here on earth".[9] That look of tenderness, Teresa says again, stirs in us a movement of surrender into the arms of the Father: "Apply yourselves to become such that you may be worthy of rejoicing with him and of throwing yourselves in his arms".[10] This attentive look also provokes

8. Translated from *Homélie sur Ezéchiel*, quoted by Henri de Lubac in *Histoire et Esprit. L'intelligence de l'Écriture par Origène*, Aubier, 1950, p. 241.

9. Translated from *Chemin de la perfection*, ch. 27, *Œuvres complètes*, p. 456.

10. Translated from *Chemin de la perfection*, ch. 27, p. 458.

in us a feeling of trust in the infinite love of the Father.

Mary's joy is also the fruit of her trust in the Father. She knows in whom she has placed her faith (2 Tm 1:10). The Lord is with her and will never deceive her: "Though I pass through a valley of darkness, I fear no harm for you are with me" (Ps 23:4). These words of the angel, "The Lord is with you" (Lk 1:28) must be understood in their strong sense. The Lord not only journeys beside her, but he makes of her his own abode: "The Holy Spirit will come upon you and the power of the Most High will cover you with its shadow" (Lk 1:35). She takes her place between the Father and the Son who has taken flesh within her and, in the power of the Spirit, she participates in the triune embrace. She takes part in a mysterious way in the embrace of love which the Father gives to his Son and which is the Holy Spirit. This is why her joy is the fruit of the triune love present and living in her.

Was Mary aware of this joy which permanently dwelt in her? We cannot have any doubts about that when we hear the hymn of the Magnificat breaking forth from her lips at the Visitation. The Word of God is always effective and operates what it declares to do in the heart of the one who receives it. Thus, when the angel invites Mary to rejoice at the declaration of the Good News, he awakens her heart and stirs in her a prayer of praise and thanksgiving: "My soul proclaims the greatness of the Lord and my spirit exults in God my savior because he has looked upon his lowly handmaid" (Lk 1:46-48). The effect of God's word is to provoke this prayer of praise in the heart of Mary. Her prayer is truly a cry of joy for God, her Savior: "Shout for joy to honor God our strength" (Ps 81:1). It is not too bold to think that Mary lived in an atmosphere of prayer made of praise and thanksgiving since she was totally surrendered into the hands of God.

But we must well understand that this state of prayer blended itself, as a habit, with a state of great peace and profound silence. Mary's joy was all the less external for being purer. She led her existence quietly, in service to others, always peaceful and in joy. We have already said so: Mary was a simple woman who did not express her experience. The joy of God is as far beyond our thinking as God himself. What Mary experienced was therefore beyond our mind and our senses. Thus her prayer of praise merged with silence within her: "For you, O God, even silence is praise".

The same goes for our prayer. How many times do we complain that we feel nothing and that our prayer is dry and austere! Some days, we really experience the presence of God and of his love in us; happiness dwells in the depth of our heart and echoes in the powers of our senses; this joy is felt and experienced. As Nicolas of Flue says: "We go to prayer as to a dance" and we are overjoyed by God. But on other days, "we go there as to a battle", for the joy of God does not resound in our faculties anymore. This is what we call unfelt joy, so deep is it that it is blended with silence. It is then truly that we "touch" God, for we cannot say anything more about him. As long as we can speak God or experience him in some way, it is dangerous, for we still risk being in the center of the picture, while at the moment all experience of the senses disappears, we live uniquely of faith and, in a certain way, God merges himself with this silence.

God's presence in us cannot be identified with any other experience of God we may have and we cannot give it any name: it puts us at peace without our knowing it. Now is the time to assert with Saint John of the Cross that faith is the surest means, the best adapted device to touch God and to meet him. The way in which we react to this weaning will be decisive for our life of prayer. When the "felt joy" does not irrigate our heart anymore to spring again in our intelligence, then is the time to lean on the "unfelt joy", that is, on pure and naked faith, which is also pure joy since it is expressed in silence.

Here is another danger we must avoid, that is,

asserting that the dryer and the more austere our prayer is, the better it is! Let us say that as a rule dryness is not a normal condition and that, if it is prolonged, we must search for the causes which do not necessarily come from God; they can also stem from a degeneration of our spiritual affection which is unable to let itself be moved and shaken. In prayer, we must ask for the "spiritual gifts" which make us taste God and appreciate his presence at the very level of our spiritual senses. Insofar as we can see, to experience a void, an emptiness or a desire is already a sign that the Spirit has left some traces in us since we experience a nostalgia for him. We would not suffer from the absence of God if we had not tasted his presence one day or another. As is expressed in a hymn: "In the measure of your immeasurable immensity, we miss you, Lord. Your place remains marked in us like a great void, a wound". This is where we find again the cry of the psalmist's prayer and of all God seekers: "Where are you, my God? I seek you at dawn, my soul thirsts for you" (Ps 63:2).

There we find Mary again. Like her, we know that God casts a look of tenderness on us, even though this look is veiled in a discreet silence. We greet this look in faith: it awakens in our heart an ardent desire to give our love to God in return for his love. It is time to go into contemplative prayer with the one purpose of expressing our love to the Father whatever may be the feelings we experience in ourselves, to be solely the joy of God, to "please" him, as Thérèse of Lisieux would say, she who spent almost seven years dozing during most of her prayers of meditation and thanksgiving. This arid and dry prayer, especially if it is painstaking, develops in us what the Fathers called an "affectus fidei", a love in faith which urges us to bind ourselves to God alone and to pray him for his own sake.

Such a love is confirmed in our life of relationships with others, for it urges us to love our brothers gratuitously and for their own sake, whatever may be the feelings of friendship we may have for them or they for us. It is in this free love for God lived in prayer and also in the love for our brothers that we really experience grace and that we become perfect like our heavenly Father: "But I say this to you: love your enemies and pray for those who persecute you; in this way you will be sons of your Father in heaven, for he causes his sun to rise on bad men as well as good, and his rain to fall on honest and dishonest men alike. For if you love those who love you, what right have you to claim any reward? Even the tax collectors do as much, do they not? And if you greet only your brothers, are you doing anything exceptional? Even the pagans do as much, do they not? You must therefore be perfect just as your heavenly Father is perfect" (Mt 5:44-47).

4. Mary poses a question to God

It is not a matter here of making an exhaustive commentary on the account of the Annunciation — this concerns especially the exegetes — but to approach the mystery of Mary's answer to the Lord and, therefore, to contemplate her prayer that it may become "a norm" for ours. The angel first reassures her by saying: "The Lord is with you" (Lk 1:28), that is, "he takes you to his service to do whatever he wishes with you". This expression often recurs in accounts concerning vocations (Ex 3:12; Jg 6:12; Jr 1: 8 and 19; 15:20; cf. Gn 26:24; 28:15). Every time God encounters a man to entrust him with a mission, he wants to reassure him in the strongest sense of the word for he knows that his presence brings about a feeling of dread and fear in the heart of man. In the same way, when Jesus sends forth his apostles, he promises them the Comfort of the Spirit who will defend and sustain them in their tribulations.

A few verses later, we see that the angel again says to Mary: "Mary, do not be afraid; you have won God's favor" (Lk 1:30). Each time God "telephones" the earth and before uttering any word, he gives an advice: "Do not be afraid". As soon as God approaches man, the latter is frightened; we could define a saint as someone who is not afraid of God anymore, for he has placed all his trust in him. Here it is not only a matter of a psychological fear, nor of a sentimental or emotional problem, but of the sense of the sacred. When man finds himself face to face with God, he becomes unsteady and discovers with dread that he is a sinner (cf. Is 5:7 and Peter's reaction after the miraculous fishing trip: "Leave me, Lord for I am a sinful man" Lk 5:8). We shall come back to this on the subject of the "God-fearing" of the Magnificat.

What the words of the angel want to stir in Mary's heart is a feeling of trust in God and a move to surrender herself in his hands. We find here again all the pedagogy of Jesus in the gospel: why worry and be afraid since the Father sees our needs and provides us with food and clothing? (cf. Lk 12: 22-32). This is a discreet invitation to live in the present moment, the only spiritual "place", the only point of contact where the sphere of God meets that of man: "So do not worry about tomorrow: tomorrow will take care of itself. Each day has enough trouble of its own" (Mt 6:34).

It is in this atmosphere of trust that we must greet the question which Mary asks God: "But how can this come about, since I am a virgin?" (Lk 1:34). We have there a clue for our prayer: when we seek to know the will of God, can we question him and in what atmosphere must we do it? It is not a matter here of dwelling on the content of the question asked by the Blessed Virgin which may mean that she does not have any marital relations with Joseph to whom she is promised in marriage, but that it can also mean she has taken the decision to remain a virgin within marriage. We should reread here the commentaries by Augustine and Cajetan on this subject.

For the time being, we shall remain on the problematic question, that is, on the manner of asking the question to suit our own behavior. Mary's attitude will direct us to the answer. What is given importance here is Mary's intelligence, her wish to know the will of God: she seeks to know his plans for her. The angel will greet her question with kindness for it is legitimate and of worth to God. Her interrogation is good while that of Zechariah, stemming from his lack of faith — as we shall see later — remains without an answer; moreover, God offers her a goal of non-receiving. Let us keep in mind for the present that Mary's question proceeds from her intensity of faith.

We can ask God all the questions we wish and even challenge him as long as we do it in a certain harmony whose dominant note is trust and love, for the tone of objection is not that of a humble request. Job questions God and Jesus, on the Cross, asks his Father why he has abandoned him but, in short, both of them surrender themselves into the hands of God. The "theologians" of Job are the ones who spoke ill of God, since they sought to explain everything; God invites them to go and find his servant Job so he may intercede on their behalf. Similarly, Jesus prays on the Cross for the executioners who put his faith to the test and crucify him. God prefers those who challenge him through love to those who keep silent through a sense of resignation.

Indeed, there are ways and ways of posing a question to God. There are those who subject God to an "interrogation" and who summon him to answer their questions. They put up objections because they do not understand. That prevents God from speaking. God needed thousands of years before he could "say" himself. The ungoldly are the ones who discuss and require God to render accounts: "Come and let us discuss"... In a certain way, to discuss with God is already to treat him as an equal, to refuse to be on one's knees before him and to wrangle with him. God does not answer as Jesus does not answer when the Pharisees want to put him to the test by asking malicious questions.

At the other end of the scale, there are those who pose a question to God in an ardent "interrogation of love", as the Blessed Virgin did. They do not understand what is happening to them, like Jesus on the Cross and Job on his pile of manure, but they place their trust in God for they know in whom they have put their faith. They are, as it were, hanging on the lips of God and they beg him to kindly tell them a word of light and comfort. They ask God to open wider his heart to them. They have the boldness of Abraham who questions the Lord about the just of Sodom and Gomorrah. Sooner or later, God always answers them even if he does so in an enigmatic way, for he loves their questioning. To Job, God asks: "Do you know how I make a flower?" To Jesus, the Father answers by giving him the strength to persevere to the end and to surrender himself into his hands. Finally, he gives him a magnificent answer by raising him from the dead. Everything is in knowing how to speak to God with the humility of Samuel: "Speak, Lord, your servant is listening!"

When we have posed a question to God, we must also question the Church, for she is our Mother: she has received the Holy Spirit and she is, with the Blessed Virgin, the perfect listener to the Word of God. Since the Blessed Virgin is invisible, we must address ourselves to the Church, for, we can say, she is the "geographical" place where we find the answer to our questions. The Holy Spirit speaks within and sends us back to the Church which is his voice speaking in the open. This is to say that we cannot be content with an inner response; it must be authenticated by a word from above and which resounds in the Church. This is the role of the spiritual father.

5. The Holy Spirit will come upon you

Mary asks God for a sign, she will receive two of them: "The angel answered her: 'The Holy Spirit will come upon you and the power of the Most High will cover you with its shadow. And so the child will be holy and will be called Son of God" (Lk 1:35). For the moment, the first sign is hidden and interior. The second sign, an outer one, is Elizabeth's fecundity, she who was called barren (Lk 1:36). Mary receives such an answer because of her faith in God, while Zechariah does not believe and he becomes dumb.

Thus begins what we might term as Mary's education. God speaks to her in the depth of her heart in a mysterious manner, through the acting presence of his Holy Spirit, but he also communicates with her to reveal his plans through the people around her or whom she meets. Thus Elizabeth will reveal to her that she is blessed among women and that her child will also be blessed. It is from this meeting with her cousin that the prayer of the Magnificat will spring forth. This is God's pedagogy. He does not always inspire us what we must do in an extraordinary manner, in such a way that we could say: "God has told me, God has inspired me", but after having spoken to us in our heart, he confirms externally his plan for us through the instrumentality of others and through events. That also is "to meditate in one's heart".

Here is not the place to speak about the virginal motherhood of Mary who does not expect her fulfilment as a woman from a mortal man to whom she would give herself, but who receives her fecundity from the Holy Spirit. He is the one who makes of Mary's virginity a sign of new times and proclaims the espousal of God with humankind in the Church (Is 54:5). We shall rather examine the way in which Mary takes her place before God in the worship and obedience of faith, asking him to kindly enlighten her as to the direction of her life.

In other words, we ask ourselves how Mary questions

God, with love and respect. As the little Anna in "Mister God"[11] understood so well, it is not the answer that is difficult to find, it is the right questions; for the answer is immediate when we have found and asked the right question. That is why it is very difficult to ask a true question in truth; for most of the time, we lack silence and availability to allow God a space of freedom where he can answer us. We ask a two-dimensional question and the answer we receive is naturally two-dimensional. This is a touchy point in our prayer and our relationship with God for our life depends on it. If someone manages to ask the right question — which supposes the extinction of questions of no interest which are stirring within us, in other words, the ascesis of silence — then the answer comes right away; it is dazzling and liberating. The difficulty lies in asking the right question.

Let us ponder for example on what we call the "problems" of life, problems touching upon spiritual life, surely! I am thinking here of the many conflicts which come up at the dividing line between psychology and spiritual life, or of other tensions we all know. Then we ask God the following question: "How will that be, since there is this or that?"

We must know that these problems have no solution at the level at which we ask them. There is the light of the Spirit and the darkness of sin, and we must let the enlightening power of the Holy Spirit touch the depths of our being to heal them. The Holy Spirit comes upon us and covers us with his shadow: he gives birth in our heart to the new man who is free of all obstacles and restraints, even psychological and social.

When Mary asks her question, the angel answers her very simply: "The Holy Spirit will come upon you..." There is nothing superfluous in this answer, nor any psychological explanation, but the simple declaration made to Mary on behalf of God of what will be accom-

---

11. Fynn, *Anna and Mister God*, Seuil, 1976.

plished in her. In the innermost depth of herself, Mary has had the experience that she is loved of God; all is simple. She will conceive in an extraordinary manner but through a particular action of God. On the part of God, it is the expression of the power of his Spirit which by-passes all our logical arguments. On the part of Mary, it is the acceptance and the total availability in the simplicity of a faith that baffles.

It is the same for us. The Holy Spirit has this in particular: he is beyond our reach; we can neither imagine him, nor understand him and still less represent him to ourselves: "He reaches the depths of everything, even the depths of God. After all, who knows the depths of man if not the spirit of man within him? In the same way no one knows the depths of God except the Spirit of God" (1 Co 2:10-11). But at the same time, he is the one who is the most intimate with us; he is "the blessed light which fills the heart of the faithful to its inmost depths"[12]; without our knowing it, he touches our se-cret wounds to heal them, bends our stubbornness by his gentleness and straightens what is devious in us, says again the same sequence. He especially makes us understand the gifts which God gives us, first the great gift of prayer: "As for us, we have not received the spirit of the world but the Spirit that comes from God, in order that we may know the gifts he has given us" (1 Co 2:12).

The Spirit always urges us to find our roots again and to assume the real in our life, for it is there that he can act at the heart of our existence in the throes of birth: "For we know that up to the present time all of creation groans with pain, like the pain of childbirth. But it is not just creation alone which groans; we, who have the Spirit as the first of God's gifts, also groan within ourselves, as we wait for God to make us his sons and set our whole being free" (Rm 8:22-23). The breath of the Spirit makes the gentle dew fall on the hardened soil of our heart and

12. Translated from the sequence *Veni, Sancte Spiritus.*

of our body, and the two hands of the Father, the Son and the Spirit (the expression is from Saint Irenaeus), mould us again into the shape of the new man created in the image and likeness of the God-Father.

In this sense, he does not destroy our nature, but he rebuilds it more marvellous yet, as is expressed in the collect of the feast of Christmas. To refashion us as we were would attest to a "lack of imagination" on the part of God. He takes us again in the depths of our humanity to bring it to its fulfilment in perfection. Man deified by the Spirit remains fully man with all his powers of lucidity, activity and tenderness, but he is totally transformed by the uncreated light and the fire of the triune love, as Mary preserved her original nature.

Basically, our questions have no answers. It suffices to allow the light of the Spirit to enlighten our darkness and to kill the impure root which nourishes our problems. This is the root which stirs and feeds our anxiety. That is why Christ rarely answers the questions we ask him. On the contrary, he always gives another answer: he promises to send forth the Spirit which transforms everything. Similarly for us: when we are blocked in a dead end, we pray and beg for light and deliverance. Apparently, God stays silent at the level where we were expecting the answer and, one fine day, the problem ceases to torment us without our knowing why, and we are at peace.

To conclude, I would simply like to explain how things really go on when the question remains but our problems do not bother us anymore. Often the one who is confronted by such difficulties which upset his life at the human as well as at the spiritual levels directs himself into paths without any outlets. He sets about reflecting on problems in order to evaluate them, study their causes and find solutions if possible. Without being aware of it, he escapes from his real life, flies into an imaginary world and comes out of the difficulty to look at it from the outside. The true attitude is much simpler:

it consists in "sitting" in the difficulty without denying it, but accepting to live it from within.

And this is where prayer intervenes, because prayer, the encounter with Christ and the supplication to the Holy Spirit are always a return to reality. But it is not a matter of just any prayer, it is a matter of supplication as Christ teaches us in the gospel: "Ask and you shall receive" (Lk 11:9). I would like to quote here the example of someone who received an interior message in prayer. I do not claim that these words came from the Spirit, for God often speaks to us in a mediate manner and we translate what he says in our language and in our way of thinking. But this man told me that he had received this word: "I will heal you through prayer and only through prayer". Undoubtedly, God made him understand that prayer was the only means of obtaining his healing.

He therefore set about to implore without giving so much as a form or a precise purpose to his prayer; he simply wanted to pray to answer the words he had heard and to be healed as the Lord wanted it. This prayer of supplication lasted for years; it was supported by the prayer of the Church and of his brothers whom he had asked to pray with him. And one day, without his knowing neither why nor how, he noticed a beginning of healing. The psychological handicap remained but the wounds of his memory gradually disappeared to give room, in the area of his conscience, to another actual experience uniquely made through prayer.

Indeed, when the Holy Spirit heals someone, he deeply respects the make-up of his nature and of his freedom, in such a way that the psychological wound remains, but the joy and the power of prayer have so flooded the heart of the man that he is no more there where suffering is. Saint Augustine speaks on this subject about "delectatio victrix", that is about a joy so strong that it easily overcomes all temptations. Aeschylus had already said: "Whatever is divine is easy".

The one who has found the precious pearl of prayer is entranced with joy.

Teresa of Avila says that in order to understand that, one must have experienced it a little himself. Man is no more in himself, says she, nor in his passion, nor in his suffering; he is completely taken up by prayer, as if he were magnetized and attracted towards God. It is heaven on earth: "Here now, in my opinion, is the immense happiness we taste, among many others, in the Kingdom of heaven. The soul takes no more heed of the things of the earth: it finds rest and glory within itself; it rejoices in everyone's joy, it possesses a perpetual peace; it experiences satisfaction as it sees that all creatures bless and praise the Lord and that his Name is hallowed while no one offends him".[13] "That happiness, adds Teresa, rebounds into the body which experiences a profound delight, and into the soul with as great a happiness".[14]

---

13. Translated from *Le Chemin de la perfection*, ch. 30, *Œuvres complètes*, p. 468.

14. Translated from *Le Chemin de la perfection*, ch. 31, p. 470.

Chapter III

PRAYING WITH MARY
AT THE ANNUNCIATION

II. THE PRAYER OF MARY TO GOD

We are undertaking now the last part of the account of the Annunciation (Lk 1: 36-38), the one where Mary gives her answer to God's proposition delivered by the angel Gabriel (Gabriel = strength of God). Until then, she has listened to the Word of the Lord, scrutinizing it in her heart and questioning Gabriel in a thoughtful attempt to understand it. In the first part of the account (vv 26-35), it is especially a question of God's wonders for the Blessed Virgin. God shows her all he has done for her, all he intends to accomplish yet and he asks her the permission to take flesh in her. It is as if God thrice Holy was addressing a prayer to Mary saying to her: "Will you say yes to the incarnation of my Son?" God is "timid", he does not impose himself for he knows that "to will" always implies a certain "power"; and since he is a helpless God, he prefers to state his wish in the fear and hope of being accepted.

Apparently, the words of the Blessed Virgin at the Annunciation do not sound like a prayer as they do in the Magnificat, but if we examine them closely, they set in motion, in a strong sense, Mary's "dynamism of faith", her openness to the Word of God and her unlimited adherence to God's proposition. This amounts to saying that she discovers her name at the same time as her vocation and mission. In Mary, one cannot dissociate prayer from mission: they are imbricated one in the other. For her prayer, formulated in a few words, expresses the deep movement of her being; her total adherence to the Father's will, all along her existence, is already a prayer without her needing to accumulate words. She realizes fully the words of her Son: "None of those who cry out, 'Lord, Lord' will enter the kingdom of heaven, but only the one who does the will of my Father in heaven" (Mt 7:21).

Jesus was the first to live this osmosis between his prayer and his consecration to the Father. He lives in an active "laissez-faire" of the Father's will in order that the Name of the Father may be hallowed and that his kingdom may come on earth as it is in heaven. By consecrating himself to the good will of the Father, he is, in the strictest sense of the words, this "worshipper in spirit and in truth that the Father seeks" (Jn 4:23). His submissive existence abandoned in the Holy Spirit to the eternal will of the Father, is thus the purest and most silent expression of his prayer.

1. Annunciation. Agony. Resurrection

It is both significant and interesting to establish this parallel between the prayer of Jesus and that of Mary; we will come back to it when we examine the mystery of Jesus' prayer in his relationship with the Father. For the moment, we limit ourselves to asserting the fact especially in order to shed light on what we will say about Mary's prayer. In a very beautiful typewritten article, the exegete M. F. Lacan, O.S.B., shows that "the structure of the Rosary is a contemplation of Jesus, center of the events in which he reveals himself as he is saving us; he is prayer brought forth by these events and expressing itself in words whose purpose is to denote to whom we are speaking and to direct us towards his presence". From this fact, there is a bond which links the events in Jesus' life to those of Mary's. After the five joyous mysteries follow the five sorrowful mysteries, then the five glorious mysteries. But if we place the three series in parallel, we notice that the three mysteries which hold the same place in each of the series have a particular relationship among them: they enlighten and complete one another. There is, therefore, an advantage in bringing them together for prayer.

To convince ourselves of this, it would suffice to bring together the Annunciation, the Agony and the Resurrection. Let us simply examine how the first joyous mystery is clarified and finds its ultimate answer in the first glorious mystery. At the Annunciation, Mary is the first to receive, in joy, the message of the Good News of the Incarnation and she greets it by giving it her faith. At the Resurrection, she sees Jesus in Glory and understands the mystery of his redemptive suffering for the salvation of Adam and Eve. There again, she is the model of our faith, she who never doubted the word telling her of the birth of God within her and of the kingdom without end of Jesus. Jesus is the source of this faith justifying us in the mystery of his Resurrection which fulfils the reality of his Name: "God saves".

At the matins of Good Friday, when they are reading the twelve pericopes of the Gospel of the Passion, our orthodox brothers sing a hymn by Romanos the Mélode which stresses well this bond between the Annunciation and the Resurrection. It comes after the reading from John 19:35. This poem introduces us into the sufferings of Christ to make us hear his answer. It takes the boldness of the Fathers to put on Christ and Mary's lips words which are not in the Scriptures and to establish a parallel between these two events: "Since you were the first to rejoice at the Annunciation, you will be the first to rejoice at the Resurrection." Romanos makes the Blessed Virgin say the following words:

"May I not fear for myself
Of never seeing you again?
For I greatly dread that once you are in the tomb
You will not return, my Child...

At those words, the one who knows all things,
Even before they ever existed, replied to Mary:
"Set your mind at ease, O Mother: after I come out of the tomb,
You shall be the first to see me;
For I shall come back to show you
from what an abyss of darkness
Adam will have been freed,
And how many sweats it will have cost me."[1]

The parallelism between the mystery of the Annunciation and that of the Agony is even clearer. To convince ourselves of this, we just have to place in parallel the two series of words of these mysteries:

1. "Nothing is impossible to God. (Lk 1:37)   "Abba (Father)! Everything is possible for you." (Mk 14:36)

2. "Let it be done to me as you have said" (Lk 1:38)   "Yet not what I want, but what you want." (Mk 14:36)

Between the prayer of Jesus and that of Mary, the relationship is clear. If we did not fear to appear pedantic, we could say that, in the two cases, we are dealing with a dialectical prayer which sets in motion

---

1. Translated from *Hymne de Marie à la Croix*, in *Hymnes* by Romanos the Mélode, in the translation by J. Grosdidier de Matons, Vol. 4, S.C.n. 128, Cerf, 1967.

two movements, apparently contradictory: on the one hand, a prayer of trusting supplication which is sure to obtain everything, for nothing is impossible to God; on the other hand, a similar prayer of faith, all relaxed, surrendered and placed in the hands of the Father: a cry of supplication and a cry of surrender. We are touching here the paradox of faith and prayer at its ultimate peak: we pray with trust and perseverance as if we were expecting everything from God and, at the same time, we surrender ourselves unconditionally to the Father's will.

No Christian prayer will relate so closely these two movements which we could compare to the two stages of breathing. On the one hand, the aspiration could be the wish we express to God in utter assurance that we will be answered. On the other hand, the expiration or the giving out of the breath is that we hand ourselves over to God. The adoration of the Father in the Holy Spirit cannot be dissociated from the always renewed "yes" to the accepted mission. The two movements are linked in a eucharistic attitude where Jesus and, after him, Mary and the believers allow themselves in the will of the Father to be yielded over to the world in thanksgiving.

When Saint John speaks of Mary in his gospel, he never names her in any other way but as the "mother of Jesus", a title which reminds us that the Father wants to give us Jesus through her. Similarly, if we wish to return to the Father in prayer, we must unite ourselves to the prayer of Jesus, the only Mediator; but the prayer to Jesus will also be given to us through the prayer to Mary, granted the completely privileged bond she has with him. We must never lose sight of that when we speak of the prayer of Mary, and especially when we pray the Rosary. This prayer makes us contemplate the life of Jesus with the eyes and heart of Mary, "Mother of Jesus", to make us one with him in his prayer to the Father. That is what "praying with Mary" means.

2. "Blessed is she who believed" (Lk 1:45)

Let us come back now to the last part of the account of the Annunciation concerning Mary's answer, what we have currently called her "Fiat". We prefer using Saint Paul's expression in the epistle to the Romans: "obedience in faith" (Rm 1:6 and 16:26). This is the very obedience of Mary and, in a broader sense, her trust which is referred to here.

Let us ask ourselves first: "Why did God love the Blessed Virgin?" There is no hesitation in the answer: it is surely not because of the numerous gifts he has given her. He filled her with grace in her Immaculate Conception, he made her the Mother of his Son and of men, not to mention the title which was given her at the end of Vatican Council II: "Mother of the Church", and raised her in a glorious Assumption in heaven. All these gifts are gratuitous and none of them is at the root of the "charm" which she exercised on the heart of God. He filled her with grace because he loved her, and not the opposite. We have seen this about the Immaculate Conception which is a fruit of this love and not its explanation.

One antiphon to the Magnificat for the feasts of the Common of the Blessed Virgin says: "I pleased the Most High because I was so lowly." The Blessed Virgin's humility attracted the eyes of the Father upon her: "He has looked upon his lowly handmaid" (Lk 1:48). She received everything from the Father without any merit on her part, for the gifts of God, fruits of his love, are gratuitous and given without any regret. But that does not mean that this love is arbitrary: in Mary, a certain countenance pleased the Most High. That countenance is, of course, that of humility, poverty and meekness. It is in this sense that we may speak of the collaboration of the Blessed Virgin who, totally emptied of herself, offered God a space of freedom so that he might fill it with his blessing.

To humility, we should immediately add its corollary which is faith. This is not the time to show the intrinsic bond between faith and humility: we will come back to this later. But let us say that the one and the other, in a same movement, urge the believer to prefer God and his will to himself. Humility, like faith, is a withdrawal of self before the God thrice Holy and an unconditional adherence to what he expects of us. To believe and to be humble is to accept to be on one's knees and in second place.

Thus Mary knew how "to do so" with God, because she could offer him a heart totally empty and poor, overflowing with trust. It is not so much our virtue, our merits and our efforts which interest God, but our poverty. He gives us everything, even the love with which we love him. In his relationships with men, God especially seeks humble and broken hearts which invoke his holy Name. All the rest poses no problem for God, and he is ready to pour on us all the gifts of his love on the condition that we be humble and poor. Saint Thérèse of Lisieux said that if God had found someone more humble and poorer than the Blessed Virgin, he would have showered yet greater blessings upon that person.

When God addresses the Blessed Virgin, he calls her his "Beloved"; that is her name and her mission. When the believer addresses the Blessed Virgin in prayer, he could call her "She who believed" (Lk 1:45). The heart of Mary is the meeting place of the two excesses: the excess of the Father's Love which turned to her and the excess of trust in him. It is the union of these two excesses which make of Mary the All-Pure and the All-Holy par excellence. She fully makes real the words of Paul about the just who is sanctified through faith: "The life I now live in this body I live in faith: faith in the Son of God who loved me and who sacrificed himself for my sake" (Ga 2:20).

To have a better definition of the quality of Mary's faith, it suffices to compare the two accounts announcing the birth of John the Baptist and that of Jesus. The parallelism is striking; however, one must note that the angel does not greet Zechariah.

Zechariah, *do not be afraid*, your prayer has been heard. Your wife Elizabeth is *to bear you a son and you must name him John.*

He will be your joy and delight and many will rejoice at his birth, for *he will be great* in the sight of the Lord; he must drink no wine, no strong drink. Even from his mother's womb he will be filled with the *Holy Spirit* and he will bring back many of the sons of Israel to the *Lord their God.*

With the spirit and power of Elijah, he will go before him to turn the hearts of fathers towards their children and the disobedient back to the wisdom that the virtuous have, preparing for the Lord a people fit for him.

Mary, *do not be afraid*; you have won God's favor. Listen! You are *to conceive and bear a son, and you must name him Jesus.*

He will be great and called the *SON of the MOST HIGH.*

The Holy Spirit will come upon you... And so the child will be holy and will be called *SON of GOD. The Lord God* will give him the throne of his ancestor David.

He will rule over the House of Jacob for ever and his reign will have no end.

It is clear that Luke wanted to emphasize the transcendent greatness of the Son with respect to the precursor and, meanwhile, their relationship; this is what explains all the dissimilarities and similarities: "He must grow greater, I must grow smaller" (Jn 3:30); and this radical distance breaks out particularly between the two reactions of Zechariah and of Mary. One evades the issue, hesitates to believe the Word of God, while the other gives her full assent. We have already examined the question Mary asks the angel; let us now examine in parallel Zechariah's reaction:

Zechariah:
How can I be sure of this? I am an old man and my wife is getting on in years?

Mary:
How can this come about, since I am a virgin?

Once again, the sequence is identical, the question being followed by the declaration of the difficulty (for Zechariah: old age, for Elizabeth: barrenness, for Mary: virginity). Starting from this identity, the disbelief of Zechariah (representing the stiff-necked people of the Old Covenant) opposes the faith of Mary (representing the new "Daughter of Sion"): "For Zechariah finally demands, as did so many before him, for example, Gedeon with his fleece, a sign which credits and justifies the disturbing words which nevertheless answer his prayer; he wants a reason to believe and to hope, while Mary only waits until the angel tells her how God will act in her very own circumstances. Perhaps people will say that I strain the difference, but let them tell me how to explain the following otherwise: 1) what Elizabeth will declare at the Visitation: "Blessed is she who believed that the promise made to her by the Lord would be fulfilled" (Lk 1:45); 2) what the angel answers to the two questions". [2]

---

2. Translated from M. Corbin, *Vie chrétienne,* Nov. 1980, pp. 14-15.

"I am Gabriel who stand in God's presence and I have been sent to speak to you and to bring you this good news. Listen! You will be silenced and have no power of speech until this has happened, for not having believed my words, which will come true at their appointed time."

"The Holy Spirit will come upon you and the power of the Most High will cover you with its shadow; this is why the child you will bear will be holy and called *SON of GOD*. And behold, your kinswoman Elizabeth has also conceived a son in her old age, and she is now in her sixth month, she who was called barren. *For no word is impossible to God.*"

The difference in tone is obvious: on the one hand, a chiding colored with humor, since God nevertheless gives a sign, Zechariah's temporary dumbness, and on the other hand, a renewal and a deepening which brings about the profession of faith: "Let it be done to me according to thy word." The sign which Zechariah demands seals his lips; the sign which Mary did not request (her cousin's pregnancy) is related to the faith we expect of her.

This is why the angel greets Mary's question with kindness, a fact which shows that it is legitimate and of value to God, while Zechariah's question arises from his lack of faith. Mary truly believed and hoped "against all hope" (Rm 4:18). We can ask ourselves how these two attitudes were motivated: why is Zechariah unbelieving while Mary believes? If it is true that Zechariah and Mary personify the old and the new covenants, that this mutism is what prevents him from answering and going back on his position, that the Annunciation culminates in the Fiat, only one answer seems possible: God waits for and brings forth the "yes" from Mary as the condition for the birth of Jesus, while he brings about the birth of

John the Baptist independently from and in spite of Zechariah's answer.

3. "May it be done to me as you have said" (Lk 1:38)

Such is the Good News hidden in the account of the Annunciation: the divine Word addressed to humankind (summed up in Mary) is the ultimate word of God, because it brings about and begs the consent of its partner. The only effect of the Word is the obedient and believing response at the heart of humanity. We can well see here the role of the answer given by Mary to God's supplication, as we could say; even if this answer is also a gift of the Holy Spirit, there is a freedom in it which can accept or refuse God's proposition.

We then touch the core of Mary's faith. Speaking of faith, we would spontaneously think of a subjection of the intelligence to a revealed truth. Without discarding that aspect of faith, it is better for us to direct ourselves in the line of Saint Paul who speaks of "obedience of faith". Saint Thomas also says that the movement of faith points directly to the person, that is to God and Christ. To credit, to trust, to become betrothed..., so many expressions which shed light on the word and which are of the same family. To believe in the Word of God is to give our trust to God himself while adhering freely to his will.

This allows us to say that faith is the permanent preference given to a light other than our own. The spirit of faith is therefore at opposite poles to stubbornness, for it declares the retreat of our judgment in favor of trust in another. In faith, the important thing is not this or that truth, which we can always take into our possession and use to become heretics, but the unutterable flexibility of adherence. Faith dynamism must be made real at all moments in our heart: we must give up understanding all the steps in order to understand in the measure of a greater light which God will give us. Re-read chapters 11 and 12 of the Letter to the Hebrews where the author praises the faith of Abraham, Isaac, Moses..., you will see that faith opens the doors of the Kingdom.

It is enough to ponder over Abraham's sacrifice where God practically contradicts God. He asks him to sacrifice specifically the fruit of his promise: "It was by faith that Abraham, when put to the test, offered up Isaac. He offered to sacrifice his only son even though the promises had been made to him and he had been told: It is through Isaac that your name will be carried on. He was confident that God had the power even to raise the dead; and so, figuratively speaking, he was given back Isaac from the dead" (Heb 11:17-19). God does not expect heroism from Abraham and still less resignation, but a faith which prompts him to believe that God can bring even a corpse back to life. This faith is so pure and unfathomable that the least suggestion of pride in a situation like this jams the mechanism and makes such an act impossible. Mary's act of faith in the Annunciation fits into the pattern of Abraham's faith. God was promising her a son, and she knew no man. She, therefore, had to proceed against her own evidence and believe that God could make of a virgin woman the mother of his Son.

We have here a law of divine pedagogy used for men. There must be on earth a certain number of men who, in the depths of their heart, allow God to dispose of them. Until then, they conducted their life as a captain guides his ship and, one fine day, they let go the helm into the hands of the pilot who is the Holy Spirit. When a human being receives the grace to do such an act, a conflagration more fantastic than all the neutron bombs is silently brought about. This act opens the locks of heaven in such a way that all the life of God can be engulfed on earth with the merits and the treasures accumulated by Christ, the Blessed Virgin and the saints. God leads the world in order to obtain such an act and all the spiritual pedagogy aims at disposing a man to produce it.

Here we find again the very attitude of Christ which makes him cross the line towards the Passion properly so-called — "not my will" — thus revealing the fundamental law of his existence: "I did not come down from heaven to do my will, but the will of the one who sent me." Similarly, Mary gives up making decisions freely and definitely allows God to dispose of her. It is the "Let it be done to me according to your word" which has created in her a free space so that the seed of God may come to life in her.

To have a better glimpse of the admirable tactfulness of God who treats his creature in a fashion proper to it, one should reread the splendid passage by Hans Urs von Balthasar in the fifth volume of the French translation of *La Gloire et la Croix*:

"In Mary, Israel must personalize as well as surpass itself, while summing up its own identity, to be able to pronounce the perfect yes of the handmaid in the Incarnation; a yes which, made possible by the Incarnation and the Cross of the Son..., becomes at the same time one of the conditions of the Incarnation, realizes the unity of one only flesh, and through that precisely establishes a radical opposition between the Head and the Body, the Lord and the Handmaid, the bridegroom and the bride... There must, somewhere in the name of all humankind, be given *the interiorly unlimited yes* to the supereminent word of God which forever surpasses all understanding, a yes that joins this word to its limit *in an unconditional agreement* and an effort of thought to understand (Lk 2:19 and 51) and follow it, which releases in history a movement without end"[3].

All the assertions of the Church on the "privileges" of Mary rest on this total "yes" to the promise; they mean that her faith includes and patterns our own; they reveal

3. Translated from *La Gloire et la Croix*, vol. V, pp. 83-84.

the mystery of the New Covenant. The Virgin Mary has become the Mother of the Church because she is the Virgin who receives the Father's Word. Theologians tell us that, if her Fiat is normative for the Church which she personifies, and with no other possible way out for salvation, we receive the command and the possibility to do as she did by obeying to the word in faith, to "treasure with care (all these accounts) and to ponder them in our heart" (Lk 2:19), storing them in the innermost part of our being, as the only power capable of renewing us into men and women of aspiration.

If Mary's "yes" can be looked upon as a norm for the Church, we shall have to contemplate often the mystery of her relationship with God and, therefore, of her trust in order to check and purify our own relationship with God. Her mission as the Mother of the Church is to teach us to live in a union of pure faith with God. We are very conscious that we are "men of little faith", deciding on our own what is possible to God and raising barriers against his power. The more we progress in our journey towards God, the more we experience our congenital helplessness to make the life of God grow in us. We are too centered on ourselves and not dependent enough on God. We must make true the maxim of Saint John of the Cross: "Supported and yet without support". Finally, we have to believe that God is God by placing all our trust in him. It is then that we will be able to experience, as Saint Paul did, the power of his Glory in thanksgiving: "Glory be to him whose power, working in us, can do infinitely more than we can ask for or imagine; glory be to him in the Church and in Christ Jesus throughout the ages for ever and ever" (Ep 3:20-21).

4. The trial of faith

When we look rather closely at our life of relationship with God, we are forced to recognize that all is not going as well as we could wish. For example, just to contemplate Mary's "Fiat" at the Annunciation or the prayer of the Magnificat, is enough to make us humbly admit that we have not reached her level of faith: we would like to yield to the will of God, but we are incapable of doing so. As spiritual experts say: "It is within our reach to see it and to desire it, but it is not within our reach to realize it!" One of my friends often tells me on this subject: "It's not in my bag!" We have there a real difficulty and, therefore, our temptation is to fall back on the problems and complications of life. It is not the first time we come across this "problem", if I dare so express myself, since we have already broached this topic of the "problems of life" at the end of the preceding chapter. We, therefore, say to ourselves: "I am unable to yield to God because I lack the will and the generosity to do so, or because of fatigue, of a depression or even because of my environment and the circumstances of my life". One especially must not deny these problems for they exist, but we must not allow ourselves to be trapped by them, for they conceal a yet deeper difficulty which is at the same time a danger.

It is evident there that the danger exists and it does not stem only from the complications and burdens of life. This danger was there first for the angels and for our first parents who did not know all our miseries. It also existed for the Blessed Virgin in the trial of the Annunciation, for Mary was free and she could refuse God's proposition. This was surely the great trial of her life which confirmed her in grace. To the ones and to the others, God proposed something very simple: "See, I set before you today a blessing and a curse: a blessing if you obey Yahweh your God, a curse if you disobey" (Dt 11:26-27). It is as if God were saying: "Either you follow your idea or you follow mine. If you follow mine, you will receive the beatitude through faith and hope." These are the two ways of the psalm: the way of the just and that of the ungoldly. Remember what we said about

75

the faith of Mary described as "a permanent preference given to God's idea". It is at this profound level that one must search for the evil root of all the problems in life. This trial may be overcome just by being humble and remaining so.

That is where we find again the relation between trust and humility. In order to trust God, we must be humble, that is, we must not turn toward ourselves, but we must look solely to God and to what he wishes to do with us. The difficulty of faith is the same as that of humility: it is always a matter of giving preference to God and to his idea rather than to our own. That is why Jesus, in the gospel, blesses the humble and the lowly, for they only are capable of placing their trust in him in an absolute manner, since they have no alternate solution. Those who prefer their own judgment to that of God risk becoming obstinate and, therefore, unable to put their trust in him.

The prophets will describe still more clearly the two ways followed by the two types of men: "Cursed be the man who puts his trust in man, who makes of flesh his support and whose heart strays away from Yahweh... Blessed be the man who puts his trust in Yahweh and for whom Yahweh is his faith" (Jr 13:5-8). The one and only problem of life is to know whether we shall entrust ourselves to God or whether we shall rely on ourselves or on others: whether we trust God or man. One has only to read the gospel to understand that. The only attitude in man which draws exclamations of joy from Christ is that of faith. Often, he asserts that he has never found such faith in Israel (Lk 7:9). The dividing line for Christ does not lie between the sinner and the non-sinner, but between the one who believes and the nonbeliever.

On this subject, all the spiritual experts are unanimous in declaring that faith is the great trial of life, we could say the only struggle which must lead us to victory, that is, the victory of faith. We would like to quote the testimony of Father Libermann, one of the greatest spiritual "directors" of the XIXth century, before he founded the Congregation of the Fathers of the Holy Spirit. He often said: "One of the things which paralyzes souls the most and prevents them from making progress is their lack of trust. It is a point against which the spiritual director will have to struggle as energetically as possible. There are many who seem to lack generosity and who, in fact, especially lack trust, or the generosity they lack is the one which consists in trusting".

We rely then on the generosity which is based on ourselves and not on God. We want to do much for God, especially to be generous, but we do not understand that the first generosity we should have is to place our trust in God. This amounts to saying, and we will see this as we conclude this chapter, that prayer is the bridge which will allow us to make the leap into the impossible. For this reason, we must come back often to this "gift of trust", for we are always tempted to give other things to God.

What interests God and Christ is not the brazen character of our generosity — that is counterfeit money — but the gold of trust. This is what Saint Peter says in his first Epistle: in the eyes of God, "the tested worth of our faith is much more precious than gold, which is corruptible even though it bears testing by fire" (1 P 1:7). This is where he precisely points to the object of our faith: the Christ whom we love without having seen him. In contemplative prayer, we must often come back to these words of Peter: "He (Jesus Christ) whom you love, although you have not seen him, in whom you believe, although you do not now see him; so you rejoice with a great and glorious joy which words cannot express, because you are receiving the salvation of your souls, which is the reward for your faith in him" (1 P 1:8-9).

Faith is this attitude which Jesus asks of those who have already given their adherence to him. This is why he reproaches the apostles and especially Peter to be a "man of little faith" (Mt 14:31). God can give us everything else: love, generosity, virtue, even faith; but faith holds this privilege that not only does God give it to us, but that we also can place our trust in him. When we believe in him, we open up an unlimited credit for him or we sign a blank cheque. This is why the spiritual director, says Father Libermann again, must experience that faith is the first struggle and he must not allow himself to be turned away by other struggles which the "directed one" might confide to him. As long as the "directed one" has not given God a sufficient dose of trust, he must not be allowed to pose other problems, but he must be brought back to the real battle of faith and trust.

5. Walking on the waters

Let us think of Peter in particular, of the one whom Jesus chides for his lack of faith at the time of the walk on the waters (Mt 14:22-23). Peter has posed "a problem" for himself: how can he walk on the water?

He had begun to be afraid towards the end of the night, when Jesus was approaching his disciples by walking himself on the sea in the middle of the storm. Then, Jesus reassures him: "Courage! It is I! Do not be afraid" (v. 27). The operative words of Jesus establish Peter in a profound peace; Jesus repeats to him the little word Peter had already heard when he was casting his nets: "Come" (v. 29). He does not dare believe his eyes and ears too much. Now his faith is confirmed and his love urges him on. He will trust himself to the power which Jesus offers him and he leaps into the water.

What happened then? Peter had begun so well! Undoubtedly, has a little presumption slipped into his initiative? At first, he believed he could walk on the waters, but when the storm rises again, the gospel says only that Peter was afraid. He loses sight of Jesus and turns to himself. By turning his eyes away from Jesus, he has surrendered himself to his own strengths and these soon betray him. Doubt takes over and there is no more trust. There we seize to the quick what faith or rather non-faith is all about: to lean on one's possibilities and to move away from the charm of Jesus' powerful love.

Peter must understand that to walk on the waters when the weather is nice is as extraordinary as when it is stormy. So he imagines, as many of us do, that the problem is to know whether the weather is nice while in reality it is a problem of trust. He was illusioned when the weather was nice for then he was relying on himself rather than on Christ. He has now understood his lack of faith and the storm only brought his disbelief to light. What does he do then? He knows that only a surge of faith and prayer can save him and he cries: "Lord, save me!" (v. 30). Jesus was waiting just for that: an anguish and a surge of faith against all hope. Immediately, the real miracle takes place: Jesus takes Peter's hand and, instantly, the wind falls. Peter needed to be saved. Jesus, holding Peter's hand in his own, gently chides him: "Man of little faith, why did you doubt?"

We are no different from Peter. We believe that our good will and our generosity can overcome the storms we have to face. But this is only a beginning; as we progress, our generosity betrays us and all our miseries are revealed. Blessed are we if we accept to take the plunge into these miseries to call on Jesus. But very often, we shield our eyes before the light which unveils the nakedness of our being and we pose to Jesus problems of rainstorms or "no rainstorms", of fatigue or "no fatigue", of the possible or the impossible. We believe everything is going well, in certain conditions. In those moments, we have the illusion of being trustful; but then when nothing works anymore, God dispels our illusions. We discover, thanks to those happenings, that to have faith in Jesus is demanding. These moments of distress are a grace, for we cannot find God without crying out to him from the depth of our wretchedness.

In spiritual life, it is always a moment of grace to discover that our strengths are betraying us, that we have no love and that our generosity is reduced to its simplest expression. Then we admit our little faith and we say like the father of the possessed child: "I believe, Lord! Come to help my lack of faith!" (Mk 9:24). When a man begins to understand that, he does not let himself be trapped by the other problems; he goes through a trying moment as did Peter sinking like a stone, but he is virtually saved. All the wiles of the devil are to make us believe that our difficulties come from this or from that, but not from our lack of trust, especially when all goes well and we rely on ourselves. The only problem then is to forget everything, both the storm which is raging and our strengths which are failing; to turn away from everything, especially from ourselves, in order to focus our attention only on Jesus and to throw ourselves in his love. Then a cry is torn from our heart, a heart-rending cry which goes to the heart of Jesus: "Jesus, save me!" It is then that the master of the impossible can perform the miracle.

How could one not recall here the reflection of a Christian who is confronted with impossible situations in his apostolic life. His words seem to summarize Peter's experience well: "Our Lord always demands of us things of which we are totally incapable, and it is this incapacity a priori that is the basis of our trust, the divine seal of our desire and the promise of God's collaboration."

By what signs can we recognize that? I say that the infallible test is the experience of a certain despair because we do not manage to give God all the trust that he demands of us. If we do not go through this trial, we do not know anything. The man who has not been tempted in his hope knows nothing. There is only one temptation, that of despair; the rest is trivial.

And it is here that we find again the Blessed Virgin whom we never lost sight of, even if we made a detour by Saint Peter. We had to make this detour because there is an abyss between our poor faith and that of Mary, and we must touch the bottom of our distress in order to rebound to the height of Mary. What is comforting when we contemplate the Blessed Virgin is to see that she experienced the darkness of faith as much when Jesus was lost in the Temple as when she witnessed the excruciating death of Jesus on the Cross. But at the very depth of her distress, the Holy Spirit upheld her faith and her hope, and she had the certitude of contemplating the resurrection. Our brothers from the East express that in the Matins of the Passion on Good Friday. After the reading of the eleventh gospel (Jn 19:38-42), they chant this response:

> Today, the Virgin pure, seeing you, Word, hanging on the Cross, bitterly suffered in her heart as a Mother; she implores, grief-stricken, from the depth of her soul. With her face drawn and her hair dishevelled, she strikes her breast and groans: "Alas, divine Child! Alas, Light of the world! Why do you hide yourself from my eyes, Lamb of God?" and the choirs of angels tremble and say "Incomprehensible Lord, glory to you."
>
> At the sight of you hanging on the tree of the Cross, Christ, God Creator of the universe, the one who gave you birth without seed was imploring bitterly: "My Son, where has the beauty of your shape gone? I cannot bear to see you crucified unjustly. But arise soon, that I may see your resurrection from the dead, on the third day!"[4]

Near the Cross, Mary had lost all human anticipation, her hope rested solely on her faith, more precious than

---

4. Translated from orthodox liturgical texts, *Le Triode du Grand Carême*, 8, Paris, 1974, from a translation by Jacques Touraille, pp. 1387-1388.

the gold in a crucible. Like her Son, having placed all her hope in the Father, she held "firm as if she could see the invisible" (Heb 11:27). Similarly, God did not ask Abraham not to love his son or to give him up; he asked him to have faith in spite and against all odds. To reach this point, one must accept to go through moments of human despair in order to break forth in theological hope. Those are moments when "we hope against all hope", says the Letter to the Romans (4:18). Then trust is something unheard-of and totally impossible.

Those who understand that, as does the Blessed Virgin, can begin to build on rock while the others are building on sand. What interests God, like a wise architect, says Paul, is the foundation and that rock is Christ! The rest does not pose any problem for God. What matters to him is to find someone who gives him the substratum of trust. On this, he can build a solid building, that is, an authentic holiness.

That is why we must be very patient and gentle towards those who are tempted against hope; we must especially not discourage them anymore, says Father Libermann. As for the others, we must be firm. As says Father Molinié with humor: for those who suffer from this lack of trust, there is one word which we must never mention to them, it is "courage", because that is precisely what they do not have! It is somewhat as if we said to someone who has no money: "Pay, pay!" We must tell them: "Go to the source where you will receive the bread of the Eucharist and the wine of faith... precisely without paying!" If you are without courage, go to be nourished and consoled. Come and buy for nothing! Basically, before entering into a course of action, we must go to be nursed and especially to nourish ourselves.

6. "Nothing is impossible to God"

To conclude this chapter, I would like to tell you the final, concrete and practical answer to all the difficulties and especially to all the problems of spiritual life which amount to being a trial of faith: one must come out of them only through the prayer of supplication. In other words, the believer must never come out of the prayer of entreaty unless God takes him out to put him in the prayer of praise and thanksgiving. On this subject, Saint Augustine wonders whether one must first invoke God or praise him; he answers with the help of a psalm: "Those who seek Yahweh will praise him" (Ps 21:27). Whoever seeks him will find him: the prayer of invocation precedes praise. He also says that in order to praise God, we must know him and, therefore, invoke him, that is, appeal to him:

"Grant me, Lord, to know and to understand if we must first invoke you or praise you; if we must first know you or invoke you. But who can invoke you without knowing you? The one who ignores you may nevertheless invoke something other than you... Or rather are you not invoked in order to be known?... Those who seek him find him and those who find him will praise him. That I may seek you, Lord, while invoking you, and that I may invoke you while believing in you... It invokes you, Lord, this faith which you have given me... And how shall I invoke my God and my Lord? When I invoke him, I shall call him to come within me".[5]

Thus we cannot take a more useful resolution than that of supplication or invocation. It is the "Jesus prayer" of the Eastern monks: "Jesus, have mercy on me, a sinner." It is the supplication of Peter who is sinking in the waters: "Lord, save me!" (Mt 14:30). It is the cry of the penitent thief: "Jesus, remember me when you

---

5. Translated from *Confessions*, I, 1-2, 5, Labriolle Ed., Paris, 1969, pp. 3-6.

come into your kingdom" (Lk 23:42). We thus remain permanently poor, but a blessed poor who receives everything from God.

To understand that, we must go back to the attitude of the Blessed Virgin at the Annunciation. When Mary accepts the angel's invitation by responding to him with a total and unconditional "yes", she is giving preference to God's idea rather than to her own. She does not understand how she can become a mother since she knows no man, but she receives from the lips of the angel the assurance that nothing is impossible to God (Lk 1:37) since he has made of the barren Elizabeth, the mother of John the Baptist. Basically, to place in God a trust which does not argue is enough for the impossible to become possible. The apparent contradiction between virginity and maternity is transcended in a surge of trust and, therefore, of prayer.

This is exactly the surge of faith in Saint Peter which calls Jesus for help. We must touch the pit of our limitations and, therefore, let ourselves fall to the bottom of our distress in order to climb up again from the depths. This is the dialectics of the ball which strikes the ground and rebounds to the top: the more powerful is the downward pressure, the more dynamic will be the upward push. Thérèse of Lisieux particularly loved one saying of Saint John of the Cross which translates this motion well: "I went down so low, so low, that I was finally able to climb up so high, so high, that I finally reached what I was looking for." In a certain way, Mary's hope is stripped of all its somewhat human expectations that it may know distress; then she can understand the words of the angel who tells her that nothing is impossible to God.

It is not said in Luke's gospel that Mary implored, but can we imagine for one moment that having had on the one hand a glimpse of the possibility of being the mother of Jesus, and on the other hand having ascertained that she knew no man, she did not experience a certain distress? When a human being carries within himself a true desire — for God never gives a grace without its being first desired — it is not without pain that he accepts to see his desire frustrated. Normally, he experiences anguish, but when he is sustained by trust and hope, and therefore by love, God has pity on him and is merciful: "Suffering brings perseverance, as we know, and perseverance brings tested fidelity, and tested fidelity brings hope, and this hope is not deceptive, because the love of God has been poured into our hearts by the Holy Spirit which has been given to us" (Rm 5:4-5).

This is what went on for the Blessed Virgin when the Holy Spirit came upon her. But we must understand that this invasion of the Spirit in her was preceded by a distress that we can hardly imagine, for we are afraid of letting ourselves fall that low. We often think that the Blessed Virgin did not have much merit in pronouncing her Fiat at the Annunciation. To allow God to act on us without seeking any consolation on this earth and to let ourselves be sunk into this desperate thirst for God is always a source of merit, even if, as in Mary's case, that is done very simply. There is a great difference between Mary and us; it is that we are not children anymore, while Mary kept the heart of a child and, therefore, let herself be acted upon entirely by God.

She accepted to be immersed in hunger and thirst: "He fills the hungry with good things" (Lk 1:53) and this is why she was filled with joy. By accepting the darkness of faith, she knew such a desolation that God took pity on her and he cast his eyes on his humble handmaid to gratify her. When God sees that "enough is enough", he intervenes: "Invoke me on the day of your troubles and I will answer you, and you shall honor me" (Ps 50:15). In order to be visited by God, to become the mother of his Son, one must die of hunger and thirst, and especially be humble and very lowly. In a certain way, Mary was crucified at the foot of the Cross to know the Glory of the Assumption.

A prayer that rises from our depths is always answered immediately, for it springs from the abyss of our distress. God often drives us to the wall because he feels like answering us. The tragedy is that we do not know how to use our distress; we perform feats of valor to escape it while seeking the "consolations" of life which hide our deep thirst for God. However, it would be much truer to say to God: "Lord, I cannot cope anymore! Have pity on me." When God sees that we have reached the end of our tether, he responds to our plea.

7. Mary implored

We are astonished by the abundance of gifts that God bestowed upon Mary, but we do not imagine to what an abyss of poverty, humility and trust she was driven in order to seduce the heart of God. The simplicity of Mary's trust must not hide from us the spontaneous movement of her prayer. Mary was a child, and a child makes no problems about having recourse to his parents when he is in need: he naturally extends his hand to ask. We often are too proud to ask from another what we cannot acquire for ourselves. Then, we would rather die of hunger before a closed pantry than beg by asking for the key. To come out of our shell and extend our hand to accept the gift of God would be enough. When he speaks of invocation, Saint Augustine says that it is a person to person relationship, a call addressed to someone; this is the absolute opposite to staying on one's position. To invoke God is to pray and, therefore, to honor his Holiness. Our difficulty in pleading stems from the fact that we do not know how "to ask" nicely and politely from others.

That is why, at the moment we are invited to make our own the Blessed Virgin's act of trust, we must at the same time approach the mystery of supplication. One cannot dissociate these two movements which

I shall call: consecration and supplication. In Mary, obedience in faith is truly a consecration of all her being to God. Properly speaking, we should not say that we consecrate ourselves to God, but rather that we are consecrated by him. To be consecrated means to be consecrated by the fire of the triune love (which is also Glory), this fire which Jesus brought to the earth (Lk 12:49). With regards to Mary, we should rather say that she was consecrated by the anointing of the Holy Spirit which was, to begin with, an anointing of meekness and joy: "God, your God, has anointed you with the oil of gladness, above all your rivals" (Ps 45:8). God asked her but one thing: acceptance. From the moment she gave her consent by signing at the bottom of the blank sheet of her life, God took over for the rest.

It is in this openness to the action of God that Mary naturally pleaded like a child. As soon as she meets an obstacle or a difficulty, she finds it normal to have recourse to God like a child to his father who gives with as much simplicity as generosity. For this reason, we must ask the Blessed Virgin to initiate us to this science, to this secret, to this wisdom which we call supplication: "If there is any one of you who needs wisdom, he must ask God, who gives to all freely and ungrudgingly; it will be given to him. But he must ask with faith, never doubting, for the doubter is like the waves thrown up in the sea when the wind drives. That sort of person, in two minds, undecided as to what to do, must not expect that the Lord will give him anything" (Jm 1:5-7). When a man is initiated to the mystery of supplication, he comes down step by step to the heart of his distress; and when he has crossed a certain "sound barrier", his distress is transformed first into silence and then, at the very bottom of it, he finds joy! There is a certain horizon in our life where the panorama of joys and griefs becomes blurred and blends itself into a line of pure supplication; but in order to know that, we must let ourselves sink to our innermost depths.

We do not know how to implore, for "we do not know how we ought to pray" (Rm 8:26); in a certain way, there is no greater affliction for us. To some extent, it is the misfortune of the original sin which we could define as follows: by losing intimacy with God, our first parents lost, at the same time, the key to supplication. They had received the gift of praying naturally and without difficulty. It is because Mary was permanently in relationship with God in the depths of her being that this key of supplication was given back to her, and not because of the privileges we admire in her: purity, immaculate conception, love, divine motherhood, assumption, transforming union, perfect charity and glory.

All that was given to her with the grace of permanent supplication which was also the secret of Jesus, but more clearly yet, since he could see the Father. This is why the Virgin Mary was called Omnipotens Supplex, the Almighty supplicant, by the Fathers of the Church. Almighty because she was supplicant, for the good reason that when we know how to implore with faith, surely, we obtain everything. But faith itself is an object of supplication: "I believe, Lord, but come to the aid of my lack of faith!" This prayer is a supplication even if it is brief like all the invocations of the gospel: "On the cross, the penitent thief said few words. But his faith was great. In one instant, he was saved. He was the first to open the doors of paradise and to go in. You who received his repentance, Lord, glory to you!"[6]

When we discover the depth of Mary's faith, we understand to what degree we have little faith. We thought we had "spotless linen", but it did not have the whiteness of linen bleached with caustic potash, as Saint John of the Cross says when he recalls the passive purifications. Then it is better to make acts of non-faith, of non-hope and of non-charity, which basically are acts

6. Translated from orthodox liturgical texts, *op. cit.*, Matins of Good Friday, p. 1375.

of supplication: "Lord, come to the aid of my little faith!" To say that we have no faith is not entirely true, but our faith does not stand a comparison with the faith and trust of Mary. Therefore we must pray that faith and love be given to us.

Ultimately, we can implore that the key to supplication be given to us. And then Christ answers us: "You have not asked for anything in my Name yet; you do not know how to ask nor what you must ask for. You have not begun yet!" In that area, we would have to convince ourselves that we have not yet begun to invoke, whatever prayers and cries may have been torn from our heart of stone in the moments of anguish and distress of our existence.

All that is nothing beside what God expects from us, desires and would like to give us as supplication. There are some tribulations from which God would like to spare us and from which he does not spare us, for this is the only means for him to bring about, if we are not too stubborn, the learning experience of supplication. But there are ways of living these situations: those who accept not to harden themselves in face of trials but remain flexible and tender have chances of being able to cry like Christ on the cross. He did not cry out to the Father from the tip of his tongue, but in a cry which was wrenched from the innermost depth of his soul. In this sense, prayer as a cry appears like a grace which the Father grants to the one who asks him for it in the name of his Son: these cries are the groanings of the Spirit within us. Unfortunately, we do not know how to cry anymore and, by this fact, we do not know how to pray anymore.

We should never speak of Mary's consecration at the Annunciation without speaking at the same time of her supplication. Too often, we admire the perfection of Mary's total gift of herself, of her consecration to God, and we envy her generosity. Either we are dwelling in a rather dreamy imagery in face of the beauties of Mary or, if we try to scrutinize what that means, a certain despair lies in wait for us, for we are aware of the distance between us and her, between the love of God and our response. In fact, we know so poorly how to love and, still less, how to give ourselves! Therefore, we draw the following conclusions: that is not for us, this is truly impossible. The apostles had somewhat the same reaction when Christ told them that it is easier for a camel to go through the eye of a needle than for a rich man to enter into the Kingdom of God: "While gazing at them, Jesus said: 'For man', this is impossible; for God everything is possible'" (Mt 19:26).

For this reason, as we contemplate in Mary the perfection of the gift of herself, we must understand that this perfection is linked to the absence of any difficulty for her to implore. She neither hesitated nor presented any difficulty in supplication. Just to see our reaction when we are going through a period of desolation or of trial is enough for us to understand how unnatural it is for us to have recourse to supplication. We ponder, argue and especially hesitate to implore. Our reflection is often a flight into the imaginary world while prayer is truly a return to the real in Christ. In the gospel, Christ does not tell us to reflect during temptations or trials, but to watch and pray.

When Mary is in a difficult situation, for example, when Jesus is lost in the Temple, she does not lose herself in imaginary cogitations, but she prays while she stores all these events in her heart. She does not say: "Things are not going well!", but she invokes. This is the only thing she knows how to do: to pray. And it is because she implores that she receives the grace to give herself. The two attitudes hold together, of course! Her supplication is valued as a gift which God expects from her: it is the most beautiful gift and the most perfect way of giving oneself. A supplication is not pure and authentic if it is not a way of giving oneself; neither is it Christian. The most beautiful gift we can give to those we love, is to tell them: "Things are not going well, help, have pity on me!"

I have also understood that there are situations where we cannot give any other advice but: "Implore". Not long ago, I was trying to make a young man in difficulty understand that his only hope was to cry to God, since he was admitting to me that he had no will power to come out of a rather tragic situation. He also told me that prayer did not manage to come out of his heart and of his lips; it rasped his throat. He was distressed by this inability to implore. At that moment, we must ask God to forgive us for this inability to pray and tell him: "Have pity on me because I don't know how to say: have pity on me... I would like to implore, but come to the help of my inability to pray, and deliver me of it." When we do not know how to pray, but have the desire to do so, we can always ask someone else to implore for us: there are men whose mission is to do this in the Church.

We must never dissociate consecration from supplication; they are the two facets of the same movement: you give yourself while imploring and you implore to give yourself. We must ask the Blessed Virgin to teach us to entreat in order to consecrate ourselves: this is what obedience in faith is, or consecration and gift. When a man permanently implores, he is permanently consecrated. This is what Grignion of Montfort, the master of the Consecration to the Blessed Virgin says: we must learn to transform all our resolutions into requests and supplications. Ultimately, we must transform the consecration itself into supplication by making an act of non-consecration: "I am not consecrated, I have not truly given myself. Teach me, Virgin Mary, to give and consecrate myself. Have pity and teach me to implore to give myself." This resolution to implore is original only in being exclusive, that is, that I do not wish to take any other resolution.

Chapter IV

PRAYING WITH MARY
THE MAGNIFICAT

When the angel announced to Mary that she would give birth to a son and give him the name of Jesus, he let her know that her cousin Elizabeth, in spite of her being advanced in age, was expecting a son and that she was in her sixth month. Without any doubt, he wanted to reassure Mary by giving her a sign to ease her faith: "Nothing is impossible to God", the angel told her as an evidence of this fact.

Mary was then much aware that a great mystery was being accomplished in her. She was also anxious to go and see her cousin to share this great joy with her. Luke tells us that "Mary set out quickly to reach a town in the hill country of Judah. She went into Zechariah's house and greeted Elizabeth" (Lk 1:39-40). She could not wait, she had to go and share her secret — which was not her own, but that of God — with her old cousin who was living through a situation similar to hers. Mary had to confide in someone who would understand her and from whom she would receive light, solace and counsel.

It is not said that the angel intimated to her the command to go and visit her cousin Elizabeth. Mary simply pondered over what was the proper thing to do. She made her decision herself and set out for Zechariah's place. Divine pedagogy proceeds this way. God is not given to trivial talk and he does not take decisions for us. When he has said what he had to say, he keeps silent and leaves man, as Saint Ignatius tells us, to the initiative of "his natural powers". It is the same in our prayer. God tells us exactly what he has to say to us; then, after this enlightenment, it is up to us to make our own decisions freely.

The Blessed Virgin also receives from the angel what she must know about the birth of Jesus, but then she acts like all women in her condition. She ponders over the situation and understands that she must speak to someone and share her joy. Apparently, everything comes from her, but all is inspired from within by the Holy Spirit who has made Mary fruitful without her being necessarily conscious of this.

There, we touch upon another more visible and more concrete facet of Mary's prayer: indeed, it is from this encounter with Elizabeth that will spring forth the only prayer — that of the Magnificat — which Luke puts on the lips of Mary and, we must admit, is the most marvellous praise that a human being could ever give to God. It took the shock of Mary's contact with Elizabeth and her words to allow the Holy Spirit to draw this hymn of personal gratitude to God from Mary's heart.

In the name of all the people, Mary gives thanks to the Lord for herself, and then for the fulfilling of the promises of the covenant. It is difficult to distinguish what is from the Blessed Virgin and what comes from the first Christian community in Palestine. From the beginning to the end, the psalm, in the traditional form of thanksgiving, uses the language of the Old Testament which will be taken up again by Jesus in the gospel of the Beatitudes. God chooses a nation with whom he makes a covenant. His choice is free and proceeds uniquely from the obliging Love of God, without any consideration of number or power. To accept this covenant, the nation must give its faith to God and remain poor, humble and hungry for his Holiness. God chooses men like Abraham from whom he demands absolute faith in order to shower them with his gifts. At the summit of the tree of Jesse and as its most perfect jewel, buds forth the Virgin, the believer par excellence, whom God has prepared as a soil all ready to receive the dew of heaven (Si 24 and Is 45:8).

We can understand why the Magnificat, a hymn of thanksgiving, is the praise of the nation as well as Mary's praise. Some think that it took form in the first Christian liturgy in Jerusalem, and that Luke would have added verse 48: "He cast his eyes on his humble handmaid", to put it on the lips of the Blessed Virgin. [1] In any case, in its place and in its present form, we greet this hymn primarily as the great prayer of the praise of Mary, Mother of Jesus. It is by virtue of Mary's prayer of praise that we want to be tutored by her in order to educate the prayer of the Church and ours.

1. You are the most blessed of all women (Lk 1:42)

Setting out quickly to meet her cousin, Mary must have prepared carefully what she would say to her. Undoubtedly, she must have been embarrassed about how to express the angel's message, quite an extraordinary one! But the faith which had prompted Mary to say her "Fiat" also gave her the assurance that all would go well and that her cousin Elizabeth would receive her account with joy. Had not Elizabeth also experienced the power of God which turns barren women into mothers of great prophets? Elizabeth still remembered what had happened to Sarah, Abraham's wife, and to Hannah, Samuel's mother.

Perhaps had Elizabeth taken up again in her own name Hannah's prayer in the Temple of Shiloh at the

---

1. Translated from TOB (= ETB), note w, p. 193.

time she was pouring forth her soul before the Lord. "Almighty Lord! If you will take notice of the distress of your servant, and bear me in mind and not forget your servant and give her a man-child, I will give him to Yahweh for his whole life and no razor shall ever touch his head" (1 Sm 1:11).

Elizabeth had surely prayed with Zechariah to have a son since the angel clearly states: "Zechariah, do not be afraid, your prayer has been heard. Your wife Elizabeth is to bear you a son and you must name him John" (Lk 1:13). She belonged to Yahweh's poor whose only refuge was the invocation of his Name. It is, therefore, a woman of prayer that the Blessed Virgin is going to meet, she who also was a great woman of prayer. And when two prayerful beings meet, their relationship is immediately set at the deep level of prayer, there where their heart is impregnated by the Holy Spirit.

This is what is going on when Mary comes into her cousin's home. Through a simple salutation of peace and love, contact in the Holy Spirit is immediately established. It is as if the child Jesus, formed by the Holy Spirit and already living in the womb of the Blessed Virgin, was spiritually touching John the Baptist and already sanctifying him in Elizabeth's womb.

As soon as a man carries the living Jesus in his heart, he sanctifies everything he touches if he is prompted by the wish to radiate Jesus. He awakens the presence of the Holy Spirit in the heart of the other. I have often asked myself why we pray so little with our brothers in faith when we meet them: first to express our joy and then to meet in the Lord. It should also be the first thing for us to do, especially when our ideas diverge or we have difficulty in accepting the other as he is or in forgiving him. As soon as we set about praying with another or in a group, something happens and, instead of looking at each other as opponents, we raise our eyes towards the Father in heaven; then we are able "to stare at each other" as brothers. As soon as we start praying together

95

in spiritual assistance as in the sacrament of reconcilia
tion, the relationship is not at all the same anymore; we
really see each other in the light of the Spirit.

Some will say that not all Christians can manage
straight off to express their intimate prayer that freely.
It is easier than we think if one of the participants is
ready "to take the plunge" and express aloud what he
has deep in his heart. Certain spiritual experts, like
Teresa of Avila, say that spiritual sharing is a great help
for contemplative prayer; Saint John Eudes says that it
is a privileged form of prayer. It is perhaps not always
possible to pray freely and openly, but we can always
recite the "Our Father" or the "Hail Mary". It is,
moreover, the first part of this prayer that Elizabeth said
to really enter into a relationship with Mary. Why would
it not be for us the spiritual link toward a real encounter
in the Lord with our brothers?

Let us come back to Mary's salutation to Elizabeth.
The Blessed Virgin is repeating with regards to her
cousin what the angel had done for her at the Annunciation in Nazareth, since he greeted her as he entered her
home: "Now as soon as Elizabeth heard Mary's greeting,
the child leapt in her womb and Elizabeth was filled with
the Holy Spirit" (Lk 1:41). Everything is prayer and joy
in this scene of the Visitation where two human beings
meet in the light of the Holy Spirit. Have we ever sensed
how the encounter with another person in the respect
and worship of his mystery can set in us the fire of the
prayer of praise? We have been too much in the habit
of experiencing prayer solely in the context of a personal
relationship with God. Perhaps do we still have to discover today the secret of prayer shared with other
brothers? There is here a real experience of the presence
of the risen Lord in the midst of those assembled in his
name for the purpose of praying: "For where two or
three meet in my name, I shall be there with them"
(Mt 18:20).

Those who experience this shared prayer, especially

if they live it in an atmosphere of truth and transparency, perceive this presence of the Lord in their midst, by the words which they receive from him. When this prayer is also lived in a profound silence, the Face of the Lord suddenly becomes alive and, from the bottom of our heart, rise those words without our knowing where they come from: it is the murmur of the Spirit in the depths of our hearts. At certain moments of grace, we are astonished to hear our brothers say aloud the words of the gospel, words perceived in the silence of our heart; and these words are not idle words, for they refer to precise situations. One must point out, nevertheless, that this shared prayer is not a universal panacea destined to those who shun personal prayer in the silence of the heart. Only those who are used to pray in private and at length are able to share in truth their prayer with their brothers. They can then experience the power of this prayer as Jesus says: "I tell you solemnly once again, if two of you on earth agree to ask anything at all, it will be granted to you by my Father in heaven" (Mt 18:19).

Of course, this prayer together is primarily lived in the liturgical assembly: but it must also be lived in small communities in a free and spontaneous expression, where each one says in front of his brothers what he believes he can say about his relationship with his Father in heaven. When two friends manage to pray in this way, they make real a communion which fulfills their desire for union far beyond all they can imagine and, in a certain way, they can make their own what Jesus would say to his Father: "All I have is yours and all you have is mine" (Jn 17:10).

This is what is going on between Mary and Elizabeth. They both were conscious that a great mystery was being accomplished in them, and they needed to speak about it in a prayer of praise and thanksgiving. This prayer will take its place in the most natural happening in the world: a young girl goes to visit her cousin because she has just learned that she is pregnant. In this encounter, all is exultation in the Holy Spirit. All prayer of praise and blessing springs from the innermost depth of the heart, under the action of the Holy Spirit: "It was then that, filled with joy by the Holy Spirit, he said, 'I bless you, Father, Lord of heaven and of earth, for hiding these things from the learned and the clever and revealing them to mere children. Yes, Father, for that is what it pleased you to do'" (Lk 10:21).

For Jesus, as well as for Mary, Luke insists on the intervention of the Holy Spirit in their joy and in their prayer to the Father. Mary and Elizabeth are of these "mere children" to whom God reveals his mystery and who pray him naturally in joy and exultation. In Elizabeth, the cry of the Spirit can spring forth because Mary is coming there to visit her: "She gave a loud cry and said, 'You are the most blessed of all women, and blessed is the fruit of your womb. Why should I be honored with a visit from the mother of my Lord? For the moment your greeting reached my ears, the child in my womb leapt for joy'" (Lk 1:42-43). Mary's salutation is what strikes Elizabeth's ear and, at the same time, pierces her heart allowing the joyous exultation of the Holy Spirit to spring forth.

Elizabeth begins by letting out a cry. Prayer is not born in the heart of man at the end of a meditation; it traces itself a path under the impulse of a cry. A cry supposes something that makes one cry: a pain or a joy, a distress or an anxiety. For Elizabeth, it is the exultation of joy which makes her pray. Then she can pronounce over the Blessed Virgin her great prayer of blessing that we so often repeat in the Ave Maria: "Blessed are you among women and blessed is your child Jesus". The God-Creator is the first to have pronounced this blessing upon Mary, when he created her full of grace to be the Mother of his Son. He made his blessing in Jesus, his blessed Son, rest upon her: "Blessed be God the Father of our Lord Jesus Christ, who has blessed us with all the spiritual blessings of heaven in Christ" (Ep 1:3).

To be blessed by God is to be filled with the divine "yes"; it is to be imbued with this Amen which wants to be without sorrow or regret. It is therefore her turn to be able, like Mary, to say the "yes" that makes us open ourselves to all risks, but also to all the joys of God's action in us. It is, more especially, to be able, like Elizabeth and Mary, to pronounce the "yes" with regard to those who drink from the same cup of blessing as we do. As soon as a man blesses the Lord, he has the power to pass on this blessing to all those who come to him. Thus Elizabeth continues the blessing pronounced on Mary by the angel and reaches all the blessings pronounced by us.

At the same time, Elizabeth is filled with gratitude for this visit, for she does not understand why the mother of her Lord has come to her. In blessing God for all the tenderness he has shown for Mary, she also blesses the Blessed Virgin in whom is focused all the love of God, since she will give birth to the Father's beloved Son. In this prayer of blessing, she makes known her wish to recognize her as the mother of her Lord.

Finally, Elizabeth understands what so many generations of believers have so well acknowledged while contemplating the Virgin of tenderness, that Mary is the prototype of our humanity filled with blessings and also capable of blessing. She understands that her fecundity was the illustration of the power acquired by the one who says "yes". God cannot refuse her anything. At the heart of the Church and of the world, Mary is pure blessing, without the least shadow of reservation, doubt or curse. Each time we say she is blessed, we learn from her to find the music and the words, the precise tone of the blessings we should pronounce upon each other.

It is at Mary's school that the Holy Spirit will teach our heart the prayer of blessing, on condition that we receive from her a "visitation". She will greet us as she greeted Elizabeth and as she will one day greet Bernadette at Lourdes. Then our heart will exult with joy and we will be able, like her, to sing the Magnificat while blessing God for his marvels. In our turn, we shall pronounce the blessing on all those who come to see us. After Bernadette saw the Blessed Virgin's smile, she had only one wish: to die in order to see her. Henceforth, she wore this smile on her face, and her look had the gift of transforming the heart and the life of many who met her.

2. My soul magnifies the Lord, exult my spirit in God, my Savior

After hearing Elizabeth's blessing, Mary suddenly becomes aware that she is entering into the history of the people of Israel and into the history of all humankind. Much more, she becomes conscious of what has happened to her when, in her lowliness and humility, she has been chosen by God to become the Mother of his Son, the most beloved woman of all humanity. She was surely aware of this in the depths of her being, but there had to be a voice from the outside — that of Elizabeth inspired by the Holy Spirit — to reveal to her the mystery of her profound being. We all need to be revealed to ourselves by someone else. It is a great grace in the life of a man to meet a truly spiritual person who reveals him his name, his vocation and his mission. Speaking of her encounter with Dom Le Saux, a Carmelite was saying: "He 'delivered' me a word which transformed my life". We must be able to tell someone: "Do you know that you have the gift of prayer, or that you have the grace of consoling wounded hearts, or the charism of speaking of God to children and making them pray?" Suddenly, the unknown world of the life of God that we were carrying within us without knowing it, awakens in light and we become conscious that the Father is the source of all these graces. Until then, we "were consuming" the gifts of God; now we acknowledge in thanksgiving the author of these gifts.

Mary can recognize that God himself is the author of all this extraordinary experience: "Then Mary said:

"My soul proclaims the greatness of the Lord and my spirit exults in God my Savior; because he has looked upon his lowly handmaid. Yes, from this day forward, all generations will call me blessed" (Lk 1:46-48).

The only purpose of Elizabeth's word of gratitude is to prompt a confession of faith from Mary. It is the same for each one of us. We read or listen to the Word of God in order that it may touch our heart, awaken it and make the prayer of praise spring to our lips. Mary can be aware that the merciful Love of the Lord has touched her and, in touching her, this love has touched all of humanity. This is the reason why Elizabeth says that Mary is "blessed". This is the great story of salvation through the redemptive Incarnation which is coming into being in Mary. It is normal that Mary, knowing herself to be loved of God, would know herself to be also loved by humankind, for on this day, it is the whole humanity that she represents. Through Mary and in her, all men recognize the infinite and unexplainable Love of God: "Yes, God loved the world so much that he gave his only Son, so that everyone who believes in him may not be lost but may have eternal life" (Jn 3:16).

Mary perceived at that moment all the love which men would translate into prayer until the end of time. This is why her spirit exults in joy and all her being is vibrant with gladness under the action of the Holy Spirit. When we say that the "soul" of Mary magnifies the Lord and that her "spirit" exults in God, her Savior, we immediately represent to ourselves the prayer made by a human being when he "thinks" of God to praise or bless him. In the case of the Blessed Virgin, we must go much further and much deeper and affirm that it is the whole being of Mary — body and soul — that is caught in prayer. Yet when a woman carries a child within her,

101

she cannot dissociate her body from her spirit anymore: she thinks, acts, speaks, prays like a mother with her whole being.

Even more so in Mary than in any other woman, the body and the spirit are intimately bound because she is the "perfect woman", sprung from the hands of God in the perfection of her being. She does not know this dualism between flesh and spirit which is so painful for us to bear. She did not need, like us, to "re-weave" the tenuous threads which bind the spirit to the body, to recover her harmony in the power of the Spirit. In her, the conveyer belts of transmission were never faulted. As says Father Raguin: "Mary did not come out of the purity of her original nature... She is all pure in her prime nature, such as she came from the heart of God."[2]

Mary was in the same situation as Adam and Eve, issued from the hand of God, living with him in a total and perfect intimacy. This amounts to saying that prayer flowed in her without her knowing it, and if she knew, it was as if she did not know. A spring cannot see its sparkling clarity and a light does not know that it shines. Mary does not have to make much effort to grasp the fact that she is always in prayer. What is so arduous for us is so simple for her since she has not come out from her prime nature. We can imagine what this means when the Holy Spirit recreates us in the power of the resurrection. Then we find again our original nature more marvellous yet, since it is glorified by Christ, dead and risen. We can say as this monk did when he reached the stage of perpetual prayer: "I carried prayer within myself; it was like a spring covered by a stone. One day, Jesus went by, he removed the stone and the spring started to flow, and it has flowed ever since."

Mary experienced this glorious transformation be-

2. Translated from Y. Raguin, S.J., *Le Livre de Marie,* Suppl. « Vie Chrétienne », n. 259, p. 6.

fore we did, since the Son of God took flesh in her. Then all her being can exult in joy and prayer, when she sees herself and knows herself in the light of God as the beloved daughter of the Father and of all humanity. She can say that her flesh and blood, her spirit and heart, her soul and body are vibrant with joy in God her Savior. Hers is the joy of a human being seized by the Spirit of God and made fruitful by its mysterious action. Because she knows that everything in her comes from God, Mary has not a shadow of self-complacency and her exultation is as simple as her praise is transparent.

Mary's wonderful human nature is a supple and docile instrument at God's fingertips; he makes it vibrate, while giving it the precise tone of praise. Mary's body, most pure and chaste, is perpetually integrated to her virginal heart which exults with joy at the least breath of God. We naturally think here of the prayer of the little shepherd boy in Bernanos: "What the little shepherd boy does from time to time and through a movement of his heart, says the Prioress of the Carmel, we must do night and day. Not that we hoped to pray better than he did, on the contrary. This simplicity of the soul, this tender surrender to the divine Majesty which, in him, is an inspiration of the moment, a grace and, as it were, a light of the genius, we devote our whole life to acquire or to recover if we have known it, for it is a gift of childhood which, most of the time, does not survive beyond childhood. Once grown out of childhood, we must suffer a very long time to return to it again, as at the very end of the night, we discover another dawn. Have I become a child again?"[3]

Mary can hear the praise of humanity for she knows what God has done in her and, like a crystal that reflects the rays of the sun in their full brilliance, she can render this praise which is due to God. Besides, this praise from

---

3. Translated from G. Bernanos, *Dialogue des Carmélites,* Livre de vie, n. 6, pp. 34 ff.

men is of so little significance in comparison to what the angel told her when he greeted her: "Rejoice, full of grace!" That is why we must join our praise to the one which comes to her on the part of God. Better than anyone else does Jesus know how to thank his mother for the "yes" which allowed him to become flesh.

Mary does not need to blindfold herself not to see what God has done in her. The more clearly she sees what is happening to her, the more she is aware that all this is the work of God. The more she contemplates the author of these gifts, the more she exults in him, God her Savior. And the world keeps on turning without noticing that God has become flesh in Mary. In the same way, it will continue its stupid dance on Good Friday at the moment when Jesus is dying on the Cross. But one day, finally, these secrets will be revealed and brought to light to the ends of the world, for what is said in secret will be proclaimed in public squares and at the crossroads of highways (Mt 10:26-28).

3. He has rested his eyes upon me

Finally, these words of the Blessed Virgin will forever attract those who seek the face and the eyes of God in contemplating prayer: "He has looked upon his lowly handmaid" (Lk 1:48). For this contemplation begins in a life of prayer at the moment when we know this truth from concrete experience and not from hearsay. One day the look of the Father must become real for us and we must "see him face to face" (cf. Is 52:8). Christ has not ceased to live from this look of the Father accompanying him everywhere and in everything he did: "He who sent me is with me, and has not left me to myself, for I always do what pleases him" (Jn 8:29).

Similarly, Mary will be fascinated by this look of the Father which comes to her and never leaves her. Her eyes are perfectly clear; she does not stop at the gifts she receives to cherish them in a selfish way, but she holds her gaze constantly fixed on the Giver of all gifts: "Every good gift, everything that is perfect, is given from above; it comes down from the Father of all light; with him there is no such thing as alteration, no shadow of a change" (Jm 1:17).

Mary sees herself solely in the eyes of God resting upon her. We could apply to her the words concerning Christ which Saint Augustine puts on the lips of the penitent thief: "He cast his eyes on me and, in his gaze, I understood everything". When the eyes of Mary cross those of God, she knows she is not alone anymore in this solitude shunned by all, young as well as old, not to speak of the adults who do their best to escape it. The only remedy to solitude is to experience the fact that the Father is always with us and that he watches over us at each moment of our life as he did for Mary.

If we wish to discover the look of the Father coming to meet ours, there is a very simple way, the privilege of Christians: it is to place ourselves under the protection of Christ. We are helped to do this by the Blessed Virgin. If we are humble enough to take advantage of this, to place ourselves in the shelter of the Blessed Virgin, as we will mention later, we shall reach a point when we shall never forget that a Father is waiting for us at the end of the road, and we shall never be afraid.

"Come to me, all you who labor and are afraid!" We must develop the instinct of seeking refuge when temptation and suffering are lurking at our door. If we do not know how to take refuge under Mary's eyes, we will fly away from these moments of distress, or what is worse yet, we will try to overcome them with our own generosity or good will; and we will fall lamentably. Those who want to learn to pray must take refuge near the Blessed Virgin; otherwise, they will pray from afar, the furthest possible, and they will fly away from prayer as they fly away from eternity.

Everyone needs a place of refuge; there is no courage

or will power strong enough to hold on. Those who do not know how to take refuge in God or, in a more concrete and human way, in Mary, are forced to turn to amusements or action, but these remedies are the worst of follies. They belong to the mentality of one falling from the thirtieth storey who keeps repeating: "As long as this can go on!"

By developing the habit of taking refuge under the look of Mary and under her protection, by repeating the "Hail Mary", mechanically and perhaps wordwise, but saying it nevertheless, Mary will make us understand from within that the Father has cast his eyes upon us. She is the one who will make us catch the tender look shining on the face of Christ. If, with all the depths of our being, we really knew how to look for the face of Christ in Mary, this invisible face which we can see only by turning inward towards our own inner depths, as we would see it emerge from these depths we would understand that the Father has cast his eyes on us and we would know the same peace, the same trust and the same surrender as the Blessed Virgin does herself.

In this sense, the Blessed Virgin educates us in a prayer which leads to the silent contemplative prayer. She teaches us to seek refuge near her, like the little child near his mother, by invoking her name and telling her simply: "You have seen my wretchedness and known the miseries of my soul" (Ps 30:8) until her eyes full of the Father's tenderness shine upon us. We often need long hours of prayer to receive this visitation, but the day we receive it we are comforted and torn away from the solitude which is everyone's tragedy. We then understand that misery, distress and fear trace the authentic route of prayer towards a life of contemplating prayer, as long as we accept not to run away from them.

Let us conclude by saying that Mary especially understood God's design on her. She understood what her Son will later express in the gospel: that God is a considerate Father on the watch for the needs of his children and providing them with everything. She especially deciphers and reads the pattern of her existence in the light of her Father's look. This sets her in a deep peace from which agitation and anxiety are banished. She can say as Abraham did speaking of his son Isaac whom he must offer in sacrifice: "God will provide". She has had enough proofs of God's tenderness towards her not to distrust him. She knows that, at night, he will not "play devious tricks" on her and that, in the morning, she will receive everything from him: food, clothing and especially love and kindness. All her life unfolds in an atmosphere of peace because she feels she is borne by the Father.

In the light of her own history led by the hand of the Father, she can enter into the mystery of the history of man and of God's attitude towards humanity: "He has come to the help of Israel his servant, mindful of his love — according to the promise he made to our ancestors — for Abraham and his descendants for ever" (Lk 1:54-55). The arm of God is never too short to help his people and especially those with whom he has made a covenant. By recalling the great figure of Abraham, the Father of believers, Mary takes her place in the line of the witnesses of faith (Heb 11 and 12) who staked all their existence on the Word of God without knowing where they were going. There is, however, a great difference in the case of Mary; it is that, in the resurrection of her Son, she saw the fulfilment of the promises: "All of these (the witnesses spoken of in the Letter to the Hebrews), although they had deserved a good record through their faith, they did not obtain what had been promised. God had made a better plan, a plan which included us. Without us, they were not to be made perfect" (Heb 11: 39-40).

4. Holy is his Name

"Yes, from this day forward all generations will call me blessed, for the Almighty has done great things for me. Holy is his Name" (Lk 1:48-49). With these words of the Blessed Virgin, we are entering upon a new phase in her prayer. Until then, Mary has become conscious of the marvels God has performed on her behalf by freely showering her with all goods; she magnifies the author of these gifts in joy and exultation. The face of God which has then impressed itself upon her is his face inasmuch as it bears a resemblance to something, in the sense that she has contemplated in her heart a reflection of his beauty, his tenderness, his power and of his truth. We could extend the list of God's perfections indefinitely since he himself is the Infinite.

At this time, she touches upon a shore which extends much beyond her experience of God's wonders, for she is crossing a horizon which separates the created from the Uncreated, the finite from the Infinite, and she emerges into a world which the human eye has never seen, nor the ear heard, with things which are beyond the heart of man (1 Co 2:9). Of course, she still rests upon "the great things" that God has done for her: how could it be otherwise since she bathes in these marvels and that all knowledge takes root in "what strikes the senses"? But now, she suspects another aspect of God which she terms as the Almighty, the Whole Other, the One who has nothing in common with the earth, the Separated One. It is the face of God that bears no resemblance to anything.

How can she give a name to this face since she has never seen it? No idea, no word can express it, and yet every living thing and even all the inanimate beings reach out towards it. When a mother is expecting a child, she has no idea of what it will be since its face is still unknown to her; she cannot even give it a name since she does not know whether it will be a boy or a girl, or if she gives it a name, it will be approximate. Nevertheless, she knows it is alive for she feels it moving inside her. It is the same with the face of God whose features are practically unknown and of which we, nevertheless, recognize the impressions because of his action in us. On this subject, Saint Gregory of Nazianzus says in a cry of admiration which is at the same time one of adoration: "O You, the Beyond of everything, is that not all we can say about you?"

If Mary is unable to name this face, she can at least apply to herself the words God says to Moses when the latter asks him: "But if they ask me what his name is, what am I to tell them? And God said to Moses, 'I Am who I Am'" (Ex 3:13-14). We know that the Jews did not even dare pronounce the name of Yahweh so sacred was it, and that they had replaced it with the name of "Lord". In her turn, Mary does not name him either, but she calls to mind his reality and sings in the Magnificat: "Holy is his Name". Happily, she can say that as a confession of faith, prayer and adoration.

For Mary, to proclaim that God is Holy is the only way for her to be in relationship with the one who is beyond, infinitely beyond what she can perceive or imagine about him. To pronounce the name of a being is to enter into communion with him; it is the only way to pray him. It is from this concept that the Jesus prayer derives all its spirituality. To assert that Jesus is Savior is to utter the first name of God whose face we have never seen. All the wonders that Mary has contemplated during her life and which make her proclaim that the Almighty has done great things for her, are nothing beside this face of God which bears no resemblance to anything we know and which is that of his holiness.

In this, she reaches all the tradition of Israel which has always been fascinated by this mysterious face of God, the Whole Other, the Separate One who throws Isaiah face down on the earth in the Temple of Jerusalem. Man can recognize this face only through his own traits as a sinner: "In the year of King Uzziah's death I saw the Lord seated on a high and magnificent throne. His train filled the sanctuary; above him stood seraphs, each one with six wings: two to cover its face, two to cover its feet and for flying. And they cried one to another in this way: 'Holy, holy, holy is Yahweh Sabaoth. His glory fills the whole earth'" (Is 6:1-3).

We must be aware of Mary's initiative which leads to the most profound discovery a man could make about the mystery of God: the proclamation of his holiness. At the risk of repeating ourselves, we must see the starting point of her initiative which is also ours. The only difference between Mary and ourselves is the point of arrival since the discovery of God's holiness awakens in us the feeling that we are sinners. We will never be men of worship if we have not perceived some reflection of the thrice Holy face of God.

As each one of us has done, Mary has contemplated the Creator while meditating on his perfections refracted in the mirror of the universe and on the marvels he has performed in her own heart: Luke tells us that she pondered on all these events. She has known God in his visible works and she has rendered thanksgiving for these. This knowledge of God directs itself towards a face which bears resemblance to something, as we have said: "What is invisible since the creation of the world, that is his everlasting power and deity, have been there for the mind to see in the things he has made. That is why such people are without excuses: they knew God and yet refused to honor him as God or to thank him" (Rm 1:20-21; Ws 13:1-9). This knowledge of God is acquired by analogy. It is enough for us to see Mary's purity, truth or goodness to say immediately: "How great and powerful is the one who has created the Blessed Virgin!" This is what prompted Mary to sing her Magnificat.

But God wanted her to discover a dimension beyond his visible face: he manifested to her a few refracted facets of the glory of his face unknown to men. For Mary, he lifted a little of the veil which concealed his holiness even though it is not possible for man to see the face of God and to remain alive: "Man cannot see my face, and live" (Ex 33:20). This is what we have described as the face of God bearing no resemblance to anything we know, or better yet, the secret of God, the mystery of his holiness. God gave a glimpse of this to the Virgin Mary. He put her in the cleft of the rock while shielding her with his hand, and she saw the back of him, for his face is not to be seen (Ex 33:23). The Blessed Virgin experiences this sense of awe at the Annunciation when she learns that the most mysterious face of God will become flesh. For in Jesus dwells the plenitude of divinity and Mary will bear him in her womb. In the Incarnation, the invisible God makes himself visible so that we may be able to touch him. He conceals his Glory and humanizes it so that we may be able to bear it.

In order that Mary may have a complete revelation of this thrice holy face of God, she will have to wait until she sees the face of her Son and hears words like these: "Not that anybody has seen the Father, only the one who comes from God has seen the Father" (Jn 6:46). "No one has ever seen God; it is only the Son, who is nearest to the Father's heart, who has made him known" (Jn 1:18). Mary must have had many surprises as she listened to such words, since she herself had borne in her womb the one who is turned towards the Father's bosom. When the Son of the Holy God becomes flesh, he incarnates at the same time the most mysterious face of the Father, that of the secret of his holiness which is at the same time his face of mercy.

The purpose of Jesus' coming on earth is to make men share his secret, his mystery which was eternally his own. He came to invite them to share the secrets of the Father and to enter into his holiness, that is, in the communion of love which unites the Three Persons each to the others. Mary was the first one to share this secret;

she carried within herself, by her divine motherhood, the Son of the Most High. Can we imagine that Jesus did not often speak to his mother about this communion of love with the Father which made him live? Moreover, at twelve, he told her so clearly: "Did you not know that I must be in my Father's house?" (Lk 2:49). And if he had not told her, she would have guessed it, for one does not bear such a secret within oneself without something of it coming through in one's face and a mother always guesses the secret of her son!

Jesus has pointed the way to make us enter into this mystery of the Father's face. We must always be ready with girded loins, a lighted lamp and, especially, we must leave everything to follow him. That is when we discover again the face of God which holds a resemblance to something we know. All these good things we rely on to seek God: his love, his tenderness, his beauty, his truth, must be transcended in order to seek God himself. In a way, we must leave God under the aspect which resembles something we know to find him in his aspect which holds no resemblance to anything we know. It is as if God were telling us: "Love life, covet all goods, but covet at the same time the Author of all these goods", for someday you will be admitted to the triune banquet, to the communion of the Father and the Son in the Holy Spirit.

5. Adoration

There is the meaning of Christian self-denial and the very meaning of the word of God to Moses: "No one can see my face and remain alive". Thus, when God asks Abraham to leave his country and go to a land he will show him, he is inviting him to leave everything to set out towards the land of his face which does not resemble anything he knows; in a sense, he is inviting him to enter into the triune secret. This is the direction taken by all the witnesses of faith (Heb 11 and 12) and more especially by Mary when she obeys the Word of God at the Annunciation and gives up understanding according to her views. Those men and women do not know it, but they are journeying towards the triune secret which Jesus will fully reveal to us a few hours before he dies: "If anyone loves me, we will love him and we shall come to him and make our home with him" (Jn 14:23). "I call you friends, because I have made known to you everything I have learnt from my Father" (Jn 15:15).

When Mary says about the Almighty: "Holy is his Name", she discovers the most mysterious face of God, that of his holiness and she is introduced, without knowing it, into the mystery of the relationship of Jesus with the Father in its intimacy. She experiences it mysteriously in the depths of her being; she will have a gradual revelation of this when Jesus will unveil his mystery to her. For the time being, the discovery of the Face of the Holy One of Israel, the central theme of Isaiah's preaching (1:4; 5:19-24; 10:17-20; 41:14-16, 20), awakens in her heart an intimate feeling of her precariousness, but also a most acute sense of the holiness of God. We can understand her saying then: "His mercy reaches from age to age for those who fear him" (Lk 1:50). She really belongs to the little remnant of the "God-fearing" people.

The highest form of the prayer of the Jewish people appears here. When Isaiah is confronted with the God thrice Holy, he is conscious not only of his precariousness, but also of his condition as a sinner. Such a sudden awareness frees him from anxiety for it brings forth an inner sense of the only movement worthy of this holiness: ADORATION. The Jews were not oblivious to anxiety, but they did not make it their refuge, because they knew how to transcend it by adoration. A Jew, and consequently a Christian, is someone who, as he discovers the thrice Holy face of God, knows how to fall on his knees and pray. Or better yet, he turns his face towards God's to adore him (*ad* = towards; *os, oris* — mouth, face).

There is, nevertheless, a great difference between Mary who proclaims the holiness of the Name of God and Isaiah, and all those who, after him, will have the same experience. As soon as he saw Yahweh seated on his throne of glory, Isaiah confesses: "How wretched I am! I am lost, for I am a man of unclean lips" (Is 6:5). God's holiness requires man to be sanctified, that is, purified from sin by participating in this holiness of God. "God of Holiness, God of Strength, God of Immortality, have mercy on us", sing our brothers from the East in the trisagion. Before God thrice Holy, Mary does not proclaim she is a "sinner", for she well knows that the holiness of God has purified her from all sin and has sanctified her from the first moment of her life.

Mary has a yet deeper experience than that of the sinner's condition — for sin is still an accident in existence — she discovers the contigency and the precariousness of her being in "situation", what the Thomists call "the misery of being a creature", totally suspended on God who creates it from moment to moment. For us, it is precisely this precariousness that is at the root of all our sins and makes them possible; these sins do not reach down to the depths of our being, to the level of its goodness. Mary, on her part, discovers her poverty of being or her substantial misery while remaining free from all sin. This sudden awareness plunges her in adoration, for she experiences the fact of finding herself between two abysses: the holiness of God and her "nothingness" or her misery.

Adoration goes much beyond love. Love wants union while adoration is letting ourselves be carried away by the torrent of God's holiness and, therefore, his love, as a cork floats on the sea. The man who adores does not seek to understand; he even rejoices that he does not understand, that he is overwhelmed and transcended from all sides by this torrent which made Saint John of

114

the Cross say: "To Love which is sweeping you away, do not ask where it is going". It is a submission of the whole being to the will and wish of the Other. Thus adoration takes its place in the prolonged movement of faith and trust and allows itself to be carried away by love, as it is said of Abraham: "He set out without knowing where he was going..., for he looked forward to a city with foundations, whose architect and builder would be God himself" (Heb 11:8 and 10). This city is, surely, the Abode of God, the Holy Trinity itself. Mary will also proclaim: "Let it be done to me according to thy Word". It is always the same transcendence: "Not mine, but thy will... You, not me".

For Abraham, as well as for Mary and Jesus, to adore in spirit and truth is to surrender his life to the good will of the Father and to consecrate himself to the holiness of his Name, that is, to sanctify his own existence by introducing it totally and forever into the heart of the Blessed Trinity. Consecration or sanctification is always the work of the Holy Father: "Consecrate them (sanctify them) in the truth: your Word is truth. As you sent me into the world, I am sending them into the world, and for their sake I consecrate myself so that they too may be consecrated in truth" (Jn 17:17-19).

So Mary can experience the precariousness of her existence without any danger since she prays and adores. She does so simply by invoking the Holy Name of God. This is the only thing that allows her to bind herself to God. She has nothing, basically, but this Name. It is the richness and the poverty of the praise and adoration of the Only One, since Mary has never seen his Face. For us sinners as well, while we are experiencing the precariousness of our existence, our manner of worship will be to repeat indefinitely: "Holy God, have mercy on us." That is true adoration.

Wealth and poverty: a name is so little a thing! We could say like the Hebrews: we saw no face, we saw no shape on Sinai; we heard but a voice and the Name (cf.

Dt 4:12). Those who practise the prayer of the Name often have the impression that they are talking to a mute person. There are days when repeating the Name of God — and for us the name of Father "Abba" or the name of Jesus — seems to be a futile exercise. Yet that name is his very own; there is no other name for us to use to make ourselves heard. Thus the one who adores God, like Mary, clings to this name which sums up all his prayer. That sort of untiring repetition of God's name is like a cry from his heart where he surrenders all his being. It is a call made in trust; it is the movement of sharing through which God comes to us.

But there again, before we are able to utter this name, the first thing to ask for is to understand, experience, and "savor" the fact that we hold our existence from God, that it is hanging on him, that he gives it to us unceasingly and that if, by chance, God had a "moment of distraction", we would fall again immediately into nothingness. Such an experience can lead to despair. We see this in the life of the Curé of Ars who had asked God to show him his "misery". It is, surely, the "misery of being a creature", hanging on God, for he already had had the profound experience of being a sinner. He admitted himself that, had the Holy Spirit not sustained him, he would have had a temptation to despair. His only escape was to take refuge, like a little dog, at the foot of the tabernacle.

When we experience the contingency of our being hanging on God who gives us existence from moment to moment, we could have a feeling of anxiety or despair. The Holy Spirit alone can give us the joy of "savoring" our misery and, at the same time, inspire us the instinct of taking refuge near the Virgin Mary. She will teach us to fall humbly on our knees and make us understand the wish of the Father, who seeks worshippers in spirit and in truth (Jn 4:23).

"The worth of a life is measured by its weight in adoration."

116

"The adoration of the Trinity is our only purpose" (Father Monchanin).

"The hidden masters of history, and who are unaware of being so, are the men of worship" (Olivier Clément).

"Those who uphold humanity are not the men in government, nor the men of genius, nor the men of action: they are the worshippers. What does God ask of them? Not much: to believe in him. The whole world, says Saint John, is in the hands of the Evil one. It is a stronghold of ice which does not want to love, and God is laying siege to it. He looks for breaches: they are the worshippers" (Father M. D. Molinié).

6. He raised the humble

This is not the first time we call to mind the humility of the Blessed Virgin. We have spoken about it on the subject of her faith and trust by saying that obedience in faith was the privilege of the humble, for the difficulty of believing is the same as that of being humble. One must transcend the evidence of one's own judgment to give preference to God's judgment. In this sense, as we were saying, we measure our growth in humility by checking our growth in faith. The more we entrust ourselves to the power of the Lord, the more we mistrust our own strengths.

But as we sing the Magnificat with the Blessed Virgin, we understand why she is "the humble one" par excellence. If we did not have to set this expression aside for Christ — we will see why later — we would say that she is "personified humility", as we said that Francis of Assisi was "personified prayer". Why can we make such an assertion? Just simply because of what we have just said about Mary's adoration. The ultimate reason for her humility is in the words she says: "Holy is his Name" and in the discovery of the thrice Holy face of the Father. When a man has discovered that God is God, that he is

117

"Everything", he can only admit his "nothingness". In order to reach the Everything, Saint John of the Cross would say, you must go through "nothingness". If worship takes its place in the very movement of trust, we must say the same about humility; or rather, we must say that adoration plunges man into absolute humility.

To make that understood, I would like to use one of the most striking examples of the Bible, that of Moses. Teilhard de Chardin judged Moses as one of the four men who had the highest experience of God on earth, since he spoke face to face with him, as a friend does with his friend. We remember the burning bush and the prayer of Moses in Exodus 33:18: "Give me the grace to see your glory". Everyone knows that God answered Moses' prayer, to the point that he had to wear a veil over his face, his skin was shining so much from the Glory of God (Ex 34:30). When Miriam and Aaron question Moses about a Cushite wife he has taken, Yahweh himself will come to the defence of Moses; we have there, after the visions Moses had, the highest praise we can offer a man: "Yahweh heard this. Now Moses was the most humble of men, the humblest man borne by the earth" (Nb 12:3).

How could it be otherwise when one has seen the Glory of Yahweh on Sinai? As soon as God has passed, Moses humbles himself even more. The more a man has been taken into the intimacy of God, the more he is immersed "To the eyes" in humility. One must not really believe that this humility comes from the fear a man would experience if he stood before a king or a person of great rank; this humility comes from the very intimacy with God. When we discover to what degree God loves us and wants to unite himself to us, we are filled with embarrassment and we say, as did Angela of Foligno: "When I was introduced to Love, I became non-love." The effect of love is the adoration of God and the humbling of ourselves.

We must say the same thing about Mary. When she understood the immensity of God and his holiness, she was not able anymore to keep herself busy with anything else. Her humility comes from her spirit of adoration, itself stemming from her perception of God's holiness. It is her fascination with God that makes the Virgin Mary humble. As the face of God outlined itself to her, Mary let herself be swept by the torrent of his holiness, as she willingly accepted to be a useless handmaid.

We are touching here the very essence of Mary's prayer: her life, like her prayer, is a eucharist, a liturgy of thanksgiving. Mary is a human being consuming herself in the flame of God and expecting nothing in return. She loses herself in God and for God by proclaiming that he alone is important and that she is useless. This is the very meaning of her prayer of thanksgiving. She knows that all this is freely given, that it is extravagance on the part of God, and she sings this is an eternal Magnificat: "He has shown the power of his arm, he has routed the proud of heart, he has pulled down princes from their thrones and exalted the lowly" (Lk 1:51-52).

She realizes the words of Paul to the letter: "Rejoice, give thanks at all times (celebrate the eucharist)" (Ph 4: 4-6). She gives thanks that she is so precious in the eyes of God who casts his eyes upon her. She pours forth her strengths in libation expecting nothing in return, simply to please God, so that she may wear away and be consumed in the fire of God. Her life is a hymn to the Glory of God, and that frees her from all anxiety: "Do not worry about anything" (Ph 4:5). In the measure that a human being prays and sings the holiness of God, he perfectly fulfils his function as a creature. He is projected into existence in a state of sacrificial explosion. Mary is faithful to this oblation engraved in her being and she lets her heart sing as it was created by God. She is conscious of her profound being and all her life becomes a sacrifice of praise animated by an intense desire to lose herself for God and in God. She truly embodies praise of glory to his grace for she has been created to praise, adore and serve the God thrice holy.

At the same time, we discover that to be humble, as to love, we must be two. As long as man is not face to face with another being, whether it is the Whole Other or the other brother whose face and especially whose love he discovers, he cannot be humble. When we understand all the tenderness given to us by another and especially the little love we have for him, we become humble. Humility is not, therefore, displeasure with ourselves nor even the admission of our misery, our sin, and indeed our pettiness. Basically, humility implies that we look at God before looking at ourselves and that we measure the abyss which separates the finite from the Infinite. The better we accept to look at that, the more humble we become. To be enlightened on this point is to become intelligent.

What gives true humility to the Blessed Virgin is her acute sense of God's holiness. When Jesus says: "I bless you, Father, for hiding these things — the mystery of the knowledge of the Son and of the Father — from the learned and the clever and revealing them to mere children" (Lk 10:21-22), he is thinking first of his mother. It is because she is lowly and humble that she can hear the second part of Jesus' message: "Yes, Father, for that is what it pleased you to do in your kindness. Everything has been entrusted to me by my Father; and no one knows who the Son is except the Father, and who the Father is except the Son and those to whom the Son chooses to reveal him" (Lk 10:22).

Mary had the true intelligence, that of the lowly which makes one humble. Humility is as far from inferiority complex (it is even the opposite) as it is from superiority complex. Both are centered on oneself and not on the other. It is not a question of being conscious of oneself which is inevitable; Mary had this to a very lucid degree since she gave thanks to God for his wonders. It is rather a matter of stopping oneself, of dwelling at length one oneself, and of reflecting on one's miseries as well as on one's joys. A pure and humble heart is a heart which does not taint itself with the good or the evil it accomplished: it remains fixed on God. A humble heart is fascinated by something other than himself and, thereby, is free from all its complications.

The day we will see God face to face, we will be truly humble. Meanwhile, the nearer we come to God in prayer, the more we are in touch with him, the more he grows in us and the lesser we become. This is why Jesus is the perfect model of humility as man; as a matter of fact, he constantly gazed upon the Face of the Father for he was always with him. We understand that Christ would say: "I am meek and humble of heart" (Mt 11:29). The humility of the Blessed Virgin, says Father Molinié, is very little compared to the annihilation of Christ before God. For this reason, Saints affirm that true humility is that of Jesus within us. When a man has seen the humility of Christ, says Silouane of Athos, he experiences an indescribable joy; he forgets the earth and tends always more fervently towards God. "If the world understood the power of the words of Christ: Learn from me meekness and humility, he would set aside all other science in order to acquire this heavenly knowledge".[4]

God alone can force us down to our place by offering us his intimacy: humility is the measure of our intimacy with God. This brings us to say that prayer is possible only to the humble, that is, to those who acknowledge that the first place in their life belongs to God and who, consequently, take the second place, that is, the last one for themselves. For there are not three or four places, but two, the first and the last. Father de Foucauld would say that Christ had been so humble that he "had taken the last place." An English writer, Charles Morgan, said something like this: "Death teaches us that we are in second place, even if we do not know who has the first... Kneeling is, therefore, morally necessary for man." The

4. Translated from Silouane, *Spiritualité orientale*, Bellefontaine, n. 5, p. 24.

proud cannot pray, because they do not accept to depend upon another and to put themselves down on their knees. They would have to become aware by suffering and by groaning that pride clings to their skin; then, they would simply have to cry to God asking him to have pity on them. As soon as a man has gone through this motion, that is, falling on his knees and sighing in prayer, he is virtually freed from his pride, or at least he does not take himself seriously anymore.

For this reason, we dare say that Mary was in a state of continual prayer because she was in her rightful place before God. Since she had her original nature, she was aware she was receiving her being from the Father, and kneeling was as natural to her as breathing, since she accepted to be dependent upon God. We all have a little feeling of that in the better moments of our life, when prayer is given to us in an almost continual manner: we suspect that our first parents prayed all the time. We then say to ourselves: "If it is thus possible for us to be in a state of prayer for a week, it should be possible to be so all the time." If we do not manage to be so, it is because there was a catastrophe in our beginnings. The saints, those whom the Fathers call men of the eighth day (that of the Resurrection) and who have found continual prayer again, take us back to the man of the first day who also prayed all the time.

Mary especially had the humility of trust which goes much further than simple submission in the sense that she lovingly adhered, as did her Son, to all the wishes of the Father. In the depths of her being, her prayer blended with her humility, her trust, and, in short, with her adoration. For Mary, to pray was to make real the truth of her being as a creature completely dependent on the Father and surrendered to him.

7. He fills the hungry with good things

A real kinship exists between the humble and the hungry: both are centered not on themselves but on another. The humble man is fascinated by the Face of the Other, while the hungry one gives up the bread that would satisfy him (or that is imposed upon him by the circumstances of his life) to nourish himself solely on the other's word: "Man does not live on bread alone but on every word that comes from the mouth of God" (Mt 4:4). Reference to the other always forms the basis of the beatitude of the humble and the hungry. God dwells in the heart emptied of itself, because a man filled with the love of self cannot be filled with the Love of God. Thus is it for Mary in whom the Word of God could fix his abode for she was completely emptied of herself. This is the reason why God brings down the powerful and gives an astonishing power to those who know how to make themselves the humblest and lowliest of all beings. Who would suspect that the humility of Love is a terrible force, the most powerful of all, says Dostoïevski?

The words of the Magnificat: "The hungry he has filled with good things, the rich sent away with empty hands" (Lk 1:53) find their parallel in the first two beatitudes and curses: "How happy are you who are poor; yours is the kingdom of God. Happy are you who are hungry now: you shall be satisfied... But woe to you who are rich: you are having your consolation now. Woe to you who have your fill now: you shall go hungry" (Lk 6:20-21 and 24-25). It is clear to Luke that this is about the poor of material goods of this world, while to Matthew, it is about the poor of heart. Similarly, the hungry is the one who has nothing to eat like poor Lazarus who "longed to fill himself with the scraps that fell from the rich man's table" (Lk 16:21).

Both of them, the poor and the hungry, are in a situation of "want": one of consumer goods, the other of food. When Jesus addressed his message first to the poor, he aims it at the lowly and humble in the midst of whom he was born. His father and mother belonged to this class of humble people who often experience indigence and sometimes hunger. Thus, when Mary speaks of the hungry, she calls to mind the meaning of what is tragic in her own life or especially in that of others. Berdiaev would say: "When I am hungry, this is a physical fact; if my neighbor is hungry, this becomes a moral issue." There is the tragedy as it appears in the Magnificat and the Beatitudes. Our neighbor is always hungry. He is not necessarily hungry for bread, but often for a friendly word, an affectionate look or an act of tenderness.

Beyond physical hunger and material poverty, there is always a hunger for love at the psychological level and at profound levels of the being and the heart; there is the great chasm of hunger and thirst for God. We experience it in our countries of overconsumption where the abundance of food, pleasure and distractions hide and blank off the great hunger for God and the thirst for the meaning of life. This explains the present thirst for prayer. Basically, the great suffering of man is to be in exile, far from God, to be seeking without finding him and, especially, to experience solitude: "Where are you, my God? I seek you at dawn, my soul is thirsting for you" (Ps 63). Whether we want to or not, thirst for prayer is what torments the people of our contemporary world, even if they refuse to admit it! The only answer to solitude, the anxiety of the heart, to the thirst for love, the only one which is as a rock, is Jesus Christ dwelling in our heart since the Resurrection.

This is where the Blessed Virgin reveals to us her experience of God. It is as if she were telling us: "You will never know the joy of receiving Christ in your heart, of being the Abode of the Father and the Temple of the Spirit, if you seek food other than the word and the will of the Father." Jesus was already saying this clearly to the disciples who were urging him to eat after he had

124

spoken of the living water with the Samaritan woman: "My food is to do the will of the one who sent me, and to accomplish his work" (Jn 4:34). If you turn to other nourishments, even spiritual, such as activity, intellectual pleasure, even the exploits of ascesis or escape in prayer, you will fall under the gospel curse cast on the rich who want to find consolation on the earth.

To receive the normal consolations of life (the joy of friendship, of a meal or of a trip), or to use them to while away the time or to avoid the great penance of life or to cheat it are quite a different thing, for the promise of Jesus to the hungry who will be satisfied has an eschatological resonance. It would be using other foods to stave off one's hunger for the return of Christ. Let us think of two friends who must go separate ways for a long time and who decide to have a good farewell meal: nothing is more legitimate. But if one of the two tries to forget this parting by drowning his grief in food or alcohol, he is cheating the exile. Those who stop up the wound of their heart thirsting for God by things other than living water cheat the exile of penance. We must accept to carry our cross lamentably without cheating the grief of absence by saying each day: "My soul yearns and pines for the Lord's courts! My heart and my flesh sing for joy to the living God (Ps 48:2).

The hunger and thirst for God draw from us a cry which does not manage to come out and spring forth, because our heart is cluttered with riches and glutted with counterfeit foods. It is wrapped up in such a protective shell that the groanings of the Spirit do not find a way out. But by repeatedly striking our heart with the Ave Maria prayer, as Moses struck the rock, this cry will manage to come out someday and the living water will spring from our heart. Mary shows us a way of poverty and detachment, and beckons us to submit our heart to a real fast so that someday we may be able to know the great consolation of the Holy Spirit which will fill us with joy and peace.

For whenever the paradox appears, it is about the great consolation, a foretaste of heaven, promised and given by God. It was never said: "Woe to those who seek that consolation!" On the contrary, Jesus tells us again and again in many ways: "If any man is thirsty, let him come to me!" (Jn 7:38); "He who eats my flesh and drinks my blood lives in me and I live in him" (Jn 6:56); "He who comes to me will never be hungry; he who believes in me will never thirst" (Jn 6:35); "I have told you this so that my own joy may be in you and your joy be complete" (Jn 15:11). "My yoke is easy and my burden light" (Mt 11:30); "You will receive a full measure, pressed down, shaken together" (Lk 6:38). It is nevertheless for today and not only for tomorrow. There we come to the paradox of the Beatitudes: it is for now and not for now! How can we reconcile this apparent contradiction? Faith is bearable only if we possess in the bottom of our heart a burning feeling that the reward of faith will come.

Let us explain ourselves on the subject of the Blessed Virgin. With Christ, she asserts that those who hunger now will be satisfied and blessed later. To hunger is to experience a void, a hollow space; but to have a hollow space now must mean that it was filled before. We would not know what it is to hunger if we did not have the feeling of the joy of being satisfied. A blind man who has never seen the light does not know it. Thus there is no absence of joy without joy. Joy cannot be painfully absent without it being secretly present. So it is in the life of Mary: at the time of the Annunciation, she was filled with joy. This joy left its imprint as a red hot iron on her heart; it left a mark, a wound, a nostalgia, so that at the foot of the Cross, at the moment when the joy of the senses has disappeared, this joy is still secretly present. Mary will be able to say "yes" in the peace of God and the anointing of the Holy Spirit. This is what allows us to say that we may hunger and, at the same time, be filled with a secretly permanent joy hidden for the time being.

Let us take the example of Bernadette who saw the Blessed Virgin eighteen times. Once the apparitions ceased, everything was over, but she kept the taste, the nostalgia and the memory of them. She never recovered from these; she wished to die in order to see the Virgin Mary again. It is not only a question of the psychology of a human memory. If she was never able to recover from the sweetness of heaven, it is because this sweetness never left her. Later, her joy was hidden by the cross, but it was there nevertheless. We should never speak of the cross, of penance without speaking at the same time of glory and joy, as Jesus speaks of heaven to the penitent thief who is dying on the cross. In order to bear the cross and to live in hunger like Mary without becoming hardened or seeking consolations, we must have tasted the Glory of the risen Christ a little and have had the feeling that eternal life can fill us beyond all our desires.

In conclusion: The presence of Mary

We have now reached the end of Mary's prayer in the Magnificat. We could still question ourselves on the Blessed Virgin's poverty of heart at the very level of her desires and of her desire, for it is at this depth that we must seek the source of prayer of a human being and ask ourselves how to reconcile the desire with hunger and poverty; but we will approach this topic in the following chapter. For the time being, let us try to sum up in one word the movement of Mary's prayer in her relationship with God as well as with Christ living in her, and with Elizabeth. The word which seems to sum up Mary's secret the best at this stage is that of presence: Mary is present to whatever there is.

Mary is present first with regard to Elizabeth. Traditionally, the Visitation is considered to be the mystery of fraternal love. Some will perhaps be surprised to see that we have not spoken much about the charity of Mary for her old cousin Elizabeth. It is obvious that she went to her to be useful and to help her on the material level. One only has to go to the East to see how these people have the sense of family and of mutual help at all levels. But is seems that Luke wanted to lay emphasis on the simple presence of Mary to the reality of her cousin. He concludes the Magnificat in this way: "Mary stayed with Elizabeth about three months and then went back home" (Lk 1:56). The three months of her stay extend to the time of the birth of John (1:36), and Mary was surely present for that event.

I believe that we must especially contemplate Mary's charity at the time of the Annunciation and all along the sorrowful mysteries where the mystery of love displays all its folly. But the Visitation shows well that this folly does not consist only in "throwing one's body in flames or in giving away one's possessions to the poor" (1 Co 13:3 ff.). This folly is not primarily an "action" in the sense often understood by the moderns: to accomplish works, great and good, which are worth more by their content and their results than by the harmony, that is, by the spirit that prompts them. The mystery of the Cross is not an action but a passion: the Passion.

As much must be said about the Visitation which is not primarily an action but a presence: the presence of Mary to Elizabeth's happiness which makes John the Baptist leap with joy in her womb; the presence to John which sanctifies him by the power of the Spirit acting in Mary. We could also say: the presence of Elizabeth to Mary, the former offering the most beautiful praise possible because she was divinely chosen: "Blessed are you among all women" (Lk 1:42). What strikes Elizabeth especially is not so much that Mary has come to be useful to her, but that, in Mary's visit, she receives the great visit of her Lord. In Mary, God is the one who makes himself present to Elizabeth: "Why should I be honored with a visit from the mother of my Lord?" (Lk 1:43).

128

All this scene could be entitled: the mystery of the encounter. Mary's visit to Elizabeth is really the presence of the joy of God hidden in the midst of the darkness of this world.

But we must immediately add the following: Mary who is all relative to God always directs all those she meets to the one who, within her, gives her to be what she is. Hardly has she received Elizabeth's salutation that, by associating her with the prayer of the Magnificat, she brings her cousin into a movement which makes her present to God. She also directs John the Baptist to the Holy Spirit. But above all, Mary is present to the eternal Presence. She does not have to recall the presence of God to herself as we do. We used to say: "Let us put ourselves in the presence of God and adore him", as if it were possible for us to put ourselves in the presence of God or to remove ourselves from it. Dom Le Saux expresses this well: "The absence of that presence would be for us a return to nothingness, to that which never was."

We are not aware of the air we breathe; consciously or not, we breathe: this is the very condition for life. It is the same for the holy and divine Presence for Mary. It is enough for her to live and to be with all the gifts she has received, to say with the psalmist: "It was you who created my inmost self..., for all these mysteries I thank you: for the wonder of myself, for the wonder of your works. You know my soul through and through... when I was being formed in secret, fashioned in the depths of the earth" (Ps 139:13-15). As Saint Irenaeus says, "she supports the hand of her craftsman, the trace of his fingers, and keeps the model of it".[5]

In the same way that Mary is all present to God because she experiences his action, she is also present to Jesus living in her. She never loses touch with him since he is "incarnate" in her flesh. She does not cease thinking of him as he does not cease thinking of her and

5. Translated from *Contre les Hérésies*, IV 39, 2.

making her exist since he is the Word in whom all things were made (Jn 1:3). Because she is present to the Father and to his Son, she is present to her brothers. She listens to Elizabeth; she is attentive to her joy and also her difficulties, as she will also listen to the shepherds, to Simeon and to Anna. She does only that: listening with a quality of presence which has never been equalled.

But at the same time and in the same movement, she is present to her Lord. She is able to allow herself to be perturbed by the misery and the suffering of others (this is evident at Cana!). She knows how to attend to material details like the lack of wine, and do her work like everyone else, but at the first moment of freedom, she comes back to be in touch with the one who is her breath, her joy, her reason to live, and even, in short, her life. We feel that she is inhabited by the Father, the Son and the Spirit, and that this is why she can offer the only praise that is worthy of them.

Since she is all relative to God, Mary never holds back those who come to pray her. As Father Marie de la Chapelle expresses so well: "If the Blessed Virgin reveals Christ to us by what she is, she unites us to him by what she does".[6] If you are looking for a master of prayer, go to her, simply pray her by reciting the rosary and she will make you present to God and his Son. Let us conclude with a well-known passage from Grignion of Montfort which can help us to understand all the scope of Mary's activity towards us and how those who pray her are introduced in her Magnificat:

> You never think of Mary, that Mary, in your place, thinks of God; you never praise or honor Mary that Mary praises and honors God with you. Mary is all relative to God, and I would very well call her the relation to God; she is but relationship with God,

---

6. Translated from Dom Marie Lamy de la Chapelle, *Présence de Marie*, p. 180.

or the echo of God, which says and repeats nothing but God. If you say "Mary", she says "God". Saint Elizabeth praised Mary and called her blessed because she had believed; Mary, the faithful echo of God, breaks into praise: "Magnificat anima mea Dominum: my soul glorifies the Lord." What Mary did on this occasion, she does everyday: when we praise her, love her, honor her, or give to her, God is praised, God is loved, God is honored; we give to God through Mary and in Mary.[7]

---

7. Translated from *Traité de la vraie dévotion*, n. 225.

Chapter V

PRAYING WITH MARY
IN BETHLEHEM

When Saint Luke sets out to write "an ordered narrative" of the events which have taken place since the beginning, he intends to do the work of a historian since, after he has carefully taken information about everything, he submits the result of his discoveries to historical criticism. But for all this, he has no intention of writing a life of Jesus in the sense understood by modern biographers. His gospel is not lacking in biographical points of reference, but the scenes of Jesus' life are put at the service of a catechetics of faith after the event of Easter, starting from the experience of meeting Christ, dead and risen.

The person of Christ remains at the center of the gospel, but Luke has also spoken to us of the Blessed Virgin; he did not wish to retrace her life but, having lived in contact with her, he has collected her memories about Jesus and the manner in which the Blessed Virgin acted with him. He is the only one to have spoken so abundantly of Jesus' childhood since the first two chapters of his gospel are devoted to him, while Matthew speaks especially of the declaration made to Joseph, the visit of the magi, the flight to Egypt and the return to Nazareth.

We have also looked especially at Mary's faith and, consequently at her prayer, that is, what she has disclosed about her feelings towards God and Jesus, it being well understood that the best of her prayer is what she does not say. This is what Luke suggests when he says that she "stored all these events in her heart". So there is a "beyond" in the prayer of Mary as there is a "beyond" in the Word of God. We are here on the threshold of the mystery of the relationship of a human being with God and we can only question our own heart to discover the prayer that the Spirit suggests to us and, therefore, to contemplate from a distance the prayer that he brings forth in Mary's heart.

Having dealt with Mary's prayer at the Annunciation and in the Magnificat, we shall now confine ourselves to the contemplation of all the accounts which start from the birth of Jesus until the first words in the Temple, what has been commonly called the infancy narratives. This is why the title of this chapter should be broadened and include the presentation in the Temple, life at Nazareth and the first words of Jesus in Jerusalem.

But in a first point, we would like to go back to this phrase which I will call "the silence of Mary carrying Jesus within her" and go back still further to the desire she had of the divine motherhood. We could have treated that on the subject of Mary's prayer at the Annunciation but it appeared preferable to us to look at the event in itself and at Mary's answer of faith in order to understand the trial to which she was subjected and in what depth of desire the Son of God became flesh. In the same way that God prepared a nation during thousands of years through the trials of the desert and the captivity to have his Son born within it, so he prepared Mary's heart by focusing in her the power of the desire aspiring to the coming of the Lord.

1. The desire of the Spirit in Mary

Like all women who are expecting a child, Mary carried Jesus nine months within her, in her womb. His generation was really carnal but it was also and especially a mystery of faith. As the Christmas liturgy says: Jesus was conceived "non ex virili semine, sed mystico spiramine", which means: "not from male seed but from a mystical spiration", with the Holy Spirit coming down and covering Mary with its shadow. In the same way, Saint Leo will declare that Mary first conceived Jesus in her heart through faith before she conceived him in her flesh. Mary, therefore, waited for and conceived the Messiah in faith as Elizabeth proclaims: "Yes, blessed are you because you believed: the promise made to you by the Lord will be fulfilled" (Lk 1:45).

As the Christmas liturgy contemplates the child of Bethlehem (in-fans: the one who does not speak) in whom are manifested "the kindness of God our Savior and his love for mankind" (Tt 3:4), it contemplates during all of Advent not only the expectations of the People of Israel, but especially the anticipation of the Daughter of Sion, the Virgin Mary. Destined to center in her person all the desires of Israel, Mary was in her heart the focal point where all the People's desires, which she had made her own, would be brought to a degree of incandescence that would make them fruitful. It is the Spirit which brings forth the desire in her; it also makes this desire efficient because it operates "the will and the act" in us. This long wait in Israel found in Mary a heart so poor and humble that she could be set aflame to a degree that God could not resist Mary's wish.

We must not believe that only the Blessed Virgin's wish would bend the Lord's thought and will. We do think that the desires of the People of Israel, concentrated in Mary, were taken over and assumed by the Holy

Spirit to the point that it is God himself, by his Spirit who, in the heart of the Blessed Virgin, yearns for and attracts the coming of the Word. It is as if there were a face of God impressed in Mary which begs and pleads for another face of God, more hidden and mysterious, the one of his merciful holiness. The Blessed Virgin was thus borne by the strength and joy of the Holy Spirit in a gentleness which was the one of eternity, in a thirst unique in the world. This was also for Mary the source of an unfathomable suffering largely due to the darkness of her faith which produced this thirst in her.

We should linger on this active presence of the Holy Spirit in the depths of Mary's heart to grasp a little how it was refracted in her psychology at the level of her desires. As the dwelling of the Spirit in us arouses spiritual interests (Rm 8:1-17) and, therefore, prayer, so the presence of the Spirit in Mary brought about a total upheaval, not only in her profound being, but also in her clear conscience, in her way of seeing, thinking, acting and, therefore, praying. The desire to pray betrays the presence of the Holy Spirit in our hearts, as an underground pool of water present in the geological strata of a terrain manages to break open the soil some-day and becomes a spring... Let us examine more closely how the sanctifying intervention of the Spirit in the Virgin of Nazareth was a culminating point in the history of salvation, since Mary sums up in herself all the interests accumulated by the People.

We should reread here the Apostolic Exhortation on the cult of the Blessed Virgin by Pope Paul VI, in particular the passage speaking of the action of the Spirit in Mary from which we take our inspiration.[1] The Fathers of the Church attributed to the work of the Holy Spirit the original holiness of Mary "almost moulded by him and formed like a new creature".[2]

---

1. Translated from the Apostolic Exhortation, *Marialis cultus*, n. 26.

2. Translated from *Lumen Gentium*, n. 56.

While reflecting on the following gospel texts: "The Holy Spirit will come upon you and the power of the Most High will cover you with its shadow" (Lk 1:35) and "Mary found that she was with child through the Holy Spirit... what is conceived in her comes from the Holy Spirit" (Mt 1:18 and 20), they discovered, in the intervention of the Holy Spirit, an action which consecrated and made the virginity of Mary fruitful and transformed the Blessed Virgin into a Dwelling for the King or a place of rest for the Word, the Temple or the Tabernacle of the Lord, the Ark of the Convenant or of sanctification, all titles rich in Biblical connotations.

As they deepened even more the mystery of the Incarnation, they saw in the unfathomable relationship between the Holy Spirit and Mary a marital aspect poetically described by Prudentius: "The Blessed Virgin who was not married was espoused by the Holy Spirit",[3] and the Fathers called her "Sanctuary of the Holy Spirit", an expression which stresses the sacred character of the Blessed Virgin, she who had become the permanent abode of the Spirit of God. As they penetrated still further into the doctrine of the Paraclete, they understood that he is the source from which springs the plenitude of grace (Lk 1:28) and the abundance of gifts which beautify Mary. It is, therefore, to the Holy Spirit that they attributed the faith, hope and charity that inspired the heart of the Blessed Virgin, the strength that stimulated her adherence to the will of God, the energy that sustained her in Compassion at the foot of the Cross. The Fathers also note the influence of the Holy Spirit in the Magnificat, as well as her special presence in the Church of the Upper Room.

According to the doctrine of Saint Paul in chapter 8 of the Romans, it is not possible that a human being inhabited by the Spirit would not aspire to what is

3. Translated from *Liber Apotheosis*, vv. 571-572, CCL 126, p. 97.

spiritual (he "aspires"). When we understand the extent to which Mary was literally possessed by the Holy Spirit from the moment of her conception, we cannot doubt for one moment that the presence of the Spirit nourished aspirations in her which we cannot imagine since no man on earth — Christ excepted — has been possessed by God to this extent. I cannot help but set up here a parallel with Saint Thérèse of the Child Jesus whose countenance is so close to that of the Blessed Virgin and who resembles her. Her sister Marie was writing on the 9th of October, 1896: "Do you want me to tell you this? Well, you are possessed by God, but I mean *possessed*, the real thing... absolutely as the ungodly are by the evil one".[4]

On the other hand, we know that Thérèse spoke of her aspirations, which revealed the possession of her being by the love of God, in a passage which has become famous, a "lieu" of spiritual theology, the "B" manuscript addressed to Sister Marie du Sacré-Cœur. It is precisely in the context of prayer that she will be able to voice her desires, somewhat as if her aspirations were constrained in her heart and were just waiting to be exhaled in her prayer and gush forth like a geyser. In the course of her retreat, she experiences, besides her vocation as a spouse, a Carmelite and a mother of souls, the desire to be a warrior, a priest, an apostle, a doctor, a martyr and a prophet: "Ah! forgive me Jesus, if I am raving when I try to express again my desires, my hopes which border on the infinite; forgive me and heal my soul by giving it what it wishes!!!"[5] "O my Jesus, what will you answer to all my nonsense?... Is there a soul more lowly, more helpless than mine!... However, because of my weakness, you pleased yourself, Lord, in fulfilling my

---

4. Translated letter from Marie du Sacré-Cœur to Thérèse, 17.9.1896, in *Lettres de Thérèse de l'Enfant-Jésus*, Lisieux, 1948, p. 339.

5. Translated from Ms B, 2 verso, *Manuscrits autobiographiques*, p. 226.

small childish wishes, and today you want to fulfil other wishes, greater than the universe".[6] And she goes on, alluding to her contemplating prayer, consumed by her desire: "At prayer, my aspirations made me go through a real martyrdom".

If Thérèse's desires made her suffer a real martyrdom, can we not suppose that this same possession by God plunged Mary, in whom dwelt the plenitude of the Spirit, in the explicit desires which consumed her heart, especially at the moment when she was initiated to the mystery of Israel. These aspirations, incomprehensible to her, placed her in a situation of suffering similar in many ways to that described by Thérèse but much more profound because Mary, "almost moulded by the Spirit", was just pure desire having no means of staving off her thirst.

There is no doubt that Mary wanted and desired the coming of the Messiah, as did John the Baptist when he sends his disciples to ask Jesus: "Are you the one who is to come or should we expect someone else?" (Mt 11:3). Mary bore this burning desire even though she did not understand the depth of its demands; these, she will soon discover with a certain dread when the angel visits her.

Mary necessarily desired the motherhood of Jesus for the Holy Spirit gives nothing without making us want it in an unconscious and inchoative way. We receive from God what we hope from him and, if we expect nothing, the Holy Spirit cannot fulfil a nonexistent aspiration. Only our desire can attract God in us; he comes only to those who ask him with intensity, trust and perseverance. We have a feeling of what this law of desire means while training for prayer: we cannot teach methods of prayer to someone who does not have an intense wish to learn. If Mary desired motherhood, we must add immediately that she did not know what she was wishing

---

6. Translated from Ms B, 3 recto, *Manuscrits autobiographiques*, p. 228.

for, because being inhabited by the Infinite, she was also moved by the Infinite. On the other hand, having resolved to keep her virginity, she could not desire "something" in the area of motherhood. Her hopes were along the line of those of the People of Israel but without knowing what they involved because she was not fixed on her own little ideas.

It is not easy for us to understand that, because desire does not exist in a pure state in us; it is always fragmented by particular wishes. We should reread here the beautiful little book by Jean Lacroix: *Le désir des désirs* which makes us understand that well. For us, to desire always means to desire something: a lemonade if we are thirsty, a friend if we are alone, a promotion if we are relegated! It is at the object level that our desire deceives us for, once satisfied, it is not silenced for all that: it wanders and clings to other objects. This is why spiritual experts ask us "to module" the images where the objects of our desires take root. This is what makes Saint Teresa of Avila express the following: "Our desire has no remedy". We can understand that easily since we aspire to the Infinite, that is, God and that nothing in this world can fulfil that aspiration. This develops into a psychology of exile for those who accept not to stave off their hunger for the Infinite by other earthly foods. This psychology plunges them into an unfathomable depth of distress which nothing in this world can soothe. If they accept not to fly away from this distress but to let themselves sink right to the bottom of it, this distress becomes the source and nourishment for their continual prayer because, while they are calling for help, they do not cease to be in communion with the Father. They become only pure desire before the Face of God: "Where are you, Lord, my soul thirsts for you... I find rest in you alone".

From what we see in saints, we can imagine a little in what situation the Blessed Virgin was finding herself on the subject of her desire for motherhood. Not only did Mary not know how to soothe this thirst, for it was boundless like that of Thérèse of the Child Jesus, but she did not even know, literally, what she wanted. Because her desires came from the Holy Spirit, she could not know "from where they came and where they were going." It is somewhat proper to women not to know what they want, says Teresa of Avila to Father Gratien who claimed he knew very well what the sisters were thinking. This is not a fault, she would say, it is even an additional asset for they do not hold on to their "little ideas" but accept at all times to be moved by the idea of the Other; this is the very definition of faith as we have seen in the case of Mary at the Annunciation.

The Holy Spirit drew the Blessed Virgin to an abyss of surrender by the play alone of her conflicting desires which he inspired her. We must admit that these desires were of an intensity great enough to make them both irresistible and incompatible. And so this is where we come to the trial of the Blessed Virgin, as there had been a trial for our first parents: no one can escape that! They were asked to give up not the forbidden fruit but the taking possession of it on their own, that is, the motion which consists in putting out one's hand and extending it to the object: the fruit of the tree of knowledge which is simply the Glory of God. It would have been sufficient for them to open wide their mouth and receive it free. Like Prometheus, they wanted to take possession of the fire of heaven on their own and they lost everything.

The Blessed Virgin knew a trial of this type and the key to the situation was obviously self-denial. We must understand the meaning of her self-denial for that goes for us too. It is not a matter of stifling or rejecting our desire; this would be mutilation and condemning ourselves to see the desire reappearing in another form, sometimes more violently. Self-denial bears precisely on the manner of fulfilling our desire: Shall we fulfil it on our own or shall we receive it from someone else? For the Blessed Virgin, the manner is expressed by these

140

words: "How shall this be?" She had to leave it all to God as to how her desire would be fulfilled. She had chosen virginity and renounced fecundity. The angel's words seem to invite her to reverse her choice; this is why she asks herself how these things will come about. Her attitude is a very active one: Paul speaks of faith put into practice or of the work of faith (1 Th 1:3). This faith amounts to a summoning up of all one's energies in a dynamism of communion to the will of another.

"In truth, in her submissive frame of mind, she had already renounced *everything*..., which is the only way of "choosing everything" as did Thérèse, daughter of Mary, two thousand years later. Mary desired fecundity as much as virginity. Unable to renounce either of her desires and to see how they could be reconciled, she had chosen not to choose anything and to hand herself over to God (even before the angel's words) as to the "Quomodo fiet istud?" "How will this be?" The unlimited scope of her thirst precisely required, by its very folly, that she take no initiative to soothe it. (That is why I am not certain she had taken the vow of virginity. She simply consecrated to God the strengths of her soul and body). Unable to find her way out of the conflicting desires in which the Holy Spirit was plunging her, she left entirely to him, in total darkness, the task of unraveling this situation".[7]

2. The silence of faith

As soon as Mary pronounces her "Fiat", that is, the act of obedience of her faith under the inspiration of the Holy Spirit — one must always remember this — there will be no more trial in her life, in the strong sense we

7. Translated from M.D. Molinié, *La Sainte Vierge et la Gloire*, Cahiers sur la Vie Spirituelle, Deuxième Série, L'Épouse, 1973, p. 102.

give to this term, like the trial of the first Adam or the Temptation of Jesus in the desert which will reappear at the Agony. According to M. Jean Mouroux, she lays down the groundwork of a new situation for herself. In the depths of her freedom, Mary reassumes all her being and reorientates it in the direction of God's will; this act creates in all her person a situation of no-return. Then, she will perform deeds which will prolong this groundwork and inscribe her existence deep into history. Teresa of Avila says that when a man enters a state in which he is espoused by the Three Persons of the Holy Trinity, that is, in the affective equilibrium of Glory, he can sin no more. This does not mean that Mary had no more struggles, nothing is ever done once and for all, but in each new situation where she will confront darkness, Mary will come back to her Fiat.

Never has a saint or a Father of the Church detected in Mary the least temptation to say "no" or to go back on her initial "yes". Whether it is in the trial of clarification with Joseph, in the Temple episode, at Cana or especially at the foot of the Cross, they have always seen in Mary an extension of the "yes" of the Incarnation. Mary's decision was a matter of course from the moment she accepted to say "yes" to the end.

That is why the Fathers never cease admiring and contemplating her "Fiat" of the Annunciation. At that moment, she performs a totally free act of the same type as Abraham's consent to sacrifice Isaac or the obedience of Jesus in the Agony, an act which prolonged the "Ecce venio" of his entrance into the world. Mary's Fiat was surely preceded and followed by other acts of obedience, but it is the Fiat of the Annunciation that definitely places her in the triune orbit where each of the Persons stands aside to allow the other in his place.

By saying her Fiat, Mary is at the top of the line of Witnesses to the faith as opposed to Satan and his refusal to submit: "I will not serve". This explains the radical antagonism between him and Mary, between darkness and light, between the meekness of God and the harsh ness of the father of lies. From desire to desire, from self-denial to self-denial, Mary was prepared to pronounce this "yes" which ushered her into the struggle of faith.

We cannot doubt that Mary subsequently lived in an obscure and naked faith. This is the reason why she is our model and intercessor. It is to her that we must have recourse in our own struggle of faith, for she lived in the same darkness as we do, while Christ saw the Father who always remained with him. Moreover, when Vatican Council II calls to mind the figure of the Blessed Virgin, it says: "She grew in faith all through her pilgrimage on earth". This amounts to saying that if her trial of faith was definitive at the moment of her Fiat, she nevertheless knew the struggle of faith throughout her life. We often think that faith is acquired once and for all; if it is a relationship with God, there is always an unpredictable aspect to it, since we never know what God will demand of us and what our answer will be.

The unpredictable aspect of God appears clearly in the life of Mary after the angel's visit: the events will follow one another to the point of surprising and, sometimes, bewildering her. In the unfolding of her history, she is perplexed by events that jostle and disconcert her in her plans, but she is never caught off her guard even when she poses a question. Since she prays and meditates in her heart, she readjusts to the will of the Father coming to her under the disguise of events. Then she can really say her Fiat again and surrender herself to God. Does she truly need to say it again since it has been pronounced in such depth? It is enough for her to be silent and to get in touch again with this source of joy and peace which dwells in her heart to face the new situations which come to her with grandeur and serenity.

Having reached this point, faith is transformed into a pure silence of adoration and that is where we find

Mary's prayer again. When one has to speak much in a conversation to preserve a contact and a relationship, we can definitely presume that this relationship has not yet reached a certain depth which keeps the speakers in true communion beyond words. It is the same with Mary's prayer as it identifies itself with silence. As soon as the angel leaves her, Mary enters into this silence which nothing can disturb. Even her visit to Elizabeth keeps her in peace and silence in an atmosphere of prayer from which the Magnificat will break forth.

It is a silence attentive to the growing Word in her. Without having known the embrace of a human being, she bears the fruit of her love in her heart: it is the work of the Holy Spirit. Thus the child which she carries in her womb is shrouded in a twofold mystery: that of any child in its mother's womb and that of its face which she cannot relate to any father. This is a substantial silence in which Mary yields her flesh and blood to her child in a marvellous exchange of love. She has no need of speaking; it is enough for her to know that the Father sees in secret.

Mary remains in this silent attitude towards Joseph when he discovers that she is pregnant and is resolving to repudiate her secretly so as not to shame her publicly. Like Jesus in his Passion, she is silent! What is most remarkable is that God intervenes only once the decision has been made; he allows all the secondary causes to come into play and especially Mary's silence: "Joseph had made up his mind to do this when the angel of the Lord appeared to him" (Mt 1:20). God does not speak idle words; he intervenes as little as possible in the course of this adventure because he lets people live according to the laws of human existence and especially in the darkness of faith. Mary was surely hurt by this suspicion weighing on her; she must have been tempted to defend herself, but she surrendered herself completely into the hands of God. She therefore left him the entire task of defending her cause. At the last moment, God intervenes and Joseph, the righteous man, understands and also gives his adherence in faith.

The following words are truly applicable to Mary: "In silence will be all your strength." Her dialogue is with the Father in heaven; it is also with her Son living within her, as says Mr. Olier: "O Jesus, living in Mary, come and live in your servants". She does not need to see his face to dialogue with him for she knows that he is the Son of the Most High, the one whose countenance bears no resemblance to anything. It is enough for her to say: "You", for an immeasurable current of human life to run through him and, at the same time, a wave of love and life sent from the heart of the Three to surge back into Mary. Her prayer consists in simply receiving these whiffs of triune air which give her a foretaste of heaven. In silence, she gives her child all the attention and love she can. Everyone knows how a child in the womb of its mother responds to all the tenderness that surrounds him: she is forming it in all its being. When Jesus will be moved with compassion before the crowds in distress, before a widow or face to face with a sinner, he will have someone to take after since his mother will have given him all the tenderness she could, or rather the Tenderness of the Father will have passed through her into his heart. It is also through this tenderness that she shows him the Father's love. Mercy is proper to God and we can only be the witnesses of this Mercy.

There will be yet another struggle of faith for Mary when Jesus will assert in the Temple that he belongs to the Father in heaven and impose a certain breach in his relationship with his parents on earth. His mother will deeply feel this wrenching and will not keep herself from asking him a question as she did to the angel on the day of the Annunciation. But she agrees since she has decided to say "yes" to God whatever may be the way he will affect her. We must scrutinize these words of Mary because they express the best in her prayer. They will teach us not to evade any question in our own prayer and also teach us, at the same time, to rejoice not to understand so that we may adore.

It is difficult for us to enter into Mary's trial of faith and also into the struggle which followed her Fiat, so pure and delicate is this trial: pure because of her Immaculate Conception and delicate because of the subtleties in the ways of the Holy Spirit in Mary's heart. In our lives, we do not place this struggle enough at the level of faith; we place it rather at the level of generosity or will power. We are obliged to admit that we have neither, whereas the subtlety of the Spirit should teach us to examine ourselves to see if we have any faith in God or in ourselves. As sinners rather roughly-hewn, we do not understand well the subtle shrewdness of the Spirit who murmurs the gentle voice of God at the bottom of our hearts. His voice is all the more imperceptible for he does not raise it because of his timidity and he remains silent when we make noise or turn our back to him. We often commit sins of superficiality in order to avoid hearing his voice. What would one day, or even one hour, lived in total obedience to the Holy Spirit be like?

The Holy Spirit did everything in Mary. He shaped Jesus' human nature by covering her with his shadow. The Spirit also inspired Mary her faith and her charity. This is the reason why the Fathers invite us to have recourse to Mary's intercession in order to obtain from the Spirit the capacity to beget Christ in us, as this magnificent prayer by Saint Ildephonsus attests: "I pray you, I pray you, holy Virgin: that from this Spirit which made you beget Jesus, I may receive Jesus myself. That my soul may receive Jesus by this Spirit which made it so that your flesh conceived that same Jesus. That I may love in this Spirit in which you adore him yourself as your Lord and you contemplate him as your Son."[8]

---

8. Translated from Saint Ildephonsus, *De Virginitate perpetua sanctæ Mariæ*, ch 12, PL 96, c. 106.

3. Adoring in silence in Bethlehem

The Messiah was to be born in Bethlehem, the city of David. To everyone, Jesus was the son of Joseph and Mary who was to be also of Davidic ancestry. Thus the birth of God's Word in flesh takes its place in the history of the Jewish people, in a human family and in a very precise location: Bethlehem. When God comes into our world, he subjects himself to the natural laws of all human births, to the circumstances of history to the point that he is totally buried right in this earth of man and no one recognizes him. We are astonished as we read the story of Jesus' birth in Luke by the scope of the framework in which the event is set: "Now at this time Caesar Augustus issued a decree for a census of the whole world to be taken" (Lk 2:1). It is the whole world that is present in the little town of Bethlehem, already so full of the descendants of David that Mary and Joseph find no room at the inn (Lk 2:7)!

But we are yet more astonished by the contrast emphasized in Luke between the whole world and the extremely modest proportions of the event. When the Word of God comes into this world, he does not even find a room to be born in but simply a manger with straw. If the inhabitants of Bethlehem had known what was going on in their little town, they would have been eager to lodge Mary and Joseph in a comfortable inn. But Jesus will be born in the company of animals unaware of the event. This is exactly what will happen at the Calvary on Good Friday: the face of the world is convulsed and yet it continues its stupid round unaware of the event of salvation: "Stat Crux, dum volvitur orbis" (the motto of the Carthusians).

"While they were there the time came for her to have her child, and she gave birth to a son, her first-born. She wrapped him in swaddling clothes, and laid him in a manger" (Lk 2:6-7). The account of these facts is so sparing in words, so discreet, so much a part of the history of the Jewish people and that of Mary and Joseph that we are astounded, amazed by these facts. "And everyone who heard it was astonished at what the shepherds had to say" (Lk 2:18). Certain manuscripts say that they were "filled with wonder". The contrast is even more striking that there is a radical disproportion between the humility of the child lying in the manger and what Luke says immediately after: "And suddenly with the angel there was a great throng of the heavenly host, praising God and singing: 'Glory to God in the highest heaven, and peace to men who enjoy his favor'" (Lk 2: 13-14). The shepherds will greet this praise and they will be able, while returning home, to give it back to God, after having made it their own: "And the shepherds went back glorifying and praising God for all they had heard and seen; it was exactly as they had been told" (Lk 2:20).

It is impossible to go any further in this account without faltering in speech and, even if this faltering is sustained by the Holy Spirit, it opens out easily into the silence of adoration, into this zone of mystery within us where human intelligence loses its footing and finds its rest in rejoicing that it does not understand. Adoration begins in us when we are confounded by the meeting of extremes: an abyss of Glory which barely touches an abyss of humility. Before this mystery, we can only remain there, in silence, trying to imagine these things with simplicity. Thus when the most mysterious face of God — that of his Mercy — becomes flesh in the world, the intensity changes into silence and we risk passing by without seeing him, so well has he espoused our human nature. In order that this mystery may become visible to our eyes, God himself must initiate us to his secrets.

For that reason, we would like to propose to you a way of praying and contemplating this scene of the Nativity in the line of the Ignatian contemplations and in a rather flexible framework, so that we may stand back and let the Holy Spirit himself put in our heart what he wishes to give us. It would also be good to go back to the Annunciation scene for the method of praying this scene proposed by Saint Ignatius is very suggestive. On the other hand, in these scenes of childhood life, we will never insist enough on the necessity of going back to the same events, for repetition helps to sink the gospel "seeds" in our heart and, through the material character of the facts, we perceive "the silent depth" of the events.[9] Little by little, these contemplations assimilate us to the Blessed Virgin and give us her taste, her ways of seeing things, of thinking, of feeling and, therefore, of praying.

The subject is the Second Week of the Exercises, after the Kingdom. Ignatius is speaking of the "mysteries of the childhood life" and he intimately links the Annunciation to the Nativity. As always, he urges the retreatant to give a full hour to prayer, taking care to begin with a prayer of request in order that his whole being may be seized by the mystery. I often advise a rather prolonged cry of pleading to the Holy Spirit at the beginning of the hour of meditation until we experience that our heart, our intelligence, even our body are impregnated by prayer. It sometimes happens that we must spend a whole hour to reach this point.

Then, when prayer has well taken root in us, Ignatius advises to approach the event of the Annunciation from a triple aspect. The manner of undertaking these contemplations is very important for it is accomplished by a slow impregnation of all our person. Before the mysteries of the Lord and of his mother, we must grasp all the dimensions of the event: the divine dimension of height, the universal dimension of length and the particular dimension of the event itself. This is never a flat contemplation, but a gradual introduction into the mystery where the event is considered in its totality.[10]

---

9. Translated from P. Evdokimov.

10. In order to follow well here, we should consult the "Livret des Exercices", numbers 101 to 117.

The first introduction places us fully in the heart of the Trinity (divine dimension) where "the three divine Persons looking over all the surface of the earth... decide in their eternity that the second Person will become man to save mankind" (102). When we examine the account of the Annunciation in Luke, we have no problem in detecting its triune structure: we are before the Father who showers grace upon Mary because he wants to make her the Mother of his Son by covering her with the shadow of the Spirit. During prayer is the time to contemplate the Holy Trinity at work in Mary (plenitude of grace, divine motherhood, assumption), then to see how the Son saves Mary, his Mother, unites with her to make her the mother of the Church and of men, finally to see how the Holy Spirit sanctifies Mary, prays in her and makes her his spouse. At the greatest depth of her human nature, Mary was already Daughter of the Father and Mother of the Word: the action of grace in Mary will take root in all her humanity. Prepared to conceive the Son of the Father, she received in her womb the eternal Word of God. We understand in this way the true sense of God's "Presence" in Mary, as in ourselves. It is not a face to face presence but an action of the Father who makes himself present by his proceedings and invites Mary to collaborate with him. It is a common activity of the one and the other in order that love may be revealed to men in the Son.

We can then suspect the intimacy with God that Mary was already living when she received her message. This is why, after having contemplated the action of the Blessed Trinity in Mary, we must also penetrate into her prayer. Here Ignatius makes us ask for the grace "of an intimate knowledge of the Lord to love him and to follow him" (104). At the end, he proposes a dialogue, that is, "to speak to God as a friend speaks to his friend" (54). "At the end, have a conversation, thinking of what I must say to the three Persons or to the eternal Word made flesh or to his mother. Ask what we shall feel within ourselves in order to follow and to imitate better our Lord newly incarnate" (109). It is interesting to note that in the triune prayer, we must always start from what we feel within ourselves. This is equivalent to saying that in our heart we can experience what went on in Mary, for it is the same Spirit who acts on the one and the other. To enter into this triune prayer, we must feel very free and go in by whatever door opens the best and the fastest! For some, it will be enough to go through the Blessed Virgin so that she may beseech the Holy Spirit to come and pray in them. Others will prefer to unite themselves to Christ living in Mary, and sometimes it will be sufficient to stay with her under the eyes of the Father. It matters little which Person we address, for each of them sends us to the other two: "Whoever sees me sees the Father", says Jesus (Jn 14:9). Little by little, we penetrate into this immense movement of love and knowledge which is the triune dance.

The second introduction places us in the universal dimension. It is to save the entire mankind that the Word becomes flesh: "To see the vastness of the world where live nations so numerous and so diverse" (103). We must note the all-embracing character of the prayer by linking the second introduction to the first. The Word comes from the Holy Trinity and is directed to all of mankind. Thus all is given to us in one single movement and we never separate the Son from the Father nor from men. There is always a twofold temptation lying in wait for us: the first one is not to see the divine origin of Christ anymore and the second is not to measure the full implications of his human deep-rootedness. We know that the twofold error entails serious consequences for our apostolic action, which can degrade itself into spiritualism or into secular humanism.

The third introduction aims at the event itself, that is, the visit of the angel to Mary. Ignatius insists on the role of the eye, especially in the second contemplation of the Nativity. We must impregnate ourselves with the persons, see their faces, listen to their words in view of an intimate transformation of our being through "the eye of the imagination" (112). We will come back to this on the subject of the Compassion of Mary (chapter VII) to lay emphasis on the role of the "spiritual senses" in prayer. It is an impregnation of the whole person; because of this, it requires time before the mysteries may come down in us. We must never anticipate, but come back often to the mysteries already contemplated to move from a human level to a spiritual one in order that everything be bathed in the gentleness of the Holy Spirit. Ignatius' reflection in this domain displays a great psychological finesse: "I must read uniquely the mystery that I will have to contemplate without reading any other for fear that the consideration of one mystery might disturb that of the other" (127). One of the great temptations in the life of prayer is to adopt the accumulation style rather than live at the profound level of assimilation. We "consume" spiritual goods as we consume material goods and that prevents the unification of the self in the contemplation of a single reality. As a remedy against that temptation, we must consider one mystery after the other in an atmosphere of great peace.

Finally, the deep spiritual attitude of Mary and Joseph before the child of Bethlehem is that of the shepherds, of the poor and the lowly, admitted to a great feast which they do not understand: "As for me, to make myself a little pauper and a little unworthy slave who looks at them, contemplates them and serves them in their needs, as if I were present, with all the reverence and respect possible" (114). We must go down even deeper in the humility of Bethlehem to see the Cross silhouetted against the background. Ignatius makes us see the mystery of the Redemption as a whole: the Cross is already present in the Nativity scene since the contemplation of the Incarnation makes us enter into the history of salvation. It is the intuition present in the stained glass in Chartres representing the Nativity:

Jesus's cradle becomes an altar: "And at the end of so much pain after the hunger, the thirst, the heat and the cold, the injustices and the insults, he will die on the Cross; and all that for me. Then, while reflecting, we must draw some spiritual benefit" (116).

The joy of Christmas is the very presence in flesh, in Bethlehem, of the one who has neither a beginning nor an end, a frail presence of the Almighty. It is the discreet arrival of the Creator introducing himself into the world "in the middle of the silence of the night." It is especially the incarnation of the most hidden face of God, that of tenderness and of his Mercy. Jourdain de Saxe says: "The name of Jesus is Mercy". But we know, at the same time, that the birth of Jesus will unleash the powers of darkness and from that moment he is in danger of death. If God had not taken action with the Magi, Herod would have quickly done away with him. Thus the hidden life of Jesus will become that of a hunted man, until the day in Cana where he will manifest his Glory by offering himself to the Cross under the impulse of Mary.

On this child lying in a manger is the wound of God who offers himself silently to us. He asks us absolutely nothing, simply to see and to understand to what point he is on his knees before us to love us, as he will be at the feet of his disciples on the evening of the Last Supper to wash their feet. The understanding of that love must be given to us from above, exactly as for the Eucharist: "this is why I told you that no one can come to me unless the Father allows him" (Jn 6:65). The purpose of Mary's supplication before the manger is to make all our resistances fall before this love so that our heart may be broken and melted. This is the time to ask him, as well as to Saint Joseph, for the grace to be touched by this child, so poor and so vulnerable. We must come to Bethlehem to contemplate the wound and the suffering of God who makes himself a small child. By placing our hand in that of the Blessed Virgin, something will break the hardness of our thoughtless heart, as a child is upset at the sight of his parents in distress: it is the only way of being initiated to the science of love.

4. "And he was named Jesus"

Luke concludes the story of Jesus' birth with the circumcision and the assigning of the Name: "When the eighth day came and the child was to be circumcised, they gave him the name of Jesus, as he had been named by the angel before his conception" (Lk 2:21). Usually the parents choose a name: it is up to the father to assign that name to single out the child from the others and to be able to engage in a dialogue with him. As for Mary and Joseph's son, the name came from above, and each of the parents received from the Father through the instrumentality of the angel, the mission to assign him the name of Jesus (Lk 1:31 for Mary, and Mt 1:21 for Joseph). Thus their authority over Jesus is mediate and they will always be for him the visible images of fatherhood and motherhood in heaven, even if Joseph confers the Davidic filiation upon the child by giving him his Name.

To emphasize the bond between Jesus and God, there is the meaning of the Name. The word "Jesus" means "the Lord saves". At no time can we dissociate Jesus from God, for since the Incarnation, the destiny of God is inextricably linked with that of man, to save him. As we have already said, Jesus is the Name blessed among all names, the "first name" of God. In order to be able to pronounce this name, one must be under the influence of the Spirit: "No one can say, 'Jesus is Lord' unless he is under the influence of the Holy Spirit" (1 Co 12:3). Moreover, since Jesus has become Christ by the anointing of the Spirit, God puts this same Spirit in our heart to introduce us into the triune communion: "God is the one who firmly establishes us along with you in Christ; it is he who anointed us and has sealed us. He has given

us as pledge, the Spirit, that we carry in our hearts"
(2 Co 1:21)

While commenting the Magnificat, we have seen that Mary prayed by pronouncing the most Holy Name of God (Lk 1:49): "Holy is his Name". We can now take another step and suspect that Mary's prayer also consisted in lovingly repeating the Name of Jesus. Each time she pronounced this word, she must have remembered that it had been given to her by God to enter into a relationship with his Son. She knew the meaning of this Name and, in pronouncing it, she was not only expressing the maternal love she bore for her Son, as all mothers lovingly like to say over and over the name of their child, but she made of it a prayer and a plea, because she knew how she had everything from her Son: "Jesus, save me". There is not a human being on earth who could have pronounced the name of Jesus with as much respect, love and tenderness as Mary, so impregnated was her heart with the gentleness of the Holy Spirit.

As Jesus drew away from her because of his mission and especially after the Ascension when he was hidden in the glory of the Father, Mary discovered another relationship with her Son. She did not search for him in places outside of herself anymore, but the Holy Spirit attracted her to the core of her heart to find the presence of Jesus hidden within it, as he was hidden in the Glory of the Father. As she invoked his name or murmured it, she understood that he was suddenly present there, in a manner which is always new, but most profound. The name of Jesus present in the innermost part of her heart sustained her hope and life. The name of her Son was the host to her interior silence and he never was silent. Like a spring of tenderness, he murmured in the inner depth of herself the gentle message of his presence, his love and his faithfulness.

Since the return of Jesus to the Father, we are about in the same situation as Mary was. Like Peter we can say: "We did not see him, yet we love him; and still without

155

seeing him, we believe in him. We are already filled with a joy so glorious that it cannot be described, because we are receiving the reward of our faith, that is, the salvation of our souls" (1 P 1:8). His presence has branded our heart like a burn with a red-hot iron, a wound that will never heal. That is why there is an indelible sadness in us as long as he has not returned. Nothing will be able to replace that presence of Jesus. Since the return of Jesus to his Father, Mary, like the Church, teaches us to say and to murmur indefinitely: "Maranatha! Come, Lord Jesus!" The name of Jesus which we keep is the name that saves us from despair and revolt: it is the rempart of our life: "Jesus, save me; Jesus, help; Jesus, have pity!".

To take Mary with us is to place ourselves at her school where she will teach us to murmur the name of Jesus, believing that he is there to hear and to answer us. Even if Jesus seems far from us, even if he is no more on this earth, we know that by lovingly repeating his name, he will surround all our feelings from those of repentance to those of tenderness, from the need for forgiveness to a most loving and intimate communion with him. Because Mary holds the secret of how to make us sinners agreeable to God, she will know how to reach us at the moment of our deepest distress of sin and suffering to unite the loving invocation of the name of Jesus to the publican's prayer: "Jesus, Son of the saving God, have pity on me, a sinner!"

There is no Christian prayer possible unless it springs from the revelation of our sin at the moment the Father forgives us and restores us in his gentle pity. Thus what we traditionally call the Jesus prayer, if it is a threshold, already constitutes a summit of prayer, the one which remembers the merciful Father and throws us unceasingly in his arms. Jesus will become the call whose soft murmur will drown all other sounds. Little by little, the man of prayer will be settle there, seated on the curbstone of the well of his heart, with the Jesus prayer;

he will dig the ground until the rivers of living waters spring forth. From then on, he will go and inhabit the name of Jesus, dwell in his love, contemplating meanwhile his face in the deepest recesses of his heart, as we see our face reflected in the well.

But, in return, Jesus will inspire us to pronounce the name of his Mother with tenderness, as he was the only one able to do so. Never will there be a man on earth able to pronounce, like him, the name of Mary with as much gentleness, filial tenderness and gratitude. The first name which opens the lips of the little child, the beautiful word "mama" is the name given to the face of tenderness bent over him, day and night. But it is much more the name which already dwells in his heart and without which there would never be security, happiness and life for him. Thus the name of Mary has inhabited Jesus' heart; it has taken root in him and invaded him with tenderness, light and joy. It has brought with it the certitude of loving and of being loved. While pronouncing these human names of "papa" and "mama", Jesus was living another yet more intimate and deeper relationship with his Father in heaven.

To his intimate friends, Jesus reveals the secrets of Mary's motherhood; he shows them how we must take refuge in her by invoking her blessed name. On the 12th of July, 1897, Thérèse of Lisieux was recalling, with Mother Agnes, the most striking graces of her existence. She admitted that at the beginning of her religious life, she had received an exceptional grace: the one of experiencing in a very intense manner the continual presence of Mary in her life. This is in July 1889: she has received the habit and goes into the garden to pray in the grotto of Saint Magdalen, and then she knows a moment of recollection:

"There was, as it were, a veil thrown for me over all things of this earth... I felt I was entirely hidden under the veil of the Blessed Virgin. At that time, I was in charge of the refectory and I remember I was doing

157

things as if I were not doing them: it was as if I were working with a borrowed body. I remained so for an entire week. This supernatural state was very difficult to explain. God alone can put us in it and it is sometimes enough to detach a soul from the earth forever".[11]

5. "A sword will pierce your soul" (Lk 2:35)

Through these scenes from Jesus' childhood, we understand better how the Holy Spirit forms prayer in Mary's heart and makes it grow in trust and love. She listens to the words of Simeon, of the aged prophetess Anna, and then she watches what is happening around her. She does not build for herself a world of dreams, ideal and unreal, in which she would be sheltered against the reactions of the world around her. Basically, Mary never interposes between herself and the Lord the world of her dreams and phantasms. She lives in the most daily reality and integrates to her prayer and life the words, the events and the persons who come to her.

In the scene of the Presentation to the Temple, which we are going to contemplate, she lives like any Jewish mother and submits herself to the customs of the Law because she is subjected to it as is her Son (Ga 4:4): "And when the day came for them to be purified as laid down by the Law of Moses, they took him up to Jerusalem to present him to the Lord, according to the Law of the Lord: Every first-born male must be consecrated to the Lord — and also to offer in sacrifice, in accordance with what is said in the Law of the Lord, a pair of turtledoves or two young pigeons" (Lk 2:22-24).

As a matter of fact, the law of purification concerns only the mother (Lv 12:1-8). Therefore, Mary submits herself to the Law, but she goes much further than the Law. Luke simply wants to lay stress on how Jesus'

---

11. Translated from *Carnet Jaune*, II, 7, 2.

parents wanted to fulfil completely the task which God had entrusted to them. Mary makes real for Jesus the words he has said himself: "You wanted no sacrifices, offerings or holocausts, but you prepared a body for me... Here I am! I have come to do your will" (Heb 10:5-9). Mary gives us there an admirable example of submission to the Law and to events, assumed in a free decision, and lives in faith. She meditates in her heart and integrates in her human history the divine mysteries with which God associates her.

Mary does not live in a dream, but she is present to herself and to her Son, to the moment she is living and to the actions she is accomplishing. Day after day, she assimilates her vocation as mother of Jesus and understands her mission better. In this way, she teaches us to live our vocation and mission, not according to our dreams, our ideal or our ideas, but by receiving the Word of God which springs from the truth of our existence and from the events of our history. We understand why Luke insists on the meditation of Mary which always oscillates between two poles: the Word of God meditated and prayed from the bottom of her heart, and her confrontation with the unforeseen event coming from the external world and which is also a lived Word of God. It is the agreement of these two realities that authenticates Mary's prayer while keeping her head and her heart in heaven and her feet rooted to the ground.

Thus through a prescription of the Law which is imposed upon her from the outside world, she makes the deliberate act of offering all her being and that of Jesus whom she consecrates in a true holocaust, in order that the fire of love from heaven may consume it: this is prayer in action. Moreover, this submission to the Law will without delay give Mary the opportunity to hear God speak about her Son through the persons he inspires. Very simply, Mary will integrate again in her prayer the words of Simeon and Anna. If we wish to enter into Mary's prayer, we must act in the same way as we did for the contemplation of the Nativity: see the people, watch their faces, listen to their words, weigh their reactions, scrutinize their amazement, to enter into the profound attitude of their heart.

The framework here is very simple: we have on the one hand Mary and Joseph with the child Jesus; on the other hand, there are Simeon and Anna not to speak of the "Temple staff": but the latter are too taken up by the material concerns relative to the cult to be attentive to the mystery, all within, which is unfolding itself in the secret recesses of hearts. Only the lowly, the humble and the poor, those whose heart is imbued with the light of the Spirit, have a look penetrating enough to see the messianic light which shines on Jesus' face: this is the case with Mary and Joseph, with Simeon and Anna.

Once again, God uses an intermediary to reveal to Mary the mystery of her Son. As was the case for Elizabeth, it is the Holy Spirit who inspires the old man's words. On three occasions, Luke notes that the Spirit is resting on Simeon: "The man was upright and devout; he looked forward to the comforting of Israel and the Holy Spirit rested on him" (Lk 2:25). Simeon is the very type of the prophet, a man rooted in prayer: each day, this man, just and pious, comes to the Temple to wait for the visit from heaven. It is the presence of the Holy Spirit in him that urges him to wait in supplication and sustains his perseverance in prayer. To wait for and to plead with the Spirit, that is practically the only thing which depends on us and that we may do in prayer. In his heart, Simeon has a certitude: he will not die before seeing the Christ of the Lord.

We find again a rather similar formula in the gospel on the subject of the Transfiguration, that is, at the time of an anticipated vision of the risen Christ, Light of the nations: "I tell you truly, there are some standing here who will not taste death before they see the Kingdom of God" (Lk 9:27). Like Simeon, the three apostles will see the face of Jesus in Glory. There are some men on earth who receive the certitude and assurance that they will see the face of the Risen One before they die. That is why they pray and do contemplative prayer in order that someday this face may be resplendent in their eyes before it disappears leaving room for a soft warmth in their heart: "And their eyes were opened and they recognized him; but he had vanished from their sight. Then they said to each other, 'Did not our hearts burn within us as he talked to us on the road and explained the Scriptures to us?'" (Lk 24:31-32). We are reminded here of Silouane of Athos: "The Lord appeared to a young novice, and all his being, even his body, was filled with the fire of the grace of the Holy Spirit, that fire which, by his coming, the Lord brought down to the earth" (Lk 12:49).[12]

Simeon's long wait, like that of Anna, who was praying night and day in the Temple, will be rewarded beyond his hopes. Not only will he see the Light of salvation prepared before all peoples, but he will clasp the Word of God in his arms and his heart will know a peace such that, henceforth, he can greet death with joy: "Now, Master, you can send your servant forth in peace, just as you promised. For my eyes have seen the salvation which you have prepared for all nations to see, a light to enlighten the pagans and the glory of Israel your people" (Lk 2:29-32). Mary knew that Jesus was the Savior, and yet she receives a new light through the instrumentality of Simeon: "The child's father and mother stood there wondering at the things that were being said about him" (Lk 2:33). It is the amazement of faith which never ceases to discover Christ in his mystery.

But for Mary, the mystery of her son will be a mystery of sorrow as well as of joy. God uses Simeon to introduce Mary to the mystery of Jesus' Cross. Before Christ, the Just and Holy One par excellence, Israel will be divided

12. Translated from Archimandrite Sophrony, *Staretz Silouane*, Présence Ed., 1973, p. 28.

and the heart of Mary will be torn by this tragedy. When a just man presents himself, says Plato, his justice is so unbearable to the tortuous and deceitful hearts that they cannot bear him especially when he unveils the secrets of their heart. Then they decide to put out his eyes, impale him and put him to death. This is exactly what happens to Jeremiah the prophet and to Jesus. Jesus reads the depths of hearts and, at the same time, he loves men with a Passion of infinite Mercy. To resist this gaze one must shield himself securely. This is why the Pharisees decide to make him die, because they put their faith in their own justice rather than in the Father's Mercy revealed by Jesus.

This is what Simeon manifests to the Blessed Virgin: by announcing to her the Passion of her Son, he predicts at the same time her Compassion: "This child is destined for the fall and for the rising of many in Israel, destined to be a sign of contradiction — and a sword will pierce your own soul too so that the secret thoughts of many will be laid bare" (Lk 2:34-35). The light of Jesus will be a sign of contradiction and the occasion for a true judgment bringing about a revolt in hell. This will culminate in the sword of sorrow piercing Mary's heart. Simeon's prophecy heralds the Cross by first manifesting its ultimate purpose which is Glory. The light contemplated by Simeon is already the Glory of the Risen One who has triumphed over the darkness of hell. Christmas is truly a theophany. Thus the dynamism of Glory subtends and supports the labor of the Cross and the suffering of Mary in Compassion.

At the very moment when Simeon completes his prediction, comes the prophetess Anna: "She never left the Temple, serving God day and night with fasting and prayer" (Lk 2:37). This woman of prayer was so happy to speak of the child to all those willing to listen. The joy which her words pour in the hearts is a foretaste of the Glory of Easter. Then Mary and Joseph return to Nazareth with Jesus, all joyful and serious as well because of Simeon's words. This is already Mary's entrance into the mystery of Compassion. At its inmost depth, her heart is already pierced by the harshness of the heart of man; but, at the same time, as she looks upon her Son who will also be pierced, she allows herself to be initiated to the great wound of the heart of the Father in face of rebellious men who are losing their souls. She maintains without hesitation the Fiat pronounced on the day of the Annunciation as she will do later on Calvary.

At that moment, she begins her initiation to the Father's Mercy while waiting for the sword which will pierce her heart on Calvary. Still today, in the glory of heaven, she continues to beseech for Mercy for her children of the earth: "No one has experienced as much as the Mother of the Crucified the mystery of the Cross, the staggering encounter of the transcendent divine justice with love: that "embrace" given by mercy to justice (Ps 85:11). No one as much as she, Mary, has greeted this mystery as profoundly in her heart: the divine mystery of the redemption which becomes a reality on Calvary through the death of her Son, accompanied by the sacrifice of her heart as a mother, by her definite "Fiat".[13]

6. "I must be in my Father's house" (Lk 2:50)

Thirty years in Nazareth, three years of public life, three days of Passion... The gospels tell us very few details about the thirty years of Jesus in Nazareth. This sobriety of words suggests that Jesus grew up like any other child. Little by little, he awakens to the reality of the world around him: first to his family, his mother and father. Matthew uses an expression which recurs several times in the gospel: "the child and his mother" (Mt 2:11;

---

13. Translated from Jean-Paul II, *Dives in Misericordia*, V, 9, Le Centurion, p. 67.

2:13; 2:20). They are inseparable. Never have two human beings known on earth a communion so deep. Mary carried Jesus for nine months in her body and then she united herself totally to his person and to his mission. Yet Jesus and Mary remain most distinct from each other, since one is the Son of the Father by nature while the other has received everything from him, including the filiation by adoption. Jesus will stress this distinction in the episode in the Temple. As for Joseph, he is always there surrounding "the child and his mother" with a presence which for them was the perfect image of the Tenderness of the Father in heaven.

We understand that a saint like Teresa of Avila, who dedicated her life to contemplative prayer, could have written about Saint Joseph that he was an eminent master in teaching prayer. She declares that she has never prayed him and remained unanswered: "People of contemplative prayer, in particular, should always cling to him; for I do not know how we can think of the Queen of the Angels at the time when she lived with the Child Jesus without thanking Saint Joseph for having so efficiently helped them. Let those who cannot find a master to teach them to pray take for master this glorious Saint, and they will not get lost on the way."[14]

Surrounded by his parents' love and prayer, Jesus awakens also to the religious and social life of his people; along with his parents, friends and neighbors, he participates each year in the Paschal feast in Jerusalem, but he knows he belongs first to the Father. To understand how Jesus belongs to two worlds: the unbearable light of the Word, Son of the Father, and the wavering light of his journey as Mary's son, we must read again verses 40 to 52 of chapter 2 in Saint Luke and remain attentive to the two verses which frame this story and enshrine the words of Jesus: "I must be in my Father's house"

14. Translated from *Autobiographie*, ch. VI, p. 41, *Œuvres complètes*, DDB, 1964.

(Lk 2:50). These two verses 40 and 52 are approximately the same: "Meanwhile the child grew in stature and in strength, and he was filled with wisdom; and God's favor was with him" (Lk 2:40); "And Jesus increased in wisdom, in stature, and in favor with God and men" (Lk 2:52). By the way, let us note the expression which recurs twice: "God's favor was with him". We have already found it used for Mary by the Angel: "The Favored one, the Beloved of God" (Lk 1:28). Favor in its highest form rests on Jesus; the Father himself declares it at the Baptism and at the Transfiguration.

Thus Luke takes care to frame the affirmation about "Jesus in his Father's house" with two other comments on the growth of Jesus; these establish well the deep-rootedness and the incarnation of his being as Son in his human person. He grows, becomes stronger, and is filled with wisdom... so many words which describe a progress, a growth. Jesus was the beloved Son of the Father; he knew that better than anyone else and he had an ineffable perception of that, but he had to live this divine filiation within a human nature. In other words, his awareness as man did not develop itself in one day, not even in one year; there were phases and thresholds, from his birth to the end of his adolescence, as there normally are in the growth of any child.

We must often go back in prayer and meditation to the episode of Jesus in the Temple in order to have a glimpse of what was going on in the deep awareness of Jesus; this apparently was escaping Mary and Joseph. This episode is also very important to understand what is going on in our heart when we awaken for good to the fact that we are sons of God, that we are to live that truth within the development of our human growth. In Jesus, the condition of the Son of the Father had espoused the human condition to such a degree that he was living this harmony in the simplest way possible, in the meekness and tenderness of family relationships. Basically, Jesus prayed his Father as easily as he loved his parents on earth and obeyed them. His father and mother surely did not suspect the depth of this intimacy with the Father; that is why they could not explain to themselves the behavior of Jesus who stayed in the Temple of Jerusalem for three days astonishing the doctors by his listening quality and his intelligent answers (Lk 2:46-47). This is not surprising; Jesus was speaking of what he had seen and heard at his Father's house while we are speaking of somethinhg we do not know.

His parents cannot explain this behavior to themselves, for they do not live at that level. They will chide him for his flight: "My child, why have you done this to us? See how worried your father and I have been looking for you" (Lk 2:48). For three days, Mary and Joseph have found themselves before a void, a silence unknown to them until then, an absence which they have never experienced; similarly the apostles will be submerged in grief and anxiety for the three days of the paschal triduum. The Fathers have always assimilated the loss of Jesus in the Temple for three days to the three days Jesus spends in the tomb, in the "descent unto hell". In the same way that Jesus will appear to his own after the resurrection in a new light — that of Glory — he appears to his parents in another light.

Suddenly, after this absolute "night of the spirit", as Father Raguin so aptly said, Jesus appears in his true mystery before the eyes of his father and mother. Jesus really had to disappear and be absent for three days in order that Mary and Joseph might accede to another relationship with him. He does not belong only to them; he is also the Son of the Father. In his human nature, Jesus has experienced what he already knew, that of which he has not finished discovering the reality and the depth: "He replied 'Why were you looking for me? Did you not know that I must be in my Father's house?'" (Lk 2:49). Suddenly, his parents realize that this child, so obedient, so full of grace and tenderness, is also and especially the Son of the Father.

If this episode points to a threshold in the life of Christ, it also points to a threshold in the faith and prayer of Mary. That is why Luke notes immediately: "His mother stored all these things in her heart" (Lk 2:51), at the same time saying that Jesus resumed the pattern of his normal life in Nazareth and that he was obedient to them. Mary knew there a new trial in her faith, but since she had given her total obedience to God in her Fiat and lived in the Father, all busy with his affairs, the Holy Spirit could have given her a glimpse of something of the mystery of her child.

"Every year his parents used to go to Jerusalem for the feast of the Passover" (Lk 2:41). In the episode of the loss of Jesus in the Temple, Mary lived her "Paschal mystery"; this was not the first time, since there had been the one of the Annunciation and of the sword predicted by the aged Simeon, but here she experienced a "night of faith" of three days. We must ask the Spirit to show us how he taught Mary to pray during this night. She tells us herself that she experienced anxiety and distress; she admits it to her son when she gently chides him: "Why have you done this to us?" (Lk 2:48). Undoubtedly, Mary, in the pit of her distress, not only sought to understand what was incomprehensible to her, but cried to the Father by asking, like his Son on the Cross: "Why?". She could do only that because she knew that nothing is impossible to God; she had experienced this in the "Fiat" of the Annunciation. What she will live in silence at the foot of the Cross while uniting herself to Jesus' cry to the Father, is already beginning to be present in her anguish when she loses Jesus in the Temple.

Mary "did not understand what he meant" (Lk 2:50) because she was living in the darkness of faith even though she was profoundly united with God. She was already torn by this child who rightly belonged to her (he was submitted to them in all things) and yet who did not belong to her ("I must be in my Father's house"). She

167

knew a real night, the one we are all meant to know sooner or later. She did not come out of it except by her trust and perseverance in prayer. How can we explain otherwise the fact that she was able to keep all these events in peace in her heart and continue to pray?

Mary suffered from the fact that she did not understand; she would sadly question Jesus, as she had asked on the day of the Annunciation: "How shall this be?" Like Jesus on the Cross, she will say: "Why?" but in trust and surrender without any discussion or argument. Mary very well understood that she could not understand, that she must suffer from that fact and question unceasingly. The prayer of a saint is a constant questioning and, at the same time, a surrender and a no less unceasing adoration. As Mary had given her consent to the Father, she could not rebel. Love does not rebel and does not resign itself; love questions, as did Abraham, Job, Jesus and Mary. The paradox is that love understands at the very moment it does not understand. It accepts and adheres with all its strength at the instant when it seems to contend: "Why did you do this to us?"

As Jacob, having struggled all night, discovers in the morning, in the depth of his wound, another relationship with God made of surrender and of submission into his hands, so can Mary come now out from the night and share with her Son Jesus the awareness he had of being the child of the Father. At that moment, she is truly the Father's Daughter in her Son Jesus and she can pray in truth as she says. "Abba! Father!" As Jesus on the Cross is really praying when he yields himself into the hands of the Father and returns to him the embrace of love that his Father had given him at his Baptism, so can Mary pray with her whole being in truth and return to the Father all the love he has given her.

And then always... the hidden life

Luke feels the need to say once more in slightly different terms: "Jesus grew in wisdom, in stature and in favor with God and men" (Lk 2:52), and why not also in favor with Joseph and Mary more than with anyone else? A Son of God cannot be other than a good son on earth and a child who is the joy of his parents even if at certain times he must bring about breaches in relationships to be faithful to what he is. In concluding this chapter, we must beseech the Spirit, who is at the heart of the triune family, to make us taste the joy of the Holy Family's hidden life in Nazareth. This hidden life brings a completely unique joy, sweeter than the paschal joy itself since it is the fruit of this life. The traditional way of naming the joyous mysteries of the Rosary is thereby justified.

We must grasp well the nature of this joy of Nazareth: it will be our eternal joy when there will be no more struggle and all will be over. The paschal joy is that of the victory of God's meekness over the harshness of men, of light over darkness, of heaven over hell. It is the joy of a world freed from all struggle where we live beyond and in some way ahead of all battle and enemy. It is the joy and peace of the eternity of God.

We will know this joy in its plenitude when all will be over and when God "will wipe every tear from our eyes." But since it gives the ultimate meaning to the labors of birth of which Paul speaks, we must receive a foretaste of it, says Father Molinié, at the time when we know nothing or almost of the struggle which awaits us. At certain moments of our life, we must pick up some echoes of what our beatitude will be when the sea will be calmed and we will enter into the sweetness of God. This is a foretaste of the Glory; it creates in us a desire and especially a delicate sense of the spiritual enabling us to appreciate "the invisible unction of the Cross." In order to sustain our journey through the desert or on the road to Calvary, we need to taste this sweetness as Elijah needs bread and the light murmur of the breeze before he faces the prophets of Baal and as Jesus is comforted when he meets his mother on the road to Calvary.

Thus God proposes a hidden life before the struggle of the Cross. It is the joyous mysteries that prepare us to enter into the sorrowful mysteries. For thirty years, God offered this life to Jesus himself and in spite of the sufferings in Nazareth, an unutterable joy reigned there. Mary tasted the indescribable joy of the presence of Jesus with whom she constantly lived the very simple relationships of everyday life. She knew that a sword would one day pierce her heart and that the storm of darkness was looming over the horizon, but she lived in the present without worrying about the future: "To each day its labor!" Someday, her Son would triumph over darkness by allowing himself to be torn by it, but his human frailty, similar to ours "in everything except sin", did not disdain to immerse itself in the sweetness of family life.

This family on earth was the image of the triune family to which Jesus rightly belonged: "I must be busy with my Father's affairs." Except for these words, we know very little about Jesus' prayer and still less about Mary's. The mystery of the filiation of Jesus surpasses all human intelligence, even the most open to the Word of God. And yet the previous scenes show that Mary and Joseph perceived something of this mystery.

In the intimacy of their heart, they scrutinized the dark heavens and, like the Magi, they surely sighted a few little stars. If we know how to remain a long time in prayer on these words of Jesus: "I must be in my Father's house", there is no doubt that the Father will lift a tiny corner of the veil which hides from us the mystery of his embrace with Jesus, and the Spirit will make us enter into the embrace of love of the Son with the Father. Then we will really know, as Mary knew, that we are "at home with our Father". This will be our little star in the heavens that will sustain our journey through the night; for the "blue" of the heavens is as fascinating as the stars. Saint John of the Cross explains this very well in the Canticle of the "dark Night" where he says that this night is more lovable than dawn, for it reunites the Loved one with the Beloved, the Beloved being transformed into the Loved one:

> In the blessed night,
> in secret, for no one could see me,
> me, I was seeing nothing as well,
> with no other guide nor light
> but that which was burning in my heart.
>
> It was leading me,
> more surely than the light at noon,
> over there where was waiting for me
> one whom I well knew,
> in a land where no one appeared.
>
> O night that was leading,
> O night more lovable than dawn,
> O night which brings together
> the Loved with the Beloved,
> the Beloved changed into the Loved!

Stanzas 3, 4, 5

Chapter VI

PRAYING WITH MARY
AT CANA

Jesus came forth from his hidden life in Nazareth to begin his ministry. He first went to meet John the Baptist and was baptized by him. It is then that the Father intervened in an extraordinary manner to consecrate and authenticate the person of Jesus and his mission in the eyes of the people. Jesus hears expressed in words what he is already living in the deepest recesses of his heart, what he has made his mother understand in the episode of the Temple of Jerusalem: "This is my own dear Son, with whom I am well pleased" (Mt 3:17). The Father declares himself openly in favor of Jesus by asserting that he is his beloved Son. All the confidences that Jesus will make about his relationship with the Father are contained in seed in these words of the Father. This is also a window opened to filial prayer, night and day, all along his public life, until the time when he will clearly tell us about his prayer to the Father: "I am not alone, because the Father is always with me" (Jn 16:29-32).

After his Baptism, Christ fasts and prays for forty days in the desert. He is then tempted by the devil who invites him to perform his first miracles, but he refuses, constantly referring to the words of the Father which he makes his nourishment (Mt 4:4). He begins to preach; he has, therefore, not made any miracles yet. It is in these circumstances that he is invited to a wedding in Cana, not very far from Nazareth.

1. "And the mother of Jesus was there" (Jn 2:2)

The Cana episode is the first manifestation of Jesus: it comes about through a sign, that of the wedding. Jesus enters with utmost tact into the human reality of the wedding ceremony. With his mother and his disciples, he accepts this invitation with joy, for he is the Son of the God Creator and he "sees that this is good" (Gn 1:25). How can Jesus scorn this mystery of the marriage of human love, the image of a still greater mystery, that of his triune love: "God created man in the image of himself, in the image of God he created him, male and female he created them" (Gn 1:27). Mankind is man and woman, a symbol of the triune communion mystery which will be our eternal heritage. Every man, married or single, is called to be espoused and consecrated by the fire of triune love. Between triune love and human love, of which Saint Paul says that already "this mystery is great", is set an intermediary reality: the union of Christ and his Church.

And that is where we must be attentive to the symbolism of the words of the evangelist who opens this narrative: "Three days later there was a wedding at Cana in Galilee and the mother of Jesus was there" (Jn 2:1). There is question of the "third day", materially three days after the promise made to Nathanael, but everyone knows that in John the chronological notations must be perceived at different levels of depth. It is clear that there is question here of the third day when Christ has risen, creating within himself the new world where man and woman are introduced into the heart of the life of the Three. It is good that the mother of Jesus be invited to the wedding with the disciples, since she will be the first to live this mystery of the triune espousals at the Calvary.

In order that you may understand the presence and the role of Mary at Cana and especially enter in her prayer which will follow, I feel like inviting you to read immediately the following chapter on Mary's prayer at the foot of the Cross. It is there that the only nuptials worthy of the name will be truly consummated, that is, the espousal of Christ with the Church and, therefore, with each one of us. Thus when Jesus hands over his last breath to the Father in an ultimate embrace of love, he communicates this breath to us at the same time, and introduces us into the triune embrace of which the human embraces are a distant and approximate image. How can one not quote here this definition of prayer, so beautiful and concise, from Father Emilianos of the monastery of Simonos Petras at the Athos: "Prayer is the clasp and the sweet embrace of the monk with the Spouse and the Savior of our souls".[1] The union of Jesus and Mary at the foot of the Cross is the eminent realization and the supreme model of the union of Christ and his mystical Spouse. At Cana, the wedding is inaugurated by the prayerful presence of Mary and it is on its way to accomplishment until the moment of consummation which Jesus will proclaim as he dies.

At Cana, "John, tying up with the Old Testament, (Es 66:19) considers miracles as eschatological events which allow believers to perceive the glory of Jesus to a certain extent."[2] This is why John affirms: "He revealed his glory, and his disciples believed in him" (Jn 2:11). Here the first believer is surely Mary, the mother of Jesus. At the foot of the Cross — we will mention this later — she is espoused by the crucifying Glory of her Son, that is, she will bear in her body but especially in her heart

---

1. Translated from an homily given in the cathedral of Dramas in Macedonia, on the 24th of April, 1983.

2. Translated from TOB, p. 295, note "z".

174

and soul the invisible stigmata of her Son's glorious Passion. She is not only the mother of Jesus now; she is at the same time his spouse, because in her the reality symbolized by human weddings comes true: the espousal of God thrice holy with mankind.

On the Calvary, Mary is the new Eve espoused by the new Adam who restores to her the glory lost by the first Adam. Jesus is truly the Spouse who gives his blood to celebrate the eternal espousal at the hour set by the Father. At the same time, Jesus hands over his mother to the disciples who represent the believers in mankind (that is why the disciples are mentioned at Cana) and communicates to her the true eternal life. Mary is the one who gave Jesus a body. In his glorious Passion, this human nature of Christ is glorified by the Holy Spirit coming from the Father. The Spirit will always come to us from the glorified humanity of Christ.

On Calvary, Mary receives the ultimate light on the meaning of her virginity and she goes from the old order of the Law to the new order of grace, symbolized by human espousals. She did not expect her fulfilment from a mortal man to whom she would give herself, for "Your Creator will be your Husband" (Is 54:5). The Spirit who created her, who formed Christ in her, will now espouse her in her Son's glory. This is the order of the new creation, where the symbol becomes reality and where the Word of God made flesh is given as a spouse to the humanity he is saving.

Mary becomes the spouse at the foot of the Cross when the eyes of Jesus meet hers and make her enter into the Father's wound of love by burning her at the same time with the fire of the triune Glory. Thus the miracle of Cana comes to its full significance on Calvary, on the glorious Cross. Mary is there, silent; she gazes upon her Son in an intense prayer of Compassion and accomplishes with him the salvation of the world. It is the blood of the new covenant in which we receive the Spirit of the sons. In this work of Redemption, each has his role: Jesus and Mary, the men and women of the new creation. The Church is present through Mary. Father Ignace de la Potterie says while commenting on the presence of Mary on Calvary: "To receive Jesus or to receive the mother of Jesus (or the Church) is all one".

Here is how Pope John Paul II expresses himself in the Encyclical *Dives in misericordia*. Meanwhile, these titles (Mother of Mercy, Our Lady of Mercy or Mother of divine Mercy), which we bestow upon the Mother of God, speak of her especially as the Mother of the Crucified One and of the Risen One, as the one who, having experienced mercy in an exceptional manner, "deserves" in the same measure this mercy all along her existence on earth and particularly at the foot of her Son's Cross. Finally, they speak to us about her as one who, by her participation, hidden but at the same time incomparable, in the messianic task of her Son, has been called in a special way to bring this love close to man, a love which he came to reveal to us."[3]

To express this mystery of the relationship of Jesus and Mary in that of Easter, the Fathers have spoken of the Transfixion of Mary at the foot of the Cross, that is, of her participation, by the martyrdom of the heart, in the glorious Passion of her Son, in other words, of the piercing through of her heart by the sword predicted in the Temple by the aged Simeon. But this transfixion was preceded and prepared in a long and intense contemplation by Mary, fixing her eyes on her crucified Son, the look of the Mother induced and brought about by the look of the Son: "Seeing his Mother" says the evangelist Saint John. This is what the Fathers have called "a prayer of Compassion" which did not exclude a certain plea for all humanity, primarily for the executioners of her Son. This prayer initiated her at the same time to the wound of the Father's heart in face of those who are

---

3. Translated from *La miséricorde divine*, n. 9, Cerf, pp. 67-68.

crucifying his Son and all the men who are losing their soul. The Cana episode, prefiguring and announcing the espousals of Jesus with the Church on the Cross, is one of the pages in the gospel of John where he gives the clearest account of Mary's prayer, since she addresses Jesus to expose an embarrassing situation to him.

2. "They have no wine left" (Jn 2:3)

In the Cana episode, Mary shows us a way of prayer for our brothers and, because she went through it first, she invites us to follow in her footsteps, or rather to enter into her own prayer since, in Jesus, she continues to intercede for us. This narrative has preserved two very precise sayings of Mary which are, at the same time, two prayers: one is addressed to Jesus: "They have no wine left", the other to the servants: "Do whatever he tells you". Mary does not become "mediatrix" of all graces only at the foot of the Cross: she is already so, at Cana, at the beginning of Jesus' public life.

Mary is there, first as the mother of the Lord according to the flesh, and her presence attests to the gratitude of her Son toward her. But she is also there already as the image of the Church, therefore, as we have just said, as the bride of Christ. Mary stands for the Church in her Son's eyes; the bride stays close to the Spouse. Every time the Church invites her children to prayer, whether it is liturgical or private, she is always the bride who prolongs Mary's prayer at Cana or at the foot of the Cross. Paul VI speaks of her as the praying Virgin: "A Prayerful Virgin, thus Mary appears at Cana where, pointing out a temporal necessity to her Son and imploring him with tact, she thus obtains an effect in the order of Grace: that Jesus confirms his disciples in their faith in him by accomplishing the first of his signs". [4]

---

4. Translated from the Apostolic Exhortation *Marialis cultus*, n. 18.

Mary is first the woman who, in a brief glance, sees what is lacking in the feast and takes steps to remedy it. In this sense, we must not seek first some "highly mystical" reasons for Mary's prayer: she simply sees what is missing and asks for it with simplicity. This quality of obliging attention will always be that of Jesus' mother: she is the one who sees what is needed in the house of the Church. Her role will always be the one of showing her Son what her maternal look has discovered: "They have no wine left".

We have here a very precious clue for our prayer to Mary. In the same way that the Father sees in secret, she knows what we need, on the material level as well as on the spiritual one: bread, clothing and wishes of all kinds; she knows our concerns. Moreover, beyond these very human requests, too human sometimes, she senses a deeper thirst: that of the Holy Spirit who wants us to say: "Abba! Father!" In our prayer addressed to Mary, let us have the simplicity of telling her all our desires, even the most secret ones, those which hardly dare to cross our lips, so exorbitant they appear to be. She will know how to discern at the very bottom of these raw wishes the gold nugget of the desire for the Spirit in us; she will extract and free it from its earthly gangue to present this wish to her Son. Or very simply, let us accept to place ourselves under her gaze as we are with the cry of the psalms on our lips: "Look, see, listen, hear my laments, let your ears be attentive to the voice of my plea."

What impels Mary to expose so simply our needs to her Son is the "excessive" faith she has in him. She knows the divine possibilities of Jesus. God has filled her so well with the light and the power of his Spirit that she cannot ignore that nothing is impossible to Jesus. At Cana, she proves her perfect availability in an absolute faith. She has no doubt, demands no proof before giving her total trust. Her faith is rooted in her feminine and maternal intuition: she is the dynamism which impels to miracles.

Mary went to the limits of her conscious faith; now she hands over the decision to her Son. But Jesus replies to her: "Woman, what do you want from me? My hour has not yet come" (Jn 2:4). We can understand Jesus' reply in many ways: literally, we would have to translate: "What is there between you and me?" "In certain contexts, this would mean: 'What business is it of your?' This was a current expression among the Jews. It points to a difference of level between the speakers"[5] and has nothing pejorative. But the reply which Jesus gives to his mother: "My hour has not come yet" enlightens us on what is going on in his mind and reveals to us his pedagogical intuition with regard to those who adhere to him through faith, to begin with his mother, the believer par excellence according to Luke (1:45; 8:21).

Jesus' action will be set at a level which goes much beyond what Mary was to anticipate normally. Mary's faith is without limit, but she can and must always grow in her dynamism all along her pilgrimage on earth. This is why Jesus will make her cross a threshold, as he already has done after his disconcerting absence at the Temple. And to do this, Jesus will introduce his mother to the mystery of the hour. Jesus does not reject his mother's request, but he wants to bring her into the world of the new creation which will become a reality at the hour of his glorious passion. Man not only thirsts for wine; he especially thirsts for living water as he does also hunger for the bread of life. This is the mystery of the cup or of the hour to which Mary must adjust herself, as each one of us must do.

"For as much a Son of God as he was, Jesus had to make plans to be ushered into the gospel ministry. He has pondered over this. There remains one question for him: when will he begin to reveal himself? What opportunity will he seize? He is waiting for "his hour". When will it come? He does not seem to be in a hurry

5. Translated from TOB (= ETB), note "w", p. 295.

to make it come. He is waiting for the right moment when his first "sign" (Jn 2:11) will have all its significance".[6]

This is where Mary intervenes, through an embarrassing event: there is no more wine for the wedding. Mary wishes to help these people and she knows that her Son can do everything, for she has meditated for a long time in her heart the angel's words at the Annunciation: "Nothing is impossible to God". She knows that Jesus is the Son of God and that he too can do everything. Then the Father draws Mary toward Jesus and makes her understand that she must be a witness to him by giving him her complete trust. In the temple, Jesus had reminded Mary and Joseph that he must see to the Father's business. Now, Mary can turn to Jesus and confess her faith in his power, for she knows that he is the Son of the almighty Father.

The first step for Mary is to show her Son what is amiss. Having done that, she entrusts the rest to the Lord and does not come back to it anymore. She goes further, she accepts to let herself be brought to the place of the hour which she ignores and crosses with Jesus into the new order of her spiritual motherhood. Her faith is purified and she understands through intuition all the depth of her divine motherhood: "My mother and my brothers, Jesus will say, are those who hear the word of God and put it into practice" (Lk 8:21). Mary becomes aware that the wonder of the virgin birth of Jesus is the work of the agreement in faith she has given to the Father in her heart. She is now ready to live its consequences "to the ultimate", that is, to the Cross. This is where she will truly be Jesus' Mother by being in communion with the work of the divine mercy in an exceptional manner through the sacrifice of the heart.

---

6. Translated from Yves Raguin, S.J., *Le Livre de Marie,* Supplément à Vie chrétienne, n. 259, p. 50.

3. "Do whatever he tells you" (Jn 2:5)

Then "his mother said to the servants: 'Do whatever he tells you'" (Jn 2:5). We know what happened: water became wine... "Such was the first of the signs given by Jesus at Cana in Galilee. He let his glory be seen, and his disciples believed in him" (Jn 2:11). So Mary, by accepting to grow in faith in her Son, invites him to go to the end of his mission and provides him with the opportunity to put to work the powers the Father has placed in him. We can say that she makes her Son's hour "come" and that she collaborates with it by the power of her faith.

Mary's faith purified by Jesus shows itself in her persevering prayer when apparently her Son does not seem to have complied with her request. Yet, he has accepted her in her profound "wish" and prepares to comply with it. We cannot help but think here of the faith of the Canaanite woman who does not let herself be rebuffed by the attitude of Jesus and makes another attempt as did the persistent widow. "Then Jesus answered her: 'Woman (the same term as the one used to designate Mary at Cana), you have great faith! Let your wish be granted'. And from that moment her daughter was well again" (Mt 15:28).

Along with trust and humility, one of the signs of the prayer which is always answered is the perseverance that makes the believer come back to knock at the Lord's door to the extent of being obtrusive and violent, says Saint Gregory. We cannot know in what depth our wish to be answered may lie and what the bottom of ouf heart is worth, but we can know quite clearly what perseverance means, for us to try to put it in practice and to check that we are faithful in spite of everything. All men of prayer can testify to the fact that no prayer, sincere, trusting and humble, has ever remained unanswered, granted a minimum of perseverance, of course! This is why Jesus tells us: "We need to pray continually and never lose heart" (Lk 18:1).

Thus, as her role as woman and mother demands, Mary will persevere in her request: she now turns to the servants of the house, "Do whatever he tells you" (Jn 2:5). She knows by experience that her Son will not refuse her anything because he has received all power on earth; therefore, she does not ask him to intervene anymore. On the other hand, she knows the little faith of the disciples and also of the servants: this is why she turns to them and invites them to deepen their heart by a trustful and perseverant prayer in order that they may receive the gift of the new wine. Her meditation is twofold: after having said to the Lord what she had to say, she turns to the believers, seeking to awaken in them a stronger faith. Mary is the ecclesial supplicant. She implores her Son but she also implores us so that in our turn we may set about to beseech and to surrender ourselves totally to the Lord. Prayer always follows the same movement: "To you everything is possible... Yet not what I want, but what you want!"

Fundamentally, we discover here the ultimate reason for the prayer of request. Ultimately, it matters little what we ask for; what is essential is the deep attitude of the heart which sets about entreating the Father to obtain from him not only the gifts he wants to give us, but especially the Donor, the Holy Spirit, the Gift par excellence. From all eternity, the Father's wish is to enter into communion with men in such a way that we become only one with him, at the same time respecting our distinctive character. God thirsts that we thirst for him. The eternal question he asks men is the one Jesus asks Peter three times after the resurrection: "Peter, do you love me more than these?" He asks it until the ear of our heart is sufficiently sensitized to hear it and to answer it. Unfortunately, we are not emptied to the depth required for us to accept his wish to be in communion with us, not to speak of the superficial sins we make so as not to hear him! There is in us a fierce will to exist on our own and to refuse through fear to let ourselves be loved, invaded and "had" by the Other who comes to us from all sides.

Without wishing it to be so and without it being always through our fault, we have a hardened heart that does not allow the love of God to move freely in us. As soon as God draws near to "tell" us his love, we stiffen and defend ourselves against him. Since we do not have the humility of the Blessed Virgin who offered no resistance to the will of God, we need to undergo a whole process of refinement to reduce us to our simplest expression of poverty and nakedness. All the "skin layers" which shield us and hide our misery, as the Fathers say, must be dissolved in order that the sun of Love which brings "healing in its rays" may transform us. This is the reason why God makes us go through the desert of indigence. He lays bare the bottom of our heart so that we may understand the extreme need we have of him.

I dare say that this is the only means he has to initiate us to a true love. The more I move forward and the more experience teaches me, whether it is in my life or in my brothers', I realize that trial, the cross and often a certain wretchedness are the only means at God's disposal to draw us to him. Whether we want to or not, we must know a certain distress in order to find God! As one of my friends would say with a touch of humor: "When we do not suffer, we do not breathe the Holy Spirit either!" The absence of suffering brings about, as it were, a despondency of spirit in us. Even the psychologists say that our tensions are a dynamism tending towards equilibrium. This brings us to say that distress, trial are like "a strategy of love" used by God to draw us to the prayer of entreaty and, therefore, to union with him.

4. Distress..., God's "strategy of love"

Then begins between man and God a game of "chassé-croisé," that is, of mutual elusion of one another in supplications. God begs man to be willing to greet him in a spirit of prayer and man, experiencing his sin and his misery, also sets about to beg God from the bottom of his distress. If man does not resist this process of peeling off some "skin tunics", if he greets the gift of prayer and implements it in his continual supplication, he becomes, without knowing it, a being totally invaded by God. Ultimately, he is not fixed on a particular request anymore, but he is "recollected" completely in his prayer and uniquely turned toward God himself. Without noticing it, he becomes a man of continual prayer and makes true the most profound wish of God: that of being greeted in one's heart. Apparently, man often has the impression of failing lamentably in this work of prayer which is not answered but, at the very bottom of his heart, a small door is opened through which God enters stealthily while the wide door of his clear conscience seems irremediably closed. He has obtained then the greatest gift that a man may receive on earth: that of continual prayer which makes him live in the intimacy of the Three divine Persons.

Moreover, man was hoping that by going forward in his journey toward God, he would be freed from certain temptations and would have the peace of which the masters of spiritual life speak (in particular the hesychasts). He becomes aware that he is nothing; sometimes temptations increase, not to speak of the sharp pains coming from a wounded psyche and even from some lamentable falls. So the temptation to abandon prayer and to fall into discouragement and acedia is strong, for it is always the same cycle of trials which repeats itself. But those who persevere in humble entreaty, whatever the temptations and trials might be, enter into a rhythm of prayer which touches upon the infinite and they understand that they were wrong to "suspect" God of abandoning them. They do not notice it at first; they even have the impression they are regressing, for they are always praying without knowing it: prayer is perfect when we are no longer aware of it! That is why certain monks declare that it is the devils and temptations which have taught them continual prayer. Some, like Mother Sara, do not even ask to be freed from their temptations, but simply to have the strength to resist. There is a story told about Father Philarète of Constamonitou, who died in the Athos in 1963. A monk seeing him seated on a chair after Compline, wearing a thoughtful expression on his face, asked him: "Father, why do you look so gloomy?" And he answered him: "No temptations today, my child! Abandoned by God."

So, the spiritual man knows a peace and a joy other than those he expected: the peace and joy promised and given by Christ in the struggle of his Passion ("my peace", Jn 14:27; "my joy", Jn 15:11). This peace is not an absence of struggles — it is not a peace of cemeteries — but a peace which is born in an equilibrium of tensions between the forces of temptations and the force of entreaty. This peace does not annul tension and suffering but it invades the whole area of the conscience in an atmosphere of praise and prayer. In a certain sense, man comes to the point of not "deluding" himself into believing that all is going well. He then fears he will not go the whole way in the gift of himself by taking delight in this "state of grace". At that moment, he could have given up everything, and he did not do so. On the other hand, when he is going through a period of desolation and dereliction and that his "devils are unleashed", he knows by experience that he cannot do much anymore, but that he is agreeable to God if he invokes him in supplication. It is when we discover ourselves as lamentable sinners and, at the same time we beseech God, that we are in the truth of our being and on the way to unceasing prayer.

We should report here another testimony, that of Father Joseph the Hesychast, who died in 1959, one of the most notable spiritual personalities of this century at Mount Athos. He may be considered as the principal artisan in the present restoration of the prayer of the heart tradition and of the Holy Mountain spiritual renewal where many monasteries are directed by his disciples, direct or indirect. He knew all kinds of trials, physical, moral and spiritual, which made him undergo a veritable martyrdom. He admitted then that it was his love for the Mother of God and his trusting prayer which saved him in temptations:

"When I was in the grotto of Little Saint Anna, temptations and afflictions multipled themselves and my only consolation was our Holy Mother. One day, I went to our little chapel where there was on the iconostasis this little icon (he subsequently always wore it on himself). I set about to pray in front of her, pleading and crying: Come quickly to my help, you who are compassionate; for you can when you want to... I then saw the icon shine with a blinding light, then the face of the Mother of God grow to its normal size. It was not an icon anymore, but the Sovereign Virgin who was present there. She was holding the Lord in her arms like a nursling and I heard her voice sweeter than honey and gentler than any perfume: 'Had I not told you to place your hope in me? Why do you become discourages like this? Here, take Christ!' Our most sweet Jesus then put out his hand and caressed me three times on my forehead and my head. My soul immediately filled with light and with a love without measure, so much that I could not stand anymore. I fell on the floor and I kissed with devotion the place where the Queen of the World was standing".[7]

That goes back to what Mary's perseverant prayer at

7. Translated from Moine Joseph, *Le Géron Joseph l'Hésychaste. Vie et enseignement* (in Greek), Thessalonia, *To Perivoli tis Panaghias*, 1983, 200 p.

Cana teaches us. If we wish to quench our thirst with the new wine of the Spirit, we must live again with Mary the way of prayer which she herself opened up. In contemplative prayer, we submit to the Lord our misery and distress with those of the whole world. We draw Jesus' attention on the vast suffering of humanity, on the most heartrending problems, especially on the hunger and thirst for God which inhabit our hearts. It is enough to beg as did the Virgin Mary: "They have no wine left!"

Jesus understands, he knows what this is about. With Mary, we become intercessors and mediators. By our union with Christ, a union which comes about through long hours of prayer, we acquire power over the heart of Christ. Saint Thomas Aquinas expressed this so well: it is in proportion with our friendship with Christ that we can ask for much on behalf of others. At the end of the Encyclical on divine Mercy, Pope John Paul II says "that in no other period of history, especially in an epoch as critical as ours, can the Church forget prayer which is a cry calling on the mercy of God... The Church has the right and the duty to call on the God of Mercy 'with great cries'. These great cries must characterize the Church of our times and must be addressed to God to beg for his Mercy."[8]

All our life should be a cry of redemption and reconciliation addressed to the Father for humanity. It is through the breach made by this cry that God can give himself to men. In this sense, we can become "mediators" in the unique Mediator; Saint Irenaeus used to say that we are "sons in the only Son" with the Blessed Virgin whom the God of Mercy wants to need in the world of today.

We should often go back to the speech made by Paul VI on the 21st of November 1964, when he proclaimed the dogmatic Constitution *Lumen Gentium* and invoked Mary under the title of "Mother of the

---

8. Translated from *La miséricorde divine*, Cerf, p. 78 ff.

187

Church". He then explained that Mary could be called Mother of the Church on three scores: 1) as the divine Mother of the Word made flesh, Head of the mystical Body which is the Church; 2) by virtue of her cooperation in the redemptive mystery of the Cross and because of the title which Christ himself gave her on this occasion; 3) by virtue of the spiritual motherhood which she exercises today with regard to the constitution (birth) and the development (growth) of the Church of God, Body of Christ and Temple of the Holy Spirit. It is worthwhile to meditate on this last point of Paul VI's teaching, for it gives the reason why the cult should be not only private but also official, by which the Church honors the Virgin Mary:

"In what way does she cooperate to the growth of grace in the members of the mystical Body? the Pope asks himself. Above all through her unceasing prayer inspired by a fervent charity. As a matter of fact, although the Blessed Virgin enjoys the contemplation of the Blessed Trinity, she does not forget her sons who, like her in the past, accomplish their pilgrimage of faith. Moreover, since she contemplates them in God and sees their needs, in communion with Jesus Christ who is living forever to intercede for all (Heb 7:25), she makes herself their advocate, their aid, their helpful mediatrix. Since the first centuries of its existence, the Church has been convinced of this unceasing intercession of Mary with her Son for the People of God... And let us not think that the maternal intervention of Mary is prejudicial to the predominant and irreplaceable effectiveness of Christ, our Savior; much to the contrary, it is from the mediation of Christ that she draws her own strength and that is an eminent proof of it."[9]

---

9. Translated from *Lumen gentium*, par. 58 and 62, D.C. 1495, col. 964-965.

5. Water changed into wine

There remains the miracle of the water changed into wine by Christ in answer to his mother's prayer: this is the transfer of the gifts to the Giver himself. These "urns" of stoneware destined to the purifications of the Jews and which could hold each two or three measures — a considerable quantity — symbolize the old law in its helplessness to purify hearts and to lead men to perfection. Jesus alone is able to purify us for he is the Savior; moreover, he quenches the thirst for God who dwells in our hearts by giving us his blood in the new wine of the Kingdom. He says one word, and the water receives through him the power to communicate what it could not give. It will be the same for all the signs of Jesus, in particular for the one of the bread of life.

In order that this wonder may come about, we are asked to believe in his word: "His disciples believed in him" (Jn 2:11). At first, the meaning of this escapes the master and the servants who are amazed. But the Blessed Virgin and the disciples are not mistaken; through this sign, they discern the Glory of Jesus and confess their faith in him. This is the meaning which John gives to the event; and immediately after having mentioned the faith of the disciples, he adds: "After this he went down to Capernaum with his mother and his disciples, but they stayed there only a few days" (Jn 2:12). Thus the presence of Mary is symbolized at the beginning and at the end of the narrative. She is the one who arouses the disciples' faith by inviting Jesus to perform a miracle; she is the one who finally enters into the daily life at Capernaum.

It is silence again. As a matter of fact, we will not have any other words from Mary in all the remaining part of the gospels. Basically, Mary's role is to lead men to the threshold of her Son's mystery, then she can withdraw and say like the Precursor: "He must grow greater, I must grow smaller" (Jn 3:30). She is the bride who receives all her fecundity from the one who gives life. It is simply up to her to offer a heart available to the seed so that it may bear fruit and produce a hundredfold (Mk 4:20). When she has accomplished her mission of stirring faith in her Son Jesus, in our hearts, she can withdraw. She does not need to speak anymore because she has said everything. Like God, Mary does not speak idle words, for her Word is the Word made flesh which she carries within her and in whom she is totally immersed.

Then she withdraws in silence, after having shown us the way of faith which is first and foremost a way of prayer. Mary knows how to do only that: pray her Son and "pray" men to be willing to pray her Son. At her school, we must learn to "pray" to discover the glory of Christ present in our daily life. After Cana, she did not cease to discover God present and acting in the pattern of her existence. As soon as we begin to see as she does, in prayer, events, things and people, we never stop being in wonder, going from discovery to discovery. We have a glimpse of deeper and deeper levels where God reaches us at the very heart of our existence on earth. In one word, we learn to decipher the holy story of our life in the midst of the confusion of things.

Mary is mentioned again in another passage of the gospel but she does not say any words. She is in the crowd when Jesus is discussing with the Pharisees and when he speaks of "this evil generation" (Mt 12:45), which does not understand anything about the things of God: "He was still speaking to the crowds when his mother and his brothers appeared; they were standing outside and were anxious to have a word with him. So someone said to him, 'Look your mother and brothers are standing outside, and they want to speak with you'" (Mt 12:46-47). Jesus will take advantage of this presence of his mother and brothers to make it understood that there is a bond of kinship, other than that of the flesh: it is that of faith which gives all power over him. Undoubtedly, at that moment, he was not making any reproach to his mother, since he knew the depth of her faith, but he wanted to introduce the others to the true kinship with him.

These words from Jesus prepare the ones he will say on the Cross when he gives us Mary as our mother through the mediacy of Saint John. In the Temple, Jesus had reminded Mary and Joseph of his divine kinship. As for the Jews who made much of their title of sons of Abraham, he reminds them that there exists another kinship, a spiritual one. Here, Jesus teaches a similar lesson to all his family members who accuse him of "having lost his mind" (Mk 3:21). He does not disown his family, but he wants to introduce them to other bonds, to make them suspect another brotherhood: "And stretching out his hand towards his disciples he said, 'Here are my mother and my brothers. Anyone who does the will of my Father in heaven, he is my brother and sister and mother'" (Mt 12:49-50). It is certain that this answer from Jesus was for Mary the opportunity of a long meditation in her heart, just as the answer of Jesus in the Temple had been. That reflection prepares her to understand the words Jesus will address to her on the Cross: "Woman, this is your Son", then to John: "This is your Mother" (Jn 19:26-27).

As the water is changed into wine and the old law into a law of grace, so the bonds of kinship according to the flesh must be transformed into bonds of communion in the Spirit. Mary first conceived Christ in her heart through faith, then she will conceive him in her flesh through the action of the Holy Spirit. Jesus proclaims that she is first his mother by the "Fiat" she pronounced at the Annunciation while freely adhering to the will of the Father in heaven. At Cana, before the miracle, she remains attached to the natural relationship she has with Jesus; then she crosses over to the new order of her spiritual motherhood without rejecting these bonds. Thus each one of us, without rejecting the talents and promises nature has put in us, is invited to consent to

191

a transcendence of self into the newness that he brings, which is grace.

In our spiritual life, the action of the Blessed Virgin makes itself felt especially at this level of transcendence, where all our human virtualities must be transfigured by the mystery of Easter to become spiritual powers. In one word, the strength of our passions must be converted into fundamental tenderness and meekness, as flat water becomes a mellow wine. Those who do not go through Mary can achieve the same result, for the Spirit alone is the source of this transformation; but there is something lacking in this new humanity, a certain sweetness and an unction which is the work of her motherly tact. Saint Grignion of Montfort expresses this when he says that the Blessed Virgin coats our crosses with the sweetness of honey. With a touch of humor, he speaks of the "jam" of the cross!

This is all the difference there is between a virtuous saint and a saint transfigured by the light and sweetness of the Spirit. In the one, we feel a certain harshness which results from the great combat that he must have waged to reach holiness; this has created a tension in him. In the other, there were no fewer struggles but the suffering was borne with more ease; moreover, he knows "that he pleases" Christ and the Blessed Virgin by going through her. That is particularly evident in the area of chastity: instead of being hard, tense and self-willed, it is royal and full of tenderness for the brothers. When a man is invited to enter into the "monastery of the passive purifications", he better seek a "pass" to the services provided on the Blessed Virgin's side, says Father Molinié. He will not avoid the sufferings and humiliations any less, but they will be, as it were, smoothed and wrapped with her maternal sweetness. Saint Bernard also says that those who love and pray the Blessed Virgin taste the invisible unction radiating from the Cross.

6. Transfigured by prayer

Because Mary is the archetype of the Christian, of the new man, the model of all Christian holiness, the "lieu" for the accomplishment of the mystery of the incarnation of God and of the deification of man, she holds a privileged and almost exclusive place in our spiritual life. She is the one who unifies all our being with its emotional, carnal, intellectual powers in the new being who is Christ living in us. She makes over without destroying them but by bringing them to their perfection, all our living strengths to transfigure them with the light and the power of the Spirit. A saint is not a virtuous man (these men are often so boring!), but a man transfigured by the energies of the Spirit which make him a true man and, at the same time, a "man of the seventh day" (an expression so dear to the Fathers of the East), that is, a heavenly man.

In a certain way, we are to pursue the virgin motherhood mystery. In the same way that the Word of God came down in the immaculate body of the Blessed Virgin and took on a human nature through the action of the Holy Spirit, so do those who dedicate themselves to her and pray her, receive in themselves a divine seed by the mystical descent of the Holy Spirit. By the Spirit of filiation, Christ takes life, grows and shines in their body, their heart and their soul with all the brilliance of his divinity, spiritually and bodily. At certain moments, when the struggle of passions is more vehement and more violent and privations make themselves felt in the body and in the heart, they can say to themselves as Mary did: "How can this come about, since I am a virgin..., I know no man?" Those who go through her will hear these words said to them: "The Holy Spirit will come upon you, will cover you with its shadow and Christ will truly be born in your heart." A sweetness, a joy and a peace gradually settle in us which relax infinitely our whole being, even our body: the Fathers call this "plerophory". To understand this transfiguration of our humanity by the Holy Spirit, we must really have experienced or at least have noted the early beginnings of it in our heart; otherwise, we receive this truth like a proposition coming from the outside to which we "nod our assent", but which does not have any hold in our real life and our struggle.

When the most blessed Mother of God appeared to Saint Peter the Athonite, one of the first saints known on the Mount of Athos, she told him that all those who would come to live there would be her property and that she would be with them in their struggle with the enemy common to all. We could say the same thing about those who have taken Mary with them in their heart by making her dwell in their house, as Saint John did after Good Friday:

"I will be for them an invisible help. I will teach them what they must do and what they must avoid. I am the one who will be their tutor, their physician, their provider of food. I will take care to give them the nourishment and the remedies suitable for the body as well as those necessary for the soul, to stimulate and invigorate it so that it might not stray away from virtue. And all those who will come to the end of their days on this mountain in the love of God and in repentance, I promise that I will recommend them to my Son and my God in order that he might grant them the complete remission of their sins".[10]

Mary presents herself as the one who makes us accede to our humanity transfigured by the presence of the Holy Spirit. Her role is to intercede with her Son for us in order that he may bring about the healing and the unification of all our being in the Spirit. In our turn, we are called to collaborate in this work by uniting our prayers to hers. This is the reason why contemplative

10. Translated from St Gregory Palamas, *Vie de saint Pierre l'Athonite*, P.G. 150, c. 1005.

prayer brings to reality our own deification. It is not only a prayer which we address to God: there would be no reason for us to remain with God through the whole day if prayer were only a matter of addressing words to him. God hears the murmur on our lips and the sound of our feelings. Therefore, there would be no need to pray night and day.

As a matter of fact, prayer, before anything else, consists in eating Christ, the Lamb of God and bread of life, and in drinking the Lord's blood with the invocation of his holy Name. Nicholas Cabasilas used to tell the laymen, who, by their work, were kept from saying the Jesus prayer unceasingly, to take the Chalice and to let themselves be transformed by Jesus. The wine of Cana, this is the symbol of the blood poured by Jesus which unifies all our being in his Spirit. In contemplative prayer, we "absorb" the whole Christ and we become participants of God by reflecting his holiness as Christ did.

The only purpose of the prayer of the lips is to light up the fire of pure prayer in our heart. When we are thus visited by divine grace, the uncreated light rebuilds us from within and reintegrates all our person. The Fathers say that contemplative prayer is like the aroma of the Holy Spirit which spreads the sweet fragrance of Christ in us. For certain saints, the uncreated light spreads so much through all their body that they become shining, radiant and all transformed under the effect of this divine presence.

We need to put ourselves in the school of the Fathers of the East who were true "physicians" of the hearts and souls. While teaching their disciples the continual prayer which leads to the contemplative prayer of the heart, they did not rely so much on psychological techniques, even though they were very proficient in this area, but they wanted to help them to allow themselves to be completely restructured in the Holy Spirit. For them, "contemplative prayer is the delightful song by which the Church invites and awakens Christ, her beloved, and captures the all-shining dove, the Holy Spirit who proceeds from the Father".[11] It is always in the love of Christ that a man becomes an integrated human being.

For the Fathers, the sign that contemplative prayer is fruitful in their spiritual sons is the health of their soul, that is, that well balanced quality of their whole being. This is the reason why they say that one must be joyful to practise the Jesus prayer. This is perhaps the only sign telling us that a man is called to commit himself to this prayer. That ties in with the integration of the person of which we have just spoken.

"If you do not overcome your affliction, prayer will then be dangerous for you. You can try it, but only if it gives you joy, for a prayer is true only if it fills us with delight. An ascetic Father notes the following as well: 'Prayer is the fruit of joy and of thanksgiving... Do you wish to know if your prayer is true? Look at what it produces: if it gives you joy as its fruit and if it puts your soul in a mood to celebrate.' The same Father adds: "When someone begins to pray, if he feels a joy coming to life in him, let him then say 'Glory to God, I have prayed'".[12] Since prayer is communion with God, it always gives joy; if it does not produce joy, that means we have something else within us and our prayer is not authentic".[13]

We have already spoken of Father Joseph the Hesychast on the subject of having recourse to the Blessed Virgin in temptations and afflictions; let us now listen to how he arrived at the prayer of the heart by practising

---

11. Translated from Archimandrite Émilianos, *Le mont Athos, écrin sacré de la prière de Jésus*, Le messager orthodoxe, n. 95, February lst, 1984, p. 8.

12. Translated from Évagre, *Chapitres sur la prière*, 15 and 153, P.G. 79, c. 1179 and 1200.

13. Translated from Archimandrite Émilianos, *Art. cit.*, pp. 11-12.

the Jesus prayer. He was then leading a very austere life in the proximity of the grotto of Saint Athanasius the Athonite, a short distance from the Great Laura, fasting and going without sleep for a week. He was saying: "No ascetical practice may procure as many blessings as privation of sleep. Truly vigil dissolves the body."

"During this period, in spite of all his efforts, he did not manage to go beyond the stage of vocal prayer. As soon as he ceased to repeat aloud the "Lord Jesus Christ, have pity on me", his mind would scatter itself in various thoughts. One day, as he was gazing towards the Athos to ask God's Mother to help him in his distress, he suddenly saw a flash of light accompanied by a violent wind coming out of the Transfiguration chapel which is located at the very summit. Like a rainbow, the light came to him and penetrated into his heart.

"I immediately felt I was all transformed. I was filled with light and did not feel anymore if I had a body or not. Then the prayer began to repeat itself in my heart at a regular clocklike rhythm." He went into the grotto and sat down, chin on his chest, to follow the prayer in his heart. But then he was ravished in ecstasy. He felt he was being carried to heaven in a place where reigned calm and an indescribable peace. One only thought would come to him: "Oh! God, grant that I may no more return to the world and that I may always remain here with you." After that, prayer never ceased to resound in his heart, without his having to make the least effort".[14]

---

14. Translated from Géron Joseph, *Expression d'une expérience monastique* (in Greek), Mount Athos, Monastery of Philothéou Ed., 1979, p. 96, Letter 37.

Chapter VII

PRAYING WITH MARY
AT THE FOOT OF THE CROSS

"Near the cross of Jesus stood his mother and his mother's sister, Mary the wife of Cleophas and Mary of Magdala" (Jn 19:25). While reading this amazingly simple text, we should have before our eyes the icon of the Crucifixion. In the center, Jesus is standing on the Cross, facing heaven, facing the Father and facing men. On the right, Mary stands; also standing are the other women and John. The attitude of Jesus has a profound meaning; it tells the Father once more, as when he entered into the world: "You did not want the sacrifices, the offerings, the holocausts for sin, and you took no pleasure in them... Then I said: 'Here I am! I have come to do your will'" (Heb 10:8-9). Jesus is standing on the cross, in prayer, facing the Father, no more in the serenity of the hidden life, but in the distress and anguish of the agony. From the beginning to the end of his existence, Jesus prays unceasingly, for he loves the Father and he is surrendered to men.

Mary's attitude is also full of significance. Even though her suffering grips her heart, she is not crushed under the weight of grief. She is there standing, all selfless, looking at Jesus who is also looking at her. What holds her body erect is that she is reaching out to her

Son in a tender love of compassion; it is also her active trust and total surrender to the will of the Father in union with her Son. She is standing tall, full of gentleness, of compassion. This is what gives her strength to hold on in her suffering. She does not think of herself. The Passion of her Son is also her passion; his death becomes her own. In one word, Mary is in prayer, or rather she is united to the prayer of her Son who does not cease to intercede for us. Soon the eyes of Jesus will cross those of Mary; her heart will espouse his in the Transfixion to make her the Mother of all men. As their eyes meet, it is the triune love which joins them in the wounds of Jesus and crushes them together unto death before this very suffering explodes in Glory.

John is also standing at the foot of the Cross with Mary of Magdala and the holy Women. This is the group of disciples which has dwindled down as Jesus went up to Jerusalem and resolutely walked to his death. The ones have departed, the others have hesitated and shuffled until the moment they fled. This group of disciples has become smaller and smaller but Mary is there to guarantee its cohesion through her faith and prayer as she will be present in the Upper Room. This tiny group is the Church in prayer, in union with Mary and Jesus' prayer. It is the Church which contemplates Jesus, going over the sequence of events in her memory and her heart. It is the Church which will become Spouse and Mother in the same mystery of transfixion and of glory.

At the top of this icon, the Father is leaning with tenderness over his Son who is dying to save us from sin. If he is truly a Father, as Jesus has shown him to us in the gospel, if there is such an intense bond with his Son, how could he not be also "in Passion"? Since One of the Three is suffering in silence, the Others cannot remain insensitive to this suffering. What cuts the Father to the heart and perturbs him — for the depths of his being have always been perturbed by Mercy — is that his Son is dying not only through the sin of men but also for their sins under the effect of a malice which possesses the heart of men and to which his Son has offered himself in utter helplessness.

Between the Father and the Son, there is a secret which Jesus holds from all eternity; he has just revealed it to his friends, a few hours before entering into his Passion of love (Jn 15:15). This secret of the Father shared with the Son is the wound of God's heart and his suffering in face of those who lose their soul. There is the mystery which fascinates the Blessed Virgin and, after her, the Church of today. It is that of the clash between the malice of sin and the disarmed gentleness of the heart of God. This is the reason why the Church asks us to contemplate Jesus on the Cross and to follow the stations of the Cross.

Jesus was the first to allow himself to be initiated to this heart wound of God in face of those who lose their soul, in other words to the convulsion of the depths of Mercy. First, we will examine how Jesus was the only one to truly understand the Father's heart, infinitely wounded by our ingratitude. For that, we will direct our eyes towards his last cry on the Cross — a cry of distress from Mercy — in which Jesus gathers all his life offered to the Father and surrendered to men.

Secondly, we will see how Mary, in her turn, let herself be initiated to this cry at the foot of the Cross. She was not crucified by the hands of the executioners, but she was identified with the death of her Son, by her prayer of Compassion and in her transfixion, to become the Mother of the Church by espousing the Cross of glory.

Finally, we will turn to the Church who is also living this mystery of the espousals with Christ to bring forth in us the life and prayer of the sons. Until the end of time, she will be fascinated by the distress of her crucified Spouse and also by the immense clamor rising from the earth caught in the labors of childbirth. This is why the prayer of the Church on Good Friday before the Cross is also a universal prayer of supplication for the needs of all her sons and all men in communion with those who consume their life in a continual intercession "for those who lose their soul".

1. The cry of Jesus on the Cross

If you wish to share Mary's prayer at the foot of the Cross, you must ask her to teach you how she herself prayed at this ultimate moment when she saw her Son dying on Calvary after several hours of agony, between heaven and earth, his arms stretched on the Cross. Undoubtedly, she ignored that she was praying at that moment, so absorbed was she in watching her Son and comforting him with her attentive and loving presence. Why would she have been conscious of praying since this movement of the heart was in her the permanent breath of her being? She had eyes only for her Son and Saint John who was representing us all on Calvary.

She will nevertheless answer our request by inviting us to keep, like her, "our eyes fixed on Jesus, the initiator of our faith, he who, renouncing the joy to which he was entitled, endured the Cross, disregarding the shamefulness of it, has taken his place seated at the right hand of the throne of God" (Heb 12:2). But since no one comes to Jesus without being drawn by the Father, she will make the prayer of Saint Paul for us: "I pray, kneeling before the Father... so that Christ may live in your hearts through faith, and then you will with all the saints have the strength to grasp the breadth and the length, the height and the depth and to know the love of Christ which is beyond all knowledge" (Ep 3:14-18). If you make this prayer with Mary, not from the tip of your tongue but from the bottom of your heart, if she is the only object of your supplication, if in the course of the days of the Holy Week "you look on everything as so much rubbish as opposed to the sole knowledge of Christ" (Ph 3:8), be convinced that Jesus' cry on the Cross will one day or the other resound in your heart.

Then the Father will seize you from within and will place you at the foot of the Cross; he will take possession of your eyes and direct them uniquely towards his Son Jesus crucified. You will be there in front of him — the true Serpent of brass — with all your wounds and those of your brothers, and you will really contemplate "the one they have pierced" (Jn 19:37). If you have, like Mary, the piercing look of those who "see through", you will contemplate at the very bottom of the pierced side of Jesus the incurable heart wound of the Father who "ever thinks of his shepherd lass, heartbroken with love. He does not weep that love has wounded him, of being thus doleful; his sorrow is not there, even though grief grips his heart, but he weeps as he thinks that he is forgotten."[1]

All through the Bible, the Father does not cease to make his complaint heard, most of the time in the humble tone of the Spouse who is gently chiding his unfaithful bride, sometimes also in the anger of the jealous and wounded Love: "O my people, what have I done to you? How have I grieved you? Answer me!" But who will hear the murmur of the one who does not raise his voice, does not put up the pitch of his tone, and does not crush the rumpled reed?

The first to really hear this complaint was the Word at the heart of the Three; this is what urged him to come and set up his tent in the midst of a rebellious people who did not welcome him: it is the one who made him go up on the Cross before the world and beg men to stop their stupid dance. In the wake of Saint Leo, the Fathers understood in prayer that this complaint from God's heart was the constant subject of the dialogue between

---

1. Translated from John of the Cross, *Poème du petit Pastoureau esseulé.*

the Father and the Son under the impulse of their mutual love, the Holy Spirit, at the heart of the "Triune Council": "He had but one left, his beloved son. He sent him to them last of all saying: 'They will respect my son', But these vine growers said to each other: 'This is the heir. Come! Let us kill him and the inheritance will be ours'. So they seized him and killed him and threw him out of the vineyard" (Mk 12:6-8).

The dialogue of Jesus at the heart of the Three has "humanized" itself in the prayer of Jesus all through his journey on the earth. For Jesus, to pray is to express over and over to the Father his desire and his will to pull men away from this abyss of perdition. This cry of love haunted him day and night and when he cried on the Cross, it was to express again his love for sinners. There is the song of the Beloved for his Vine, a song which Jesus has not ceased to reverberate on earth, now by his words of meekness, then by his acts of kindness, but especially by his silence in the Passion and on the Cross.

He is the only one to have truly understood the Father's secret by allowing himself to be initiated to the wound of his heart in face of the distress of man. We must linger on this "suffering" of God, if we may express ourselves in this way; it is well understood that in God the words which contain those realities do not have the same meaning as they do for us. In God, Love and Joy identify themselves with suffering, since he suffers through excess of love and not, as it were, from a lack of it, as is the case for us.

As soon as sin entered in this world, eternal death spread its empire; the heart of God is broken by this death, wounded by a sorrow which we cannot understand because it is not the sorrow of God, but the very calamity of the reprobates "savored" by God more deeply than the reprobates themselves will ever be able to do. This is what makes the spiritual people say: "God alone knows what hell is".[2] In the very heart of the

2. Translated from Father M.D. Molinié.

triune Love, a kind of immeasurable wound develops which hangs uniquely on the fact that the Three obstinately love the obstinate beings that we are.

This is why this wound of an unfailing love which, by its nature, is at the same time the beatitude of love, entails no suffering in the sense in which we understand this word. But God himself has not found any other word but that one to express this wound, nor any other sight but that of Jesus on the Cross to make us contemplate his grief. This is what Paul will term as "Verbum Crucis" and which we will examine later in the contemplation of the Church. He says so clearly in the Letter to the Galatians: "O stupid Galatians, who has cast a spell on you in spite of the plain sight you have had of the crucifixion of Jesus Christ?" (3:1).

On the Cross, Jesus bears the stigmata of the wound of God, and it is with the Virgin's eyes and heart that we also are asked to contemplate it, on the condition that we are willing to bare our own wounds by emptying them of the venom of self-love in order that they may be healed by the wounds of Christ: "He through whose wounds you have been healed" (1 P 2:24). This is the Virgin — the one who was never bitten on the heel — who must normally dress our wounds by the sweetness of her Mercy in order that they may be cauterized by the love of Christ.

Throughout his life on earth, Jesus let this wound in the Father's heart resound in his own heart. It was permanently fixed in the heart of his being, like a sword of love. This gave him the obsession of making the Father's Name known and introducing us in the triune secret which he had come to reveal to men to make them his friends: "I do not call you my servants anymore, but my friends because I have made known to you everything I have learnt from my Father." The gospel tells us that Jesus often withdrew to the mountain to pray for the whole night; very early in the morning, the Apostles would find him still in prayer. He also prayed in front of his disciples and in front of the crowd before raising Lazarus from the dead. All chapter 17 of Saint John is a very long prayer of Christ in which he asks the Father: "May they be one in us" (Jn 17:21).

We cannot linger on Jesus' prayer during his public life, for we especially want to direct our eyes to his prayer during his Passion. Let us say, nevertheless, that Jesus' prayer was the same as his prayer in the "Council" of the Three. He was possessed by a passion of love, stemming precisely from the fact that he constantly contemplated the wound in the Father's heart. He had only one wish: cry to men this unutterable love which he nevertheless wanted to express by the "Word of the Cross", the only one able to sing the love of the Spouse for his unfaithful Bride. This is what really obsessed Jesus' prayer and inhabits the prayer of the Church today. A Christian is someone who has been introduced to the intimacy of the wound of God and who prolongs the dialogue of Jesus with his Father on the subject of sinners, "he, who during his life on earth, offered up prayer and entreaty, in cries and in silent tears to the one who had the power to save him from death, and he submitted so humbly that his prayer was heard" (Heb 5:7). Basically, when Jesus prays for all men, it is the most mysterious face of God, that of his Mercy made flesh in Jesus which pleads and intercedes with the other face of God, that one being more accessible to our sight — that of his Justice — to soften it in favor of men of hardened hearts. We see there what Mercy is: it is not "forgetting" what we have done, "wiping it away" as it were. It is really a cry that is first wrenched from the heart of Christ and then passes into ours. This cry tears the heart of God and it appeases his Justice. But if there is no cry, there is no mercy either!

In this sense, Jesus' prayer in Gethsemane is like the summing up of the prayer of all his life. In these brief words, Jesus expresses the deepest aspiration of his heart which urged him to become flesh. With all the strengths of his being, he begs the Father to spare him this cup that he dreads in anguish, but at the same time, he is anxious to drink it in order that the Father's will to which he totally adheres might be fulfilled: "And going on a little further he fell on the ground and prayed that, if it were possible, this hour might pass him by. He said: 'Abba, Father, everything is possible for you. Take this cup away from me. But let it be as you, not I, would have it'" (Mk 14:35-36).

For Jesus, the Father's will is not a "command" coming to him from outside which he should blindly obey without understanding anything of it. When we speak of the "will of God", we must include in this word his good will, his aspiration and his love, in other words, the desire which the Father bears in the deepest recesses of his heart. For Jesus, to do the will of the Father is to agree to share with him his passion of love for men. It is especially to allow himself to be perturbed by the wound of his heart in the presence of our distress. As soon as Jesus becomes flesh, he is the object of the Father's kindness and, therefore, of his will: this is the reason why he is told at his Baptism and at the Transfiguration: "You are my Son, my Beloved; my Love rests in you."

In the agony, the Father's will is first his Love that he offers and proposes to his Son. It is the Father who prays first and asks Jesus: "Will you share my love?" While Adam said "no" to the prayer of God, the new man says "yes". He totally appropriates the will of God for himself. He is the first man in whom God can contemplate the plenitude of the Love which displays itself without restraint. This is why Jesus prays. His prayer is a response to the prayer of God. In a well-knit family, we do not command but we mutually pray each other. In the triune family, each of the Persons withdraws before the other and prays it to willingly accept his love.

This is the reason why Jesus prays at the Baptism, to accept the good will of the Father. He also prays at the Transfiguration to lovingly surrender himself to this same will. Finally, he will pray intensely during the Agony so that his own will as a man be totally emptied, obliterated, and leave in him a space of complete freedom for the Love of the Father. The agony at Gethsemane goes on until the moment Jesus dies. On the Cross, he continues to pray, but his sufferings reach a paroxysm that plunges him to a level of depth surpassing all human dimension. In the midst of all that, he remains hanging on the love of the Father whether it is in the scenes of violent abuse or in the mockeries of passers-by and high priests. These mockeries bear upon a crucial point for Jesus: his relationship with the Father. It is a matter of knowing whether or not Jesus is really the Son of God and whether he can invoke, pray his Father and count on him: "He put his trust in God; now let God rescue him if he loves him. For he did say, I am the son of God" (Mt 27:43).

At this hour of paroxysm, Jesus' words must be taken as ultimate prayers, vertiginous openings over the abyss of God's Mercy. In Jesus, not a movement of complaint or of condemnation, but a prayer for his executioners: "Father, forgive them for they know not what they do" (Lk 23:24); a constant concern for his own to whom he gives Mary for Mother: "This is your Mother" (Jn 19:27); an infinite mercy for sinners: "Today, you will be with me in paradise" (Lk 23:43); a driving thirst for men for whom he is dying (Jn 19:28). From the moment God hands himself over to the decision of a created being, he is helpless before the contingent refusal arising from our freedom. Because of that, he has an indescribable thirst for our answer of love which only our freedom can give him. Jesus' thirst on the Cross refracts in the flesh of Christ the infinite thirst which God has for the happiness of all men: the thirst that we may thirst for him, as has often been said.

And then these words which seem to justify those who scoff at him: "My God, my God, why have you deserted me?" (Mt 27:46). But Jesus does not let out this cry in a void; he addresses it to the Father in a final prayer which is also a surrender into his hands: "Father, into your hands, I commend my spirit" (Lk 23:46). Jesus has stopped speaking to men, he has nothing more to say, he is now turned towards his Father. Jesus does not speak of God anymore, he speaks to the Father: "All is finished" (Jn 19:30).

Finally, there is the last cry of Jesus on the Cross: "Jesus gave a loud cry and breathed his last" (Mk 15:37). This cry will reverberate in the heart of those who have ears to hear until the end of the world. It is the cry of the distress of mercy wanting to save men and not managing to do so, but saving, nevertheless, those who let themselves be touched, shaken and converted by Jesus who proclaims that he wants to save us. He can do so if our resistance is not the strongest and if we hand all our rebellions over to him.

The first to be converted by this cry is, surely, the centurion: "Seeing how Jesus had died, he said, 'In truth, this man was the son of God'" (Mk 15:39). This man understands: for Jesus to hold on to God, to remain fixed on him at a time when God is depriving him of all protection, all joy and all defence, there has to be, between God and himself, a bond of trust so strong and a certitude so unshakable that he cannot but be the Son of God.

2. Mary at the foot of the Cross

We must now go back to Mary's prayer at the foot of the Cross. But we have never left it, for the last two words said by the Blessed Virgin in the gospel are meant to direct us towards her Son Jesus: "Do whatever he tells you" (Jn 2:5). It cannot be otherwise at the moment Jesus is dying on the Cross; she keeps her eyes fixed on him and joins him in his prayer. I have already cited the trust

208

of this old blind woman, alone and abandoned, whom one of my priest friends had gone to visit. She said to him: "It seems to me that I always hear this cry of Jesus dying on the Cross and that it has not ceased resounding in my heart." That cry is the final prayer of Jesus. After that cry, it is silence and this silence is yet more profound than the cry. There are no more words of Mary reported to us in the gospel, but there is no doubt whatsoever that the last cry of Jesus on the Cross never ceased to reverberate in her heart until the moment she breathed her last breath. Thus her prayer and her life must have stopped both at the same time.

But before we contemplate Mary's prayer at the foot of the Cross, we must watch her following Jesus from the moment he leaves her to enter into his public life. Mary would not have been present on Calvary if she had become disinterested in her Son's mission. It is first to her that Jesus addresses the words on the Beatitudes, on the spirit of childhood, on self-denial and on the Cross, for she was the first to enter into the Kingdom. Mary has always been present to her Son; discreetly, she has accompanied him through all his public life with the group of women who were following him. When Jesus decided that the time had come to go up to Jerusalem and to walk resolutely to his death (Lk 9:51), without any doubt Mary also turned her eyes toward Jerusalem. Thus we must understand the manner in which Mary took part in the unfolding of the mission of Jesus.

At Cana, she begs him to act and begin his mission. The first miracle performed by Jesus is an answer to Mary's request. But she is immediately warned that in manifesting his Glory, Jesus already knows that the hour of his Passion is looming over the horizon, from the antagonism between the Glory of God — which blends with the defenceless gentleness of Jesus — and the unleashed forces of hell. When Jesus speaks of his hour which is also the hour of the prince of darkness, Mary cannot help but make the link with the words of the aged

Simeon who predicted to her that her Son would be a sign of contradiction, for the fall and the rising of many in Israel: "As for you, a sword will pierce your own soul, thus the secret thoughts of many will be laid bare" (Lk 2:35).

As the Passion is drawing near, the secret of hearts is truly unveiled. Mary is present to this debating in the heart of those who knew Jesus. Some leave him as Judas did, others hesitate not knowing which side to take, some make him rash promises, as did Peter forgetting that Jesus had prayed that his faith might not fail. She sees especially the rift which is widening between her Son and the religious authorities, and she now knows that the Pharisees have decided to condemn him to death.

Thus she accompanies her Son, not by following him everywhere he goes, but by a constant attention to everything he says and does. She especially remains at the center of the group of friends which is becoming smaller and smaller, made up especially of women who have accompanied him from Galilee (Lk 23:55). She is the soul of this little community by her faith in Jesus' mission and by her silent prayer which assures its cohesion in the same way that she will be the soul of the small Church of the Upper Room. It is impossible to separate Jesus from his mother, the Christ, dead and risen, of Mary and of the Church.

Every time the Church commemorates Calvary, she associates, in a privileged way, the prayer of Mary and of the holy Women at the foot of the Cross with our prayer and her own. It is in this sense that we must put ourselves at the school of the Blessed Virgin so that she may educate us in our prayer and make it ecclesial. Not that she adds anything to the unique intercession of Christ, the only Mediator between the Father and men, but the Church needs her prayer to bring to perfection in extent, not in depth, what is lacking to the Passion of Christ for his Body which is the Church.

A — The prayer of Compassion

The gospel does not speak of the encounter of Christ and his mother on the road to Calvary. It was brought to us by the contemplative tradition of the stations of the Cross, but "we may consider it to be true as it is so likely."[3] On the other hand, John attests that Mary is there standing at the foot of the Cross such as we see her represented on the icon of the Crucifixion, hands open, a Virgin in prayer (the Deisis on the doors of the iconostasis). Apparently, she does not say or do anything, but she looks at her Son on the Cross and, through this event, sorrowful for her heart as a mother, she allows herself to be introduced to the contemplation of the mystery hidden since the beginning of time: the wound of the heart of God in the presence of the misery of those who lose their soul.

To draw near this mystery of Mary's presence on Calvary and her role with respect to Jesus, we must understand what Compassion is: "The sacrifice of the Cross is perfect as redemption in the person of Jesus alone and, in this sense, it is true that the redemptive Christ does not need a co-redemption coming from Mary. But as a sight contemplated by the Church allowing her to penetrate through faith into the intimacy of the Father and to be introduced to the wound of his heart, Jesus crucified would not be complete without Mary who is already here the presence of the Church associated as a bride to the sacrifice of the Lamb".[4]

To translate her participation in the Passion of Christ (compassio Passionis Christi), the Church will apply to Mary the beautiful word "Compassion" which explains well what went on in her heart and in her soul, at the moment she was journeying with Jesus on the road to

---

3. Translated from P. Raguin.

4. Translated from M.D. Molinié, O.P., *Chemin de Croix*, Lettre polycopiée, n. 18, p. 4, Lent 1975.

Calvary. Like Jesus, she had her moments of fear and her heart was troubled. If the heart of Christ was so, the same may be said of his mother. There is as much suffering for her in her own compassion as there is for Christ in his Passion. Standing near the Cross, Mary "cruelly suffered with her only Son, associated with a motherly heart to his sacrifice, giving the consent of her love to the immolation of the victim born of her flesh."[5] That is where her heart was really "pierced as with a sword":

"How great must have been the suffering of the Mother of God when she stood at the foot of the Cross! Her love was immeasurably great and we know that the one who loves more suffers more. In her human nature, the Mother of God could not have endured such a pain, but she surrendered herself to the will of God and, comforted by the Holy Spirit, she received the strength to bear her suffering. That is why she became forever the consolation in grief: 'Here I am, I am the Handmaid of the Lord, let it be done to me according to thy word!' Thus speaks the Blessed Virgin and she totally surrenders herself to the will of God".[6]

So the role of Mary on Calvary is especially one of a contemplative presence in the sense that she, with the eyes of her heart, looks at the one they have pierced through the heart. Her presence is primarily a silent presence: she does not say anything, like her Son, but the silence of the mother is infinitely more eloquent than words. Before the Cross, we must avoid idle talk and superficial feelings. We must simply look with intensity and in silence at the one who has no more the face of man, so disfigured is he by sin. It is a simple presence to what is.

But in Mary's look on Jesus on the Cross, there is

_____

5. Translated from Vatican Council II.

6. Translated from Silouane, *Spiritualité orientale*, n. 5, Bellefontaine Editions, p. 46.

infinitely more than a sharing of his human suffering. At that moment, she is wrenched from herself, and a power of attraction coming from the glorious Cross focuses her gaze completely on Jesus: "When I am raised from the ground, I will draw all men to me." Through this mystery apparently accessible to our human psychology, there is a mysterious and deeper reality. While contemplating, in the Holy Spirit, Jesus on the Cross and in glory, Mary is seized through the very simple and human sight of the dying Christ by the crucifying glorification which comes from the Risen Christ.

In the deepest recesses of her heart, she is crucified by Glory and glorified by the Cross. Her human gaze, intense with compassionate love for her Son, becomes the channel and the fruit of a purely interior holocaust. The Fathers of the East tell us in a somewhat special language that she crosses over from the order of grace to the order of glory. Since her conception, Mary was literally possessed by the love of God which plunged her into extraordinary abysses of humility, by making her accept the most hidden ordinary life. At the level of her conscience, this presence of God in her stirred desires which directed her toward a practically continual prayer.

But as she contemplated the love of Mercy burning in the heart of her Son on the Cross — this being nothing but the Glory of the burning Bush — the presence of God in her was raised to a state of incandescence that totally identified her with the death of her Son. In a certain way, the Virgin knew on Calvary a death of glory which is at the same time a death of love, all the while remaining alive.

B — The Transfixion

For Mary, what is realized in plenitude is what the liturgy makes us sing in the Stabat Mater: "Grant that my heart may burn with a greater flame of love for Christ my God and that I may please him. O holy Mother, deign to engrave the wounds of the crucified Christ deeply in my heart." This is why Mary's prayer of "compassion" at the foot of the Cross will lead her to another yet deeper mystery which liturgy calls the "Transfixion" of the Blessed Virgin. This amounts to saying that, in Mary, Jesus has reproduced wound for wound the stigmata of his Passion.

Speaking of the presence of Mary at the Cross, Saint John notes that Jesus looked at his Mother: "Seeing his mother and the disciple he loved standing near her" (Jn 19:26). This is what allows us to say that on Calvary, Jesus' eyes crossed those of Mary and that their heart was crushed and submerged in the same triune love. It is therefore the same wound of the Father's heart which reproduced itself in the heart of Jesus and his Mother. When Jesus lowers his eyes towards his Mother, he impresses upon her his divine resemblance and Mary in reality becomes the living icon of her Son. The miraculous impression of the face of Jesus on Veronica's veil symbolizes the supernatural impression of this same face in the heart of Mary and of the Church. It is the mystery of the Transfixion, which is at the same time a mystery of Glory but especially of the espousals.

As she contemplated the face of Jesus on the Cross and allowed herself to be gazed upon by him, Mary was invaded by the fire of the triune Love which Jesus came to cast upon earth, and she became a living "copy" of him. What went on in the heart of Thérèse of Lisieux when she was following the stations of the Cross, after having offered herself to the merciful Love, can give us a very faint and approximative idea of what went on in Mary's heart at the moment of the Transfixion on Calvary:

"I was beginning my stations of the Cross and behold, suddenly, I was seized by such a violent love for God that I cannot explain; it was as if someone had plunged me completely in fire. Oh! what a fire and what sweetness at the same time! I was burning with love and I felt that one minute more, one second more, I would not have been able to bear this ardor without dying. I understood then what saints say about these states which they have experienced so often. As for me, I experienced it only once and for only one instant, then I immediately fell back again in my usual dryness".[7]

Mary's unique privilege is to have suffered martyrdom in its totality without having known death. One quotation from liturgy shows well that Mary espoused fully in the darkness of faith the struggle and the death of Jesus: "Blessed are the senses of the Virgin Mary who deserved the crown of martyrdom near the Cross of the Lord without the intervention of death." By the transfixion, Mary fully became the spouse of her Son in her own right as the Church is as a community.

In the wake of Saint Paul, the Fathers have always celebrated the mystery of the espousals of Christ and the Church on the Cross. As they contemplated the pierced side of Jesus and the flow of water and blood, they saw the birth of the Church and, at the same time, its espousal with the Lamb. This is the reason why the Christian marriage appeared to them as the sacrament of the nuptials: "Husbands, love your wives as Christ loved the Church and sacrificed himself for her to make her holy. He made her clean by washing her in water and he did so through the Word. This mystery is great and I say that it applies to Christ and the Church" (Ep 5:25-33).

Thus humankind means man and woman, a symbol of triune mystery which will be our eternal legacy. In eternity, we are called to be espoused by the fire of the triune love. Human marriage is a true ladder of Jacob: it brings down the triune exchanges to the union of man

7. Translated from Saint Thérèse of the Child Jesus and of the Holy Face, *Derniers entretiens*, Desclée-Cerf, 1971, p. 241.

and woman and goes up again to the heart of the Three. Married or not, we are destined to be invaded by the Glory of Christ on the Cross who is the fire of the burning bush. Between this triune mystery and nuptial love, there is the intermediate reality which concerns Christ and the Church. For this reason, Saint Paul says on the subject of marriage: "This is a great mystery!"

It is in the mystery of the Church, of which she is the mother, that we find the Blessed Virgin. The union of Jesus and Mary at the hour of the Passion is no other than the eminent realization and the supreme model of the union of Christ and his Church, his mystical Bride. Inaugurated at the wedding of Cana, these espousals are on the way to fulfilment until the moment of consummation which Jesus proclaims as he is dying. Scheeben writes: "The Son is at the same time the spouse of the mother".[8]

The mystical espousals of Mary and the Lamb were consummated at the hour of the crucifying glorification, according to a tradition which seems quite established among the Fathers and the mystics like Saint Teresa of Avila: "Crucified spouse, I wed thee in crucifying", or yet: "You shall be for me a spouse of blood." At the very moment when she receives the grace of the spiritual espousal, Teresa of Avila also receives as a wedding gift a "nail" of the crucifixion and Jesus tells her: "From now on, I shall not answer for you only as creator, but also as spouse." In a certain sense, Saint Paul will know an experience of the same kind when he says: "I bear in my flesh the stigmata of Christ Jesus."

---

8. Translated from *La mère virginale du Sauveur*, p. 71.

3. "Woman, behold your son... Behold your Mother"

"Seeing his mother and the disciple he loved standing near her, Jesus said to his mother, 'Woman, this is your son.' Then to the disciple he said, 'This is your mother'. And from that moment the disciple made a place for her in his home" (Jn 19:27). We must now broaden our vision and, after having cast our eyes on Christ and the Blessed Virgin, we must associate Saint John with it: this "trinity of the earth" as some mystics love to call it. In addition to the mystery of divine motherhood, there is a mystery of friendship between Jesus and Saint John which has always fascinated those whom the Church of the East calls "the ones-who-stay behind". Saint John is the contemplative par excellence since he is the one who "stays behind" (Jn 21:23) and the disciple Jesus loved. John insists much on the experience he had of his friendship with Christ. He always keeps his image in sight, the inflections of his voice in his ears, and his hands still vibrate from his contact with the Word of life.

Until the end of his life, John preserved the wonder of the unsettling look of friendship which Jesus cast on him. He lived from this look while resting on Jesus' heart at the Last Supper and his eagle eye makes him guess the secret of the heart of Christ. Beyond this human friendship, tender and virile, John heard the beat of the heart of Christ and he perceived in it an echo of the heart of the Father. Like Mary and like all those who gaze at length on Jesus to listen to his heart, he has understood the heart of the Father which was beating in Jesus' chest. He understood that the cry of Jesus on the Cross refracted the cry of the Father which will not cease to reverberate in the heart of men of prayer. While contemplating the pierced heart of Jesus, he "saw" the large wound and the sorrowful break in the heart of God in the presence of the distress of men.

This is what John expresses at the beginning of his First Letter: "What has existed since the beginning, what we have heard, and we have seen with our own eyes; what we have watched and touched with our hands of the Word of life... we are telling you so that you too may be in union with us as we are in union with the Father and with his Son Jesus Christ" (1 Jn 1: 1-3). Practically speaking, John had the same experience as Mary: while contemplating Jesus, listening to him and touching him, he "touched" at the same time the heart of the Father and his infinite mercy for all those who lose their soul. In this sense, John is the very type of those who contemplate the sin of the world with the eyes and the very heart of Jesus. The purer the heart, because the Lord has delivered him from his own darkness, the more oppressed he is by the darkness of the world which comes down upon him.

We can understand that Jesus would give his mother to Saint John, for there was such an affinity between these two that they were only of one heart and soul. Their eyes were centered on the person of Jesus, as Jesus existed only for the Father; and it is this total oblivion of self that produced such a profound communion. It is not surprising that Saint John took Mary "with him" (Jn 19:27). There was in John's heart a space of freedom that allowed him to greet Mary while letting her live her own mystery. Saint John saw all beings in the light of the Word. His intimacy with the one whom God made immaculate had given him the intelligence of the heart which made him see the essential in the relationship of Mary with Christ. He never calls her "Mary" but the "Mother of Jesus", stressing thereby her exceptional and privileged relationship with Christ. At Cana, before the manifestation of the Glory, he calls her "Woman" as an allusion to the *protoevangelium*. Mary, the Mother of Jesus, is truly the new Eve taking her place beside the new Adam, her Son and Spouse at the same time.

While commenting on the "Behold your son... Behold your Mother", the Church has especially emphasized the motherhood of Mary with regard to all the disciples of Jesus, in the present and in the future. Such is the most evident meaning of Jesus' words on the Cross. But we can go another step further and consider Mary's motherhood for us in the very mystery of the Incarnation.

Mary gave Jesus the body of a man. However, Jesus, the Son of God by nature, shares this humanity with all the men of the world. Thus, in Mary, humanity finds its divine filiation again. In her, every human being rediscovers himself as a child of God. This is surely what Saint Paul, always chary on the subject of the Blessed Virgin, wanted to express when he calls to mind Jesus born of a woman, a fact which makes sons of us by his taking flesh: "God sent his Son, born of a woman, and subject to the Law, to pay the ransom for those subject to the Law and to enable us to be adopted as sons. For sons you are: God has sent the Spirit of his Son into our hearts: the Spirit that cries, 'Abba, Father', and it is this that makes you a son. You are not a slave anymore; and as son, he has made you heir; this is the work of God" (Ga 4:5-7). It is also in the perspective of the Incarnation that we must read again the words of Jesus on the Cross about the divine motherhood of Mary.

On the Cross, Jesus goes to the limit of the reality of his divine filiation. Similarly, he associates Mary with the Church in their role as spouses to make them become mothers of all the adopted sons of the Father. Mary discovers also that she is really daughter of the Father, mother and spouse of the Son by the power of the Spirit, and also "mother" of mankind. By her "yes" to the Father, she has given to the Son a human nature by which he brings about the salvation of mankind in a threefold and unique mystery of the incarnation, the redemption and the participation in the triune life.

Jesus' words to his mother and to Saint John have always nourished the faith and prayer of Christians. The danger would be to remain in a purely affective aspect of it at the risk of blocking the way to a deeper understanding of the mystery. As a matter of fact, it is certain, that Christ did not want only to touch our affectivity: never does he remain at this level. He especially wanted to make us understand the radical change of our being in his redemptive incarnation. By his glorious death, the old man is destroyed in order that baptism may invest us with the new man. This grace is conferred upon us by Christ risen from death: "If it is certain that through one man's fall so many died, it is even more certain that divine grace, coming through the one man, Jesus Christ, came to so many as an abundant free gift" (Rm 5:15). If death came to us through the first Eve, the new Adam has conferred the new life upon us. From this salvation in his blood, the new Eve was, by an unheard-of privilege, the beneficiary of this salvation from the first moment of her existence. The first "re-born" in Christ, she is placed at the source of the new life since she is "filled with grace."

For this new birth, humanity needs a mother in order that the divine life which was restored to us by Christ be accepted in an environment which favors its growth: "Christ is dead to himself, dead to his mortal life which Mary had given him. He went further: we can say that he is "dead" to his mother, that he divested himself of this filial relationship, as, to become man, he had "forgone" the Glory that came to him from the Father. In some way, he had "forgone" his Father. Now, on the Cross, he renounces his mother. He gives her to every human being so that humanity may be reborn in divine life and find itself full of grace again".[9]

In this sense, Mary is really much more our Mother than Eve was. She is close to her Son at the very root of our regeneration in the Spirit. Knowing to what depth she is united to the Father by the bond of the Spirit, we understand better that, having begotten Christ in his

---

9. Translated from Yves Raguin, S.J., *Le Livre de la Vierge,* Supplément à la "Vie chrétienne", n. 259, p. 56.

human nature, she regenerates us ceaselessly and gives us a countenance similar to that of her Son Jesus. This is the mystery which Jesus has revealed to us on the Cross and that we will contemplate later when we see Mary present at the birth of the Church.

4. The disciple took her "at his house".

Once we have asserted the ontological root of the motherhood of Mary for man, that is, the union of our being with Christ born from Mary, we can speak of her more pedagogical role in the growth of our being as sons. In what sense does Mary train our heart and conscience as sons? We touch here a fundamental point, not only of the affective order, but which aims especially at our life of prayer. We should reread in this light all the texts of the New Testament where Jesus speaks of a new birth, in Saint John, to Nicodemus (Jn 3:1-12) and in the Synoptics where he asks us to go back to the condition of children (Mt 18:1-5). This last text is a transcription in Matthew's style of the new birth in Saint John. In the two cases, Jesus aims at the same reality, more theological in John, more moral in the Synoptics: that of filial life.

When Jesus tells us that no one can enter the Kingdom unless he converts himself to the condition of a child, he does not wish to make us become infantile suggesting that we should adopt patterns of behavior made up of naïvety, of nice pretty ways or even of childishness. Christ is not "nice", he is Love and that is something else! His intention is clear. The first to have the spirit of childhood or rather the filial spirit, the source and root of the spirit of childhood, was he, Jesus. From the beginning to the end of his existence, he lived in the meekness and adaptability of the one who receives himself from the Father and who returns to the Father after having loved his own to the end. Whether it is a matter of beatitudes, of humility or of the childhood spirit, it is always his own portrait that Jesus sketches in the gospel.

He is asking us today, not to imitate him in an external manner, but to allow him once again to live his filial condition in us by adding a note of humility, lowliness and refuge. The Word alone has a filial spirit, the first component of the childhood spirit. That is where Mary intervenes in her motherly education. Not that she could have told Jesus that he was the Son of God, he knew it, since this reality inhabited the depths of his being and radiated itself in his conscience, but she taught him how a true son should live. She is the one who, the first, having pronounced her "Fiat", will teach Jesus in the day to day aspect of his existence to say: "Here I am to do your will."

There is an area where Mary must have fashioned her Son's heart, it is the one of prayer. Little by little, she taught him to say: "Abba, Dear Father!" this word which so often recurs in Jesus' prayer as recorded in the gospels. This little word "Father" was to constitute the background music of his prayer as the blessed name of "Jesus", for us, dwells in our prayers day and night. Besides, everytime Jesus invites us to pray, he asks us to place ourselves under the eyes of the Father who sees in our secret. He brings up in this advice what was for him a current habit when he prayed. We know what it cost Christ to say "Father" at the moment when, on the Cross, he seemed totally abandoned by him. Like Jesus, we will perhaps have to hold on to the end, hooked and hanging on this name alone of the Father in the darkness of the night.

It is to Mary that we will simply have recourse in filial intercession in order that she may form in us the prayer of sons, that of Jesus to his Father. When Nicodemus naively asks Jesus what he must do to become a child again: "How can a man be born if he is old? Can he go back a second time into his mother's womb and be born again?" (Jn 3:4), Jesus does not reply right away, but from the height of the Cross, he answers Nicodemus who was wandering in the vicinity of Calvary (Jn 19:39). Jesus tells him: "Behold your mother", in the womb of whom you must enter again in order to become a child again!

We will be able to take advantage of this short route into the heart of Mary only if we are willing to pray like Jesus, the Son par excellence. To assert this is to ask ourselves what bond of "devotion" will bind us to Mary. We use here the term "devotion" in the sense of being "devoted" to Mary, in short, of "consecrating" our being to her. This devotion is first a love in charity that makes us love Mary with the very heart of her Son. We are present to Mary with the love with which the Lord surrounded his mother. Also this charity will bear the stamp of filial respect and admiration which were growing in Jesus' heart at the sight of his mother.

There is more yet in our devotion to the Blessed Virgin, for it will never measure up to the love of Jesus for his mother, given our condition as sinners and as men wounded by the bite of the serpent. Let us remember what has been said about Mary Immaculate, who is at the same time Mother of Mercy. She holds a privileged bond with the sinners that we are. Our indigence places us in an extreme need and, therefore, our filial love for Mary invites us to implore her mercy. As "the Spirit himself bears witness with our spirit that we are children of God", in such a way that moved by him, we may cry: "Abba! Father!" (Rm 8:15-16), so the Spirit of Jesus wants to testify in the intimacy of our heart that we really have become children of Mary at the foot of the Cross. For this reason, while continuing to venerate her in us, the Spirit teaches us to say like Jesus: "Mother".

This is the reason why from the time Jesus gave Mary as Mother to Saint John, "the disciple made a place for her in his home" (Jn 19:27). Like him, we shall have to take her with us, that is, in our heart and live with her intimately in a presence which consecrates all our existence to her. This is the very meaning of the Consecration to Mary by Saint Louis Mary Grignion of Montfort. We, thereby, give her full power over all our being so that we be totally consecrated to Jesus Christ. We must note that this consecration is always made in the perspective of the renewal of the Baptismal promises. Here all the effectiveness of Mary's presence appears; it is to lead us, beyond herself, to her Son. Indeed, the Immaculate Virgin is a reflection of God — "Splendor of the eternal light, untarnished mirror of God's majesty" (Ws 7:26) — too pure not to lead us along to discover in her the one who is the principle of her beauty and her holiness. This stems from the very quality of her virginal consecration which makes her be all for God: "the image of God responding to the holiness of the Lord".[10]

Thus, "to take Mary in our home" will not only mean to have recourse to her protection, to call for her intercession, or to implore her assistance; it will also lead us to enter into her prayer of praise, since she will take us beyond herself into her prayer of the Magnificat. Mary is all relative to God and we cannot pronounce her name without her pronouncing in us the holy Name of God. In this light, the words of Mary assume their full significance: "Yes, from this day forward all generations will call me blessed" (Lk 1:48).

5. "When I am raised... I will draw..."

Not only must our meditation on the Virgin, spouse and mother, be made within the Church, but it is the Church alone who lives this contemplation with all the

---

10. Translated from Saint Cyprian, *De habitu virginum*, P.L. 4, c. 455. It is the word used by Saint Cyprian to depict the virginity of Mary consecrated to God.

sinews of her being, from the day of Pentecost until the end of time and for eternity. All we have said about the Compassion and Transfixion of the Blessed Virgin applies also and primarily to the Church, the true Spouse of Christ, dead and risen. Since Christ has risen from the dead, he has sent the Spirit in his Church to make the Spouse and each of his faithful live, in infinitely varied modes, something of what Mary lived at the foot of the Cross. At the same time, the Church scrutinizes the mystery of the Compassion and the Transfixion, which she lives within herself, to try to have a glimpse of what Mary must have experienced. There is an interaction between what went on to perfection in Mary and what goes on in, shall we say, a slower "combustion" in the heart of the saints and the faithful journeying towards holiness.

In the measure that a Christian contemplates Mary and allows himself to be crucified by the Glory radiating from the Cross, he becomes a true member of the Church: "When the Church attempts to understand what is happening to her — the mystery of the espousals with the Lamb being fulfilled slowly and yet without delay — she looks first in Mary's heart at the mystery of the transfixion which is accomplished to a lesser depth and purity in the tainted heart of her children: for it is the same mystery which prolongs itself, and the immaculate transparency of Mary's heart allows her to reflect with more strength than ours the mortal confrontation of light and darkness in Jesus' heart. The Bride of the Lamb is made up of saints and sinners who groan in the labors of childbirth: by looking at Mary, these sinners understand their own suffering better — and it is in their own suffering that they contemplate the mystery of Mary at the foot of the Cross".[11]

11. Translated from **P.M.D.** Molinié: *La Sainte Vierge et la Gloire*, Cahiers sur la vie spirituelle, Deuxième Série, L'Épouse, 1973, p. 112.

This is the reason why the Church contemplates and venerates the Cross on Good Friday and advises the faithful to follow the stations of the Cross so that they may let themselves be modeled on the Spouse in the mystery of the Transfixion of Mary. If we wish this contemplation to have some meaning for us, we must not limit ourselves to the sufferings and death of the human nature of Jesus; we must allow ourselves to be introduced through events to the mystery hidden since the beginning of time (Ep 3:5-6), that is, to the wound of God caused by the misery of those who lose their soul, in other words, to the perturbed heart of Mercy.

The Church hangs on the glorious Cross and claims only one thing from Christians: to allow themselves to be troubled by the heart of mercy. For the moment, she does not ask them to understand, as Jesus does not ask Peter to understand why he wants to wash his feet: this will come later. He simply asks him to let himself be shaken by this gesture of humility and tenderness: "At the moment you do not know what I am doing, but later you will understand" (Jn 13:7). To the Christian who contemplates the Cross of Christ, the Church says about the same thing: "For the moment, you cannot understand. Allow yourself to be disturbed by this love, then you will understand."

In order to be overwhelmed, our heart must be pierced by the cry of Jesus on the Cross. Conversion is always given to us by the sight of Jesus on the Cross. Thus, in his first speech in the Acts, after the effusion of the Holy Spirit, Saint Peter says to the Jews: "This Jesus whom God had commended to you by miracles, wonders and signs performed among you, as you all know, this man, who was delivered into your power by the deliberate intention and foreknowledge of God, you destroyed by making sinful men crucify him; but God raised him to life, freeing him from the pangs of death, for it was impossible for him to be held in its power" (Ac 2:22-24). Peter hurriedly adds: "Brothers, I know you acted this way through ignorance" (Ac 3:17). It is as if he were saying: "You are as much victims as guilty." But the essence of Peter's preaching is really: "God raised him from the dead." From the Cross flows a power which will pierce the heart of Peter's listeners and convert them: "Hearing this, they were deeply troubled" (Ac 2:37).

Every time the Church invites Christians to contemplate the Cross with the eyes of the Blessed Virgin, it is to bring about in them a pierced and troubled heart or a conversion, which amounts to the same thing. Remember the comment made by this old woman: "The cry of Jesus on the Cross does not cease to resound in my heart": it is the Church who stands today at the feet of the Lord in Glory on the Cross near Mary, Saint John and the holy women, and who allows the cry of Jesus to resound in her heart. It is the Church of the poor, the sick, the humiliated, the rejected and the tortured who keeps watch around the Cross on Good Friday; it is also the Church who celebrates her liturgical prayer of the Passion of Jesus, but who also commemorates the suffering of men in whom Jesus renews the mystery of his glorious Passion.

When we say that the Church continues today the prayer of Jesus to his Father for men, we first think of Mary's presence. As long as there are men and women on earth called to contemplate the darkness of the world with the eyes of Jesus — for that is what a contemplative is [12] — these will always be attracted as if magnetized by the prayer of Mary at the foot of the Cross. And when

12. "Through the concrete manner with which Mercy confronts the dark recesses of our heart, God murmurs to us the hymn of his unknown face (that of his mercy), the most difficult one for us to grasp..., the most sacred, consequently the most divine. We thus come on to this paradox: if we could contemplate sin with the eyes of God, we would be much closer to him than by gazing at his splendor" (Translated from Father

they themselves come to their last hour, after having consumed their life in supplication, they will have only one recourse: to entrust themselves to the prayer of Mary: "Holy Mary, Mother of God, pray for us, sinners, now and at the hour of our death."

We must understand why the Church is fascinated by the glorious Cross. There is not in her any morbid attraction for suffering, nor masochism, for she knows that the Father has raised Jesus from the dead; as Saint Peter says: "It was not possible for him to be held in the power of death" (Ac 2:24). Every time a Christian contemplates the Cross, in Mary's steps, he is pierced by the power of the resurrection. It is a matter of "knowing him, Christ, and the power of his resurrection" (Ph 3:10). This is what we have said about the transfixion of Mary espoused by the Glory of her Son on the Cross. All those who contemplate the glorious Cross and allow themselves to be crucified by the Glory of Jesus understand the truth of these words of Jesus which have fascinated all the fools of Christ for two thousand years: "When I am lifted up from the earth, I shall draw all men to myself" (Jn 12:32).

There are no human words to denote this power of the Cross which pulls a man out of himself and places him in the situation of Paul: "I know a man in Christ who, fourteen years ago, — whether still in the body or out of the body, I do not know; God knows — was caught up right into the third heaven... and heard words which must not and cannot be put into human language" (2 Co 12:2-4). We talk of being fascinated or seduced, yet these words are too weak to denote a reality which is not of this world but of heaven. To understand this power of the Cross, we must pray the penitent thief so that he may make us suspect a little of what went on in

Molinié, *La Sainte Vierge et la Gloire*, Cahier quoted above, p. 141.

his heart when the eyes of Jesus met his and Jesus told him in the midst of atrocious pain, which made the unrepentant thief on his left blaspheme: "Today, you will be with me in paradise" (Lk 23:43).

The day must come when, in our prayer, the skies will tear open and Stephen's experience, whose martyrdom is reported in the Acts, will be renewed for us: "He, filled with the Holy Spirit, gazed into heaven: he saw the glory of Good Friday, the Church directs her eyes on Jesus (Ac 7:55). From the beginning of Lent to the evening of Good Friday, The Church directs her eyes on Jesus crucified, as she contemplated him as a small child during the Christmas season. It is true that meanwhile she has examined closely the words and deeds of Jesus in his public life from Cana to the Palms episode; but what is especially of interest to the Church is beyond the words of Jesus, the Word of God, the unique Word of the Father, Jesus himself in person. The Church cannot draw away her eyes from the very person of Jesus who is her life and her reason to be.

Basically, what fascinates the Church and what should fascinate us as well, is God who opens his heart and utters one Word for us. And this unique word which the Father tells us, his ultimate confidence, the one he tells us when he cannot tell us anything more, is the Word of the Cross, the "Verbum Crucis" (1 Co 1:18), which will become the "Verbum Resurrectionis". "We are preaching a crucified Christ, a stumbling block to the Jews, madness to the pagans: he is the Christ, the power and the wisdom of God" (1 Co 1: 22-23).

The only power we know of as men is often aggressiveness or deterrence; but who would suspect that love, humility, meekness are a terrible force, as Dostoïevski makes the staretz Zozime say: "It happens sometimes that in the presence of sin we are baffled and we ask ourselves: Must this be overcome by force or by humble love? Tell yourself each time: By humble love! If such is your resolution once and for all, you will be able to subject the world. The humility of love is a terrible force not to be compared to any other".[13]

This is the reason why the Church contemplates the Verbum Crucis and directs the eyes of the Christians towards Jesus on the Cross during Holy Week. In her prayer, she makes us ask the Father, "that, according to the riches of his glory, he may through his Spirit, make us firm in his power in order that the inner man in us may grow strong" (Ep 3:16) and that we be granted "to know Christ and the power of his resurrection and to share his sufferings, the pattern of his death in the hopes that we may take our place, if possible, in the resurrection of the dead" (Ph 3:10-11).

Let us finally say that the prayer of the Church in the presence of the Cross is not only a prayer of compassion, but also and especially a prayer of entreaty which flows from the power of the resurrection. To convince ourselves of that it is enough to examine the liturgy of the Office of the Passion on Good Friday. Just after having read the gospel of the Passion according to Saint John, the celebrant makes a long prayer of intercession including all men without exception, who are on the surface of the earth, the Christians as well as the Jews and those who do not believe in God. This prayer ranges from the most material needs to the most spiritual aspirations.

We have here a precious clue for our personal prayer. The contemplation of Christ on the Cross must never let us forget our brothers in trial and in need, especially, those who do not know God and his infinite love, or who resist his overtures. Basically, this prayer of entreaty originates from a twofold source: the contemplation of the wound of God in the presence of the reproved and the sinners, and the awareness of the misery of these men. Only those who have been introduced to the wound of Mercy of the Father's heart are able to have compas-

---

13. Translated from *Les Frères Karamazov*, Marabout géant Edition, 1957, p. 290.

sion for sinners. It is said that when Saint Dominic was overwhelmed by God's mercy, he would groan and cry: "What will become of the sinners?" Let us think of Thérèse of Lisieux seated at the table of sinners and interceding for them and, in the East, of the staretz Silouane who kept his mind in hell and never despaired of the Father's mercy:

"Lord in the same way that you prayed for your enemies, so teach us through your Holy Spirit to love them and to pray for them with tears. However, this is very difficult for us, sinners, if your grace is not with us."

"The Spirit of God teaches us to pray everywhere, even in the desert, for all men, for the whole world. There is nothing better than prayer. The saints prayed without ceasing and did not remain one second without praying".[14]

---

14. Translated from Silouane, *Spiritualité orientale*, n. 5, Bellefontaine Editions, pp. 24 and 59.

Chapter VIII

PRAYING WITH MARY
IN THE UPPER ROOM

Pentecost is the fulfilment of the triune revelation through the gift of the Holy Spirit, so, on that day our brothers from the East venerate the icon of the Blessed Trinity. The following Monday, they venerate the icon of the descent of the Holy Spirit on the Apostles, which is that of the disciples in the Upper Room. The apostles are twelve in number. Experts in iconography will easily recognize the apostle Saint Paul who, however, was not yet converted, and the evangelists Luke (the author of the Acts) and Mark, who were not apostles. Besides, the disciples in the Upper Room were more than twelve in number. In the Upper Room, the Church is symbolized by the twelve pillars representing the apostles, but some of the seventy-two disciples have made their way among them.

This group of apostles-evangelists is seated in a half circle in the Upper Room which is truly set between heaven and earth. Jesus' place is kept free. It is the image of the Council presided by Jesus although invisible. Oddly enough, Mary is not represented on the icon of the Upper Room: this is not necessary anymore, for she is already consumed by the fire of the Spirit. Sometimes, she is represented on other icons, but she appears then as pure transparency in the incandescence of the fire of the Holy Spirit without any flame on her head. Mary fully makes real the words of Jesus: "I have come to bring fire to the earth, and how I wish it were blazing already!" (Lk 12:49). Jesus burns with zeal in his wish to communicate to all men the fire which is corporally in him — that of the burning Bush, the plenitude of divinity (Col 2:9) — his mission is there. He is ready to give his time, his life and death in order that men may know of it and also burn:

"Suddenly they heard what sounded like a powerful wind from heaven, the noise of which filled the entire house in which they were sitting; then something appeared to them that seemed like tongues of fire; these separated and came to rest on the head of each of them. They were all filled with the Holy Spirit and began to speak other languages as the Spirit inspired them to express themselves" (Ac 2:2-4).

Mary was the first to greet this fire of the Spirit which springs from the depths of her being. She opens the joyous mysteries of the Rosary and offers her body and heart so that the fire of the Spirit may set ablaze in her the burning Bush of the Word made flesh. She carries him in her womb without being consumed by it.

Mary seems to withdraw into the background at the hour of the sorrowful mysteries even though the Rosary celebrates her presence at the foot of the Cross where she receives from Jesus the burn from the fire of merciful Love. She reappears explicitly at Pentecost: "Unanimously persevering in prayer with Mary." Since she has been "crucified by the Glory of Jesus on the Cross", the fire of the Spirit which was smouldering within herself has reached the level of incandescence. Mary is interiorly consumed by this fire of Love escaping from the wound in the side of Jesus, himself being consumed by the fire of the wound of the merciful Love of the Father. The iconographers often embellish the wounds of Christ with flowers and flames. We are reminded here of the Hindu custom according to which the body of the Sadhus is not burned before being thrown in the Ganges for they have been destroyed and consumed by the interior flame of Love.

When we contemplate Mary at Pentecost, we must never cease to watch her at the foot of the Cross, for this mystery prolongs the Passion and, at the same time, introduces it into Glory. Indeed, the Passion is already the Glory of Jesus, not that of Sinai or of the burning Bush (the burden of the Glory, of the Doxa which overwhelms and causes to tremble with fear), but the infinite gentleness of the mercy of God which is more terrible than all human power, for it is a heartrending sweetness for the hard of heart which we are. An underground member in the French Resistance, who was tortured by the Nazis at Fresnes, one day told one of my friends: "On the Cross, Jesus offered a heartrending meekness to his executioners!" All through the Passion and at the foot of the Cross, Mary was "stigmatized", that is, espoused by this agony, this death and this glorification of Jesus, by the suffering and the gentleness of God. She is par excellence the unwedded Spouse; she has known the throes of agony and of death whose dart is sin — death itself being engulfed by the death whose dart is Glory.

Thus Mary is already inhabited by the Glory of Christ, dead and risen; in her, the mystery of Easter was able to deploy all the divine energies of grace and glory. Until Pentecost, her wait had a particular character. At the moment of the Incarnation, she had received the action of the Holy Spirit within her in an absolutely unique manner. On the day of Pentecost, this same spirit present in her becomes incandescent through a new effusion which makes her a "living resurrected!" But this time, she is not alone anymore; she is in the midst of the first Christian community. This manifestation sheds a new light on the action of the Spirit in her since her birth and confirms this new motherhood which her Son has conferred upon her on the Cross. Mother of Jesus, she is now Mother of the Church.

1. "A new Pentecost"

Mary is the Mother of this Church living through her first Pentecost; at the same time, she is the image, the heart and soul of this new Church. We will see later how she exercises this new motherhood of glory on the group of disciples in the Upper Room uniquely by her prayerful and pleading presence. However, her prayer has henceforth acquired a particular efficacy in the presence of the Father: "The final biographical episode of Mary's life equally presents her to us in prayer: the apostles, with one heart, persevered in prayer with a few women, among them Mary the Mother of Jesus and his brothers" (Ac 1:14). This is the prayerful presence of Mary in the Church newly born and in the Church of all times because, now in heaven, she has not given up her mission of intercession and of salvation. So is the Church, a prayerful virgin who each day presents the needs of her sons to her Father, who praises the Lord unceasingly and intercedes for the salvation of the whole world".[1]

The Pentecost of the Church will last until the return of Jesus in Glory. There remains for Mary to become the mother of the whole humanity until the end of time. Pentecost is already the Parousia. However, the coming of Jesus in glory is a mystery more mysterious than that of the Pentecost, and the apostles could hardly have had any idea of it. Mary is the Virgin, humble and patient, who waits in silence for the hour of the effusion of the Spirit. She thus teaches the Church and the Christians to accept the delays so that the Spirit may be able to bear in them all the fruits of the Easter of Christ. But her wait

---

1. Translated from Paul VI, Apostolic Exhortation *Marialis cultus,* n. 18.

is not passive; it is vigilant and prayerful like that of the servants in the Gospel who are waiting for the return of the master. While waiting for this return of Jesus, the intercession of Mary today is totally directed toward the Father to whom she asks that the Spirit may be sent in the very name of Jesus. Like her Son (Heb 7:25) and with him, Mary is unceasingly in the process of interceding with the Father so that the Spirit may be given to men. All those whom the Father wishes to stay in the Upper Room today enter into this prayer of Mary, prolong it and continue it for the Church so that a new Pentecost may become a reality in the world, according to the prayer of John XXIII before Vatican Council II.

This mystery of the Pentecost extends over two thousand years and may yet extend for a long time before it reaches into eternity. We are always in the season of Pentecost, the long series of the thirty-three ordinary Sundays when the green color of liturgy sustains our hope. For this mystery, at the same time, prolongs that of the Passion. It is true that the fire of the Spirit is smouldering in the heart of men and of the world and that a seed of glory lies buried in us; but sin and evil are still at work in "the entire creation which has been groaning in one great act of giving birth; and not only creation, but all of us who possess the first-fruits of the Spirit, we too groan inwardly as we wait for our bodies to be adopted and set free" (Rm 8:22-23).

Pentecost is thus an apocalyptical mystery that has a sorrowful and a magnificent aspect, for Christ's victory is already at work in us and in history, as it is totally realized in the Virgin Mary. This victory of good over evil, of life over death is seen only by the eyes of faith, that is, to eyes which have been cauterized by fire and bathed in the living waters of Pentecost. We are so challenged by the obstacle of the Cross in the world, not to speak of our hearts slow to trust the power of holiness which can transform us, that we believe little in the victory of the Risen One. We are like the disciples of

236

Emmaus: they are fixed on the event of Good Friday and a carnal veil covers their hearts: "Their eyes were prevented from recognizing him" (Lk 24:16).

In this sense, we do not see the signs of the new Pentecost today nor, using again an expression dear to John Paul II, the signs of the new Advent. And yet, those who have eyes to see and ears to hear understand that the Glory of the Risen One is hidden in the heart of the world, buried in our heart, and that it acts like yeast raising dough. This is God's power which raised Jesus from the dead through the strength of the Spirit: it converts sinners, sustains the courage of the persecuted and fashions saints as they go through sorrowful agonies.

This is the invisible Pentecost which sometimes becomes visible as in the healing of the lame man at the Beautiful Gate in Jerusalem. Peter explains that this man was healed by the only power of the Name of the risen Jesus who sends forth the Holy Spirit (Ac 3:1-16). In prayer, we must examine closely the signs that manifest this power of the Spirit and allow us to proclaim that Jesus is risen indeed. Thus we see small communities of prayer and sharing being formed, whether they be of the Renewal movement or as basic communities, where the emphasis is laid on welcoming the lowly, the poor, the "lame". Men and women, hurt by life and their experience of sin or bruised by the hand of man, accept to present their wounds to a brother priest in the sacrament of reconciliation, or ask the community of brothers for the prayer of intercession. Little by little, the Spirit of Jesus restores them from within; the traumatizing effects of their wounds become blurred and prayer invests them to the point that their memory and their heart are wholly impregnated by the power of the risen Jesus.

We should not think that these healings are magic, instantaneous and leave no mark in the person; often the wound remains, but instead of being a source of anxiety and paralysis, it transforms itself into the distress of a poor and a sinner. Then the prayer of entreaty can spring forth at the same time as that of the praise of joy and peace. I notice that these healings are very often brought about through the intercession of the Immaculate Virgin, often that of the miraculous medal from the apparitions at Bac in Paris. I would like to quote here the testimony of a twenty-five year old who had an unhappy childhood and was emotionally wounded; today he bears a heavy cross which disturbs his psyche as well as his body. This makes him live an ordeal which could lead him to the edge of despair. And yet, at the heart of his torment, the Blessed Virgin sustains him and heals him in a mysterious manner. Here is what he was writing on the last 25th of March after he had renewed his Consecration to Mary:

"On this feast of the Annunciation in 1984 and of this consecration of the world to Mary, I became more keenly aware of the Virgin Mother's place in the crowd of sinners and sick people... What a mistake it is to visualize one's motherhood as if on a pedestal. No! Mary is a mother especially there where life is not obvious, where it tries to emerge. She is a mother especially where non-life has gained ground, where moral decay and death have apparently triumphed. Mary is a mother especially there where sin has settled in, in my mediocrity.

I understand my Marian vocation better in this perspective, in the discovery of such a law: Mary rushes first to places of misery in order that the mercy of her Son may be manifested in all its dimensions, in its power.

Before that, my life seemed to be divided between on one side, my thirst for holiness where Mary, the Immaculate, was seducing me by her beauty and, on the other, my experience as a sinner, keener at certain times when I did not dare to look at her too much and I would place in a sort of parenthesis my relationship with her.

Today, that's over: at the very heart of the struggle, of temptation, of humiliation, I grasp her hand and I tell her while clinging to my rosary: 'This is where I want you.' And then, I pursue my contact with her in faith with her Son Jesus, disturbed by the presence of such a flaw within me. But I remain faithful.

The enemy, on his side, would drive me to sadness, to fall back on myself, to distance myself from her Son since I live in such a depressed state because of my temptations. But I refuse to fall in this trap. Since my relationship with Mary pursues itself in a dialogue in the midst of temptations and sometimes even within the experience of failure, I regain my strength and the enemy loses ground."

Some would be tempted to say that this is not a healing since the battle and the trial remain. But this is much better than a "magic" healing, for this is the mystery of evil and of sin perpetually transcended and transfigured by the power of the Risen One: "My power is at its best in weakness. So I shall be very happy to make my weaknesses my special boast so that the power of Christ may stay over me" (2 Co 12:9). This man is lifted by the force from above which sustains his weakness. It never ceases to be a weakness as is clearly shown by his falls; he will never know with certitude to what extent they are sins: "This darkness, says Father Molinié, about the first fall of Christ, must be accepted, for Jesus also could say as he fell: I should have done better... but, precisely, he did not wish to do better."

After he had given his testimony, this young man was saying how he saw and noted his healing after receiving the sacrament of reconciliation. At the very moment he perceived these pulsations in his conscience, he felt an uninterrupted prayer of praise coming up from the depths of his being. He then had the impression that his passions were seized and absorbed by the power of prayer. This is what authorizes us to say that these human beings are healed by the springing forth of a continual prayer of the heart, in praise and thanksgiving, a source of deep peace and joy.

During the Easter vigil, the liturgy boldly proclaims this mystery: "O necessary sin of Adam which the death of Christ wiped away. O happy fault which gained for us so great a Redeemer!" "Christ had to suffer and die" as "Adam's sin was necessary!" We sing that exultantly in the *Exultet* of the Easter vigil, but we accept and bear it with difficulty in our own life, when we experience our weakness and our sin.

2. The attractive invisible unction of the Risen One

We could call to mind other signs of this new Pentecost. However, reading the book "We, the converted of the Soviet Union" by Tatiana Goritchéva, should be enough to convince us, or the Acts of the martyrs of Latin America, and the martyrs of Korea, canonized by Pope John Paul II at the time of his visit in that country. Everyone knows that the Christendom of Korea is flourishing today: "The blood of martyrs is the seed for Christians". What the Spirit of Pentecost makes us finally experience is the seed of Christians in the blood of martyrs, the innocent and sinners. That Spirit is given to us by Christ seated at his Father's right at the request of Mary in the Upper Room if we really want to recite persistently the glorious mysteries of the Rosary. We must assert that before speaking of the event of Pentecost and contemplating the overwhelming action of the Holy Spirit in the heart of the apostles, the disciples and the first communities such as the Acts describe it to us. To contemplate the glory of the Risen One on earth or the Church is the same. To contemplate the Church is to see sin always at work to crucify her and to help her in this way to prolong what is lacking in the Passion of Christ, but, at the same time, it is to contemplate the power of the Love that changed Saul the persecutor of Christians into Paul, the apostle of the Gentiles, a man mad with the love of Christ.

The list of signs just enumerated could be lengthened: Mother Teresa, Dom Helder Camara, Christians active and committed at home or in Poland, renewal of contemplative and priestly vocations. That is where we touch the invisible heart of Pentecost, explained only by the power of attraction which the Risen Christ still exercises today on the heart of men. This is the conversion the Acts speak of after Peter's discourse: "You must repent and every one must be baptized in the name of Jesus for the forgiveness of his sins and you will receive the gift of the Holy Spirit" (Ac 2:38). The healing of hearts and bodies, the changes in life, the testimony of martyrdom, the commitment in the wake of Christ in celibacy... so many glaring signs of the transformation of hearts through conversion, not only a moral conversion but a turning about of the whole being under the impulse of the Holy Spirit who reveals the face of Christ. We must first convert ourselves by encountering the Face of the Risen One, then there follows an effusion of the Spirit.

It is good to reflect on the full significance of this event of the Risen Christ as a disturbing element in one's existence. There is a man who lived two thousand years ago under Pontius Pilate and dies gathering hardly a handful of people at the foot of the Cross on which he was hung. We have, therefore, a character who belongs to history and even to an ancient one. And yet, in the twentieth century, men who have never known him, women who were educated outside of any Christian system, martyrs, all claim they have "business' with him, enough to sacrifice their life and to renounce what we call human happiness. They even claim they speak to him and have a relationship with him, not only by reading the gospel, but verbally.

This is the abyss which separates the disciples of Christ (the saints) from the disciples of Mohammed, or Buddha, Socrates or Marx, disciples who believe passionately in the teachings of their masters. But these disciples cannot claim they get in touch with them;

they simply study the wisdom offered by their masters. Christians also study the gospel, but in it, they are seeking Jesus: his eyes, his love, his life, the living water he has promised, and not primarily his doctrine.

It appears so foolish to love a man who lived two thousand years ago that we must have a closer look and see if these wretched people should not be sequestered. "They often are, says Father Molinié, but in convents!" If they are not secluded, that means that Jesus Christ did not purely and simply die. He died but something happened to him which is called Resurrection and which is the heart of the Christian mystery.

He is risen and he leads a humano-divine life radiating glory and is no more subjected to the vicissitudes of earth. He is very distinct from all the others and is not to be mistaken for any of them. He lives in our midst and he seeks us today. We can also try to reach him and get in touch with him. If we succeed, we find happiness and everything else appears as a waste of time (Ph 3:8). There is therefore in him an extraordinary power of seduction which first attracted the apostles and the disciples and which continues today to fascinate men. Raised on the Cross, he draws all men to him. From his glorified humanity trickles a living water which gives a taste of eternal life. This is the Spirit of the fire of Pentecost that tries to invade and cross our own existence. For Jesus, hidden in the Glory of God, also has the power to dwell in and to inhabit the heart of those who love him, for "the love of God has been poured into our hearts by the Holy Spirit which has been given us" (Rm 5:5). Those who accept to live this life and to love him experience at the bottom of their heart through the burdens of daily life, suffering and death, a spring gushing forth unto eternal life.

But we must add that this Jesus who lives in the deepest recesses of our self has a proper and distinct face: he is not pure interiority as Renan would have told Christians: "Basically, Jesus, that's you, your ideal, your

desire, the sublimation and the projection of your love!"
He is not that at all, for Jesus is the object of our love
and not its product. This means that he is also external
to us, that we have "business" with him and that if we
do not do what pleases him, he resists us. We cannot do
as we please with him, for he is a concrete person whom
we cannot enclose within any system.

We only need to see a saint, or even a sinner seeking
holiness like the publican of the parable or the young
man whose testimony we have quoted, to meet indeed
the one who dwells in their heart. A saint is a man who
is inhabited by Jesus Christ, who always thinks of him
— that is why he prays unceasingly — and who is at the
same time shaken by the distress of men to the point of
constantly pleading for them. When Jesus announces
that the Holy Spirit will make his disciples witnesses to
the end of time, it is of men seized by the madness of
his love that he is thinking. We often invite Christians
to be apostles, that is, to radiate and witness to the Risen
Christ, but we do not radiate him by "strokes of will
power"; we do not do it deliberately. We radiate him
without knowing it because of the power of the Spirit
of Pentecost burning in us and making saints of us. As
long as we have not seen the love of Christ "functioning"
in the heart of saints and apostles, nor have had the
feeling that they have the key, the secret of happiness,
truth and life, it is useless to wear ourselves out in
talking about the Risen Jesus Christ: we would incur the
accusation of being "simply a gong booming or a cymbal
clashing" (1 Co 13:1).

If we wish to understand something about this mystery of the effusion of the Spirit which allows the encounter with the Risen Christ today, we must renounce
rational knowledge in order to let ourselves be carried
away by the "music of the Crucified" as Julian of
Norwich says: the invisible unction of the Cross which
is also that of the Risen One and of Pentecost. The
apparition of Christ to Saint Thomas should be renewed

243

for us. Jesus should make us feel his wounds while showing us that they were made by the hands of the executioners and of sin, but that they have now become wounds of eternal love. Henceforth, through them, we contemplate the great wound of the heart of the Father. As long as we have not been introduced, by the Blessed Virgin at the foot of the Cross, to this mystery of the wound of God in the presence of the sin of men, we will not be able to bear the shock of the Cross and of the Crucified. We must accept to be crushed not by the executioners, but by the very gentleness of the victim: "Love is what nailed me to the Cross, said Jesus to Catherine of Sienna, and not the nails." If we do not take sides with the victim, we shall topple over on the side of the executioners.

The first Pentecost was spectacular because of the violent wind, the tongues of fire and the spiritual inebriety which invaded the heart of the apostles on that day to the point of converting three thousand men. Such a commotion was necessary to give a great thrust to found the Church and allow all the nations to hear the gospel and the praises of God in their own language. But this was somewhat the external facet of the event. There is today, in the Church, an invisible Pentecost which will last until the Parousia: it is the soft and light murmur of the Holy Spirit, the light breeze that caresses the face of Elijah at Horeb and changes hearts, obstinate and slow to believe, into saints with a heart melted by meekness. It is this meekness that inspired Peter to say to Jesus, not "I shall give my life for you" anymore, but an unutterable sigh, "You know everything, you know very well that I love you." This allowed him to fall no more but to give his life in the manner we all know, with all the apostles, those forgiven sinners.

Pentecost goes on today in the same way that Stephen lived it by forgiving his executioners and by praying for them. Let us but think of Saint Maximilian Kolbe who took the place of a prisoner in the bunker of starvation in Auschwitz and displayed a disarming and harrowing meekness towards his executioners to the point that they begged him not to look at them, so much did his gaze burn their heart. Is there any need to add that the effusion of the Spirit was for Father Kolbe the fruit of his love and of his prayer to Mary Immaculate, mediatrix of all graces?

The fire of the Spirit which burns in the heart of the saints is always the merciful Love that springs from the wound of Christ on the Cross. When we have understood that, we dread the fire of the burning Bush more than we would like and we take refuge near the Blessed Virgin in the Upper Room so that she may introduce us to this meekness and this humility. In a beautiful homily on spiritual sacrifice, Saint Peter Chrysologus opens to us the secret of the heart of Christ during his passion:

"But perhaps the enormity of my Passion of which you are the authors covers you with shame (Peter will not speak in any other way to the Jews assembled in Jerusalem on the day of Pentecost: Ac 2:23 and 37). Do not fear. This cross was fatal not for me but for death. Those nails do not penetrate me with pain, but with a yet deeper love for you. These wounds do not draw groanings from me, but they make you enter more deeply into my heart. The stretching of my body on the Cross opens my arms to you, it does not increase my torment. My blood is not lost to me but it is poured for your ransom".[2]

3. "Unanimously persevering in prayer" (Ac 1:14)

Thus when we call to mind the event of Pentecost, when the apostles were invested with a Spirit of power and of strength, we must never forget that this is about

2. Translated from St. Peter Chrysologus, *Homélie sur le sacrifice spirituel*, P.L. 52, c. 499-500.

the "invisible unction of the Cross",[3] all of meekness and humility. This is the reason why the waiting for this Spirit passes through the heart of the Blessed Virgin who possesses the secret of God's meekness. In praying, we are initiated by patience and perseverance to this mystery and are taught to convert our desire, forcibly bitter and self-willed, to unutterable groanings of meekness and humility. When the Father sees that we have reached the depth of our distress, when "enough is enough" and we can no more live without this "sovereign Comforter", then he sends this "most gentle Host of our souls" who is at the same time "a refreshing sweetness". The true purpose of prayer to Mary, if it is assiduous and perseverant, is to rend our heart and wrench from it an immense clamor which will rise to the heavens and tear the Father's heart as the cry of Jesus on the Cross shook Mary's heart. Our heart must be inhabited by this vehement desire to receive the words of Jesus promising us the Holy Spirit: "And now I am sending down upon you what the Father has promised. Stay in the city then, until you are clothed with the power from on high. Then he took them out as far as Bethany, and lifting up his hands he blessed them. Now as he blessed them, he withdrew from them and was carried up to heaven. They worshipped him and then went back to Jerusalem full of joy; and they were continually in the Temple praising God" (Lk 24:49-53). There are some good reasons to think that Mary was present at the last meal that Jesus took with his own (Ac 1:4) before leading his disciples to the Mount of Olives to be witnesses to his Ascension: "Before their eyes he rose and a cloud took him from their sight" (Ac 1:9). This cloud symbolizes another world into which Jesus is entering where he will live an existence different from the one he had on this earth.

The cloud is the image of Jesus in glory. Henceforth,

---

3. Translated from St. Bernard.

divine realities are hidden from his apostles and also from us. The time has not yet come for the friends of Jesus to go through this cloud and enter into the light of God. They cannot penetrate this cloud except by an act of faith. It is to stir them on to this faith that Jesus left them his mother. She is the believer par excellence who has kept her act of faith to the end, since we see her standing at the foot of the Cross. After Calvary, Mary disappears again from the gospels. She is not with the women at the tomb on the morning of the Resurrection. In none of the apparitions do we find any mention of her presence, but she lives so close to the Risen Jesus present in her through faith that the evangelists do not think it is useful to mention her: for them, this goes without saying. Jesus is surely thinking of her when he says to Thomas: "You believe because you can see me. Happy are those who have not seen and yet believe" (Jn 20:29).

However, we know that she is not far since she now lives at John's home. It is highly probable that she is with the apostles and the friends of Jesus when they gather together. We must, nevertheless, wait for the definite departure of Jesus before we find her mentioned again (Ac 1:14). It is significant that the evangelists, always discreet on the subject of the Blessed Virgin and on the events of her life, note her presence at that time. In this lies a design of faith for the community of the apostles. Luke's intention is clear: he wishes to show that Mary's presence in faith was absolutely necessary for the Upper Room as it was in Nazareth on the day of the Annunciation.

It is, therefore, in an atmosphere of joy, praise and prayer that they come back to Jerusalem. Mary leads them to this new joy of which she has the secret because Jesus, glorious from now on, has promised them the Holy Spirit which will inhabit their heart and will instruct them on all that the Lord has told them. Once Jesus has disappeared, the apostles and his friends come back to Jerusalem to wait for the promise of the Father:

"You will receive a power, that of the Holy Spirit which will come upon you" (Ac 1:8). And this is where Luke's text on the presence of Mary in the Upper Room comes in: "When they returned, they went to the Upper Room where they gathered together; ... All these unanimously joined in continuous prayer, together with several women, including Mary the Mother of Jesus, and with his brothers" (Ac 1:13-14).

Mary is there in the midst of the first disciples, relatives and friends, as the mother of the Lord whom they respect and venerate because of the privileged bond she had with him, but also for her presence and unshakable trust on Calvary. By the power of the Spirit, in union with the Father, she begets and conceives the mystical Body of her Son. Having given her son his body and his human nature, she continues this role in a mystical way as humanity enters in communion with her Son. She is the Mother of the Church until the end of time.

"It is through the most Blessed Virgin Mary that Jesus Christ came into the world and it is also through her that he is to reign on the world". Thus speaks Grignion of Montfort at the beginning of the *True Devotion to Mary*. In this sense, Pentecost is strictly the counterpart of the Annunciation and the fruit also of a fecundation of Mary by the Spirit. I shall compare the latter to a parabolic mirror at whose focal point the Sun by reflecting itself can reach temperatures of 2000 to 3000 degrees. The Upper Room appears thus as an extension of the virginal womb of Mary, an enclosed garden reflecting the flame of the Spirit like an untarnished mirror in the interior of which the apostles "unanimously persevering in prayer" remained exposed to this warmth for about ten days... at the end of which very naturally they took fire".[4]

4. Translated from M.D. Molinié, *Lettre n. 21 sur le Rosaire*, May 1976, p. 14.

The icon of the Ascension by Andreï Roublëv[5], in the absence of the icon of Mary in the Upper Room, can draw us near this mystery of Mary's mediation in the descent of the Spirit. She is always placed on the side of the Church who, in a prayer of entreaty, is waiting for the Holy Spirit while Jesus, the only mediator, is in heaven seated at the right of the Father, a fact which denotes his equality with the Father, and meanwhile he is interceding for us. Thus all the top part of the icon is made up of the cloud, a sign of the presence of God and, at the center of this cloud, Christ is carried by two angels dressed like the apostles. He brings our humanity to the Father. In his left hand, he holds the scroll of the gospels and with his right hand, he is blessing the Church.

Jesus is asking his Father for the effusion of the Holy Spirit for his Church on Pentecost. The icon of the Ascension is the one of Jesus' prayer to his Father that each of his disciples — the Church — may be filled with the Holy Spirit. It is the fulfilment of these words: "I shall ask the Father and he will give you another Paraclete (protector) to be with you forever" (Jn 14:15). We must note that these words of Jesus come immediately after he has said to his disciples: "Whatever you ask for in my name I will do, so that the Father may be glorified in the Son" (Jn 14:13). This is truly Christ's intercession for the Church of today: it is the one which gives worth and efficacy to the prayer of Mary and of the Church. In each of our liturgies we commemorate this prayer of Christ who is asking the Holy Spirit for us. It is he who consecrates the oblates and consecrates us at the same time in the communion to his Body in order that we may become an "agreeable offering to the Father", that is to say, that we be transformed "into prayer".

On the icon, half of the apostles look towards the heavenly Christ and the other half look towards Mary.

---

5. Tretiakov Gallery, Moscow.

To everyone, the two angels (who were already at the tomb) are saying: "Do not weep, he will come again in the same way, he is always there." In prayer as in life, we cannot restrict faith for Christ belongs to two worlds: he is near the Father and he is with us. The apostles are in motion for they must evangelize the whole world. On the other hand, Mary, standing out from the whiteness of the angels, appears as the motionless supplicant. In the animated group of the apostles, Mary is the supplicant, the one who truly has faith and trust in God.

The effusion of the Spirit is a gratuitous initiative of the Father; it, therefore, does not depend on us and still less on our personal merits: "It is not for you to know times or dates that the Father has decided by his own authority, but you will receive a power, that of the Holy Spirit which will come upon you" (Ac 1:7-8). Meanwhile, we must collaborate with this effusion of the Spirit for it is not arbitrary even if it is gratuitous and Jesus forever invites us to ask, to plead and to seek. To believe in the power of the Spirit and to ask for it is our way of collaborating towards the acquisition of this free gift. If this desire does not take form in a request, there is no gift either. To make us understand that, Jesus uses the parables of the troublesome friend and of the insistent widow to show how the Father is generous and gives the good Spirit to those who pray for it (Lk 18:8).

"When he was at table with them, he told them not to leave Jerusalem, but to wait there for what the Father had promised" (Ac 1:4). Jesus cannot make himself any clearer in the instructions he gives to the apostles: they must not leave the place where they are but wait for the Spirit. In order to understand how apt and reasonable this "order" is, we must have experienced what the monks who have dedicated all their life to prayer have to say. They do not cease to repeat to their disciples that the most difficult and the most austere work of their life is the struggle of prayer in their cell: "Persevere in your cell and your cell will teach you everything",[6] It is not only a question of staying in one's room, for we can be more or less gifted for solitude, but to yield ourselves continually to the labor of prayer, if not in acts, at least in desire and in intention.

This is where, I believe, the intercession of the Blessed Virgin is necessary to teach us to persevere in prayer. At the Annunciation and each time she was confronted with an impossible situation, she discovered by experience that nothing is impossible to God. For her, there was no door of escape but that of prayer; she could only "have recourse to her usual resource", which was to call for help. The Blessed Virgin is one who does not have an alternative solution but the prayer of entreaty.

She has thus taken the habit of pleading at every moment when God has invited her to say "Fiat". We must admit that she did not find within herself any resistances against pleading nor any complications in yielding herself totally to the Father in heaven, so lowly and humble as she was. The prayer of entreaty was in her as permanent as breathing itself. We can see that in certain saints who cannot stop pleading anymore so much has their cry gathered a momentum touching upon the infinite. The situation is different for us. We would willingly ask but we also want some "alternative solutions" for the difficult cases where the prayer of entreaty would not work.

It is exactly for this reason that our supplication does not have that desperate strength which overturns mountains and makes them throw themselves into the sea. To understand that, it is sufficient to try, to say "we must do it"! Precisely, we must hope that all might not go as well as we wish in our life, otherwise we would have no opportunity to plead. We must not look for opportunities, but use all the ones that present themselves to cry to God: it is in this way that one becomes a person of prayer. We must have recourse to the Blessed

6. Translated from *Apophtegmes*, Moïse 6.

251

Virgin and ask her to teach us how to implore. I admit that one critical moment in spiritual life occurs when we notice that we will not be able to stop praying anymore. Indeed, we find it good to plead from time to time, especially in difficult moments or when we have been able to get started in prayer, but when the impulse of the Holy Spirit becomes such that we cannot stop anymore, we discreetly go off on a tangent admitting to ourselves that this is somewhat exhausting!

To understand that is perhaps the greatest grace which can come to us in spiritual life. We must often go back to the Upper Room to ask the Blessed Virgin for this grace, for it is not enough to understand it, nor even to experience it, so great is the instability of our nature. There are moments in our life when prayer is "given" to us or when the prayer of entreaty is a matter of course; but very quickly we let go this grace — we lose grace, says Silouane — and we rebuild new circuits more conforming to our wish of realizing ourselves on our own, until the day God breaks down these circuits and puts us back in uninterrupted prayer. Basically, the only grace to ask of the Blessed Virgin is never to stop pleading: by dint of asking for this grace, we obtain it, for already we do not cease to be in prayer:

"The rosary is an insistent prayer addressed to the One who is the highest expression of humanity in prayer, the model of the Church in supplication and entreaty in Christ, the Mercy of God. In the same way that Christ is 'living for ever to intercede for us' (Heb 7:25), so does Mary continue her mission as Mother in heaven and becomes for every man the voice of all men until the definite crowning of the elect.[7] When we pray her, we implore her to come to our aid in the entire course of our present life and above all at this moment decisive for our eternal destiny, the hour of our death".[8]

7. Cf. *Lumen Gentium*, 62.

8. Translated from John Paul II, Angelus of October 2, 1983.

4. "Living forever to intercede..." (Heb 7:25)

Some would be tempted to be fastidious with regards to the prayer of entreaty of the rosary for they claim that the summum in prayer is praise or thanksgiving and they look upon those who are still in the phase of demand with pity! They are not altogether wrong for far too many Christians have recourse to prayer only when they need to obtain this or that favor. As Saint Thomas says, this prayer is called a prayer of request for it has definite things for its object. But the prayer of which we are speaking here is rather indeterminate as in the following invocation: "Lord, come to my rescue" (Ps 69:1). It is properly speaking an entreaty which can become an insistent adjuration!

This prayer of entreaty rests uniquely on the words of Jesus who lays its foundation and gives it all its effectiveness: "Without me, you can do nothing" (Jn 15:5). While commenting on these words, theologians like Saint Basil, Saint John Chrysostom, Saint Augustine, will say that prayer is necessary for all, not only as a necessity by precept but also as a necessity of means. This means that we are able neither to conceive the good nor to realize it, nor to bring it to completion, nor even to desire it "without being predisposed by the inspiration of the Holy Spirit and without his help".[9] "Without the help of grace, we can do nothing; on the other hand, God usually gives such a help only to the one who prays. Who can fail to see the conclusion that emerges from this: prayer is absolutely necessary for our salvation".[10]

Thus prayer is a question of life or death; in this sense, it is totalitarian. It is not a question of whether we should pray much or little: neither is it a question of time or formulas, nor even of contemplative prayer,

9. Council of Trent.

10. Translated from St. Alphonsus of Liguori, *Le grand moyen de la prière*, Apôtre du Foyer Ed., 1945, p. 19.

for we can be more or less gifted for this exercise. The stakes are much higher, for they pertain to the situation of man before God and to the decision man takes of expecting everything from God or of getting everything on his own. Basically, do we accept to be on our knees before God, our Creator and our Father? Are we ready to do as Jesus said in the gospel: "You must pray continually and never lose heart" (Lk 18:1). Either we pray all the time or we never pray: between these two extremes, there is no middle line. Let us repeat it: it is not a question of being "stuck on prayer", and devote hours to contemplative prayer... That will come later. It is a question of the heart's movement which takes but a quarter of a second and which could be translated into one only word: "Help". As soon as a man has let out this cry from the bottom of his heart under the effect of grace or of tribulations, he is threatened by continual prayer, for this cry will be followed by many others, more and more frequent; these will transform his life into a prayer. Yet he must not resist the impulse of the Holy Spirit by going on a tangent. For then, he goes off the orbit of prayer which should have carried him off at an infinite speed to the heart of the triune life.

Basically, prayer makes us realize the great commandment Jesus gave on the evening of the Last Supper: "Remain in my love". If Jesus insisted so much on prayer, it is because he himself first prayed unceasingly in order to remain in the Father's love: "As the Father has loved me, I also have loved you. Remain in my love. If you keep my commandments you will remain in my love just as, by keeping my Father's commandments, I remain in his love" (Jn 15:9-10). Note that it is in this passage that Jesus says the words quoted above: "Without me, you can do nothing" (Jn 15:15); thus he links the necessity of expecting everything from him in prayer to his commandment to remain in the Father's love. It is somewhat as if he were saying: "I ask you to heed to my words that you may remain in my love, but I well know that you will not manage this by your own strengths. Therefore, by giving you my commandment, I give you at the same time the key to take heed of it, that is prayer." Saint Augustine used a formula that will be taken up again by the Council of Trent: "God does not command things impossible to do but when he commands, he warns us to do what is possible for us, to ask him for what is not possible for us, and he helps us that this may become possible." In other words, when we experience our helplessness to keep the Word of Christ, we must ask him for help in prayer.

We must also point out that it is the same context of the entrance into the triune life that Jesus reminds us on two occasions of the power of prayer made in his name: "If you remain in me and my words remain in you, you may ask what you will and you shall get it... Anything you ask the Father in my name, he will give you" (Jn 15:7 and 16). Basically, if there had not been the triune revelation, Christ would not have been able to speak to us in this way about the prayer of entreaty. And if he had not invited us to share the secret which he holds with his Father, he would not have invited us to implore with so much insistence: "I call you friends, because I have made known to you everything I have learnt from my Father" (Jn 15:15).

This is the reason why we must never say that entreaty is a phase that must be transcended even if we are within God's love. What is a friendship relation that does not plead? This is the most divine attitude and we do not transcend the divine attitude and the triune habits. The Father forever asks his Son to accept his love and thanks him for his response: "You are my son, today I have become your father" (Ps 2:7). The Son offers himself to the Father at all times pleading him to kindly accept him and, at the same time, he thanks him for his love: "You, my Father, my God and rock of my safety" (Ps 89:27). As for the Spirit, he is the very supplication of the Father and the Son, thereby becoming a person;

he is the fruit of their mutual love. He proceeds from the Father and the Son, theologians say, as a child is the fruit of the love of a father and a mother. We understand why Saint Paul will say that the Spirit prays in us with unutterable groanings since he is "prayer in person". To call the Spirit in our hearts is to make the entreaty of love, which the Father and the Son mutually address to each other while giving thanks, come down on us or rather spring from the depths of our being.

It is not easy for us to grasp that idea for we live in space and time and we cannot escape these in order to understand the relationships at the heart of the Trinity. Eternity is a "yes" which has an eternal dimension; it is the triune dance described by Lewis in which each person stands aside not only to allow the other to exist but to make him exist, or in a rather uncouth term, it is a "subsisting relationship". We understand that in his humanity, in the course of his life on earth, Jesus would have entreated the Father "With cries and tears" (Heb 5:7); this attitude was natural for his being as Son. Similarly, he gives thanks to the Father when his prayers have been answered: "Father, I thank you for hearing my prayer. I knew indeed that you always hear me, but I have spoken for the sake of all those who stand round me, so that they may believe it was you who sent me" (Jn 11:41-42).

In the same way that the Persons of the Blessed Trinity mutually entreat and accept each other, so does Christ implore us to kindly receive his friendship and thanks us for our "yes", as Mary was proclaimed blessed because of her "yes". Every time we enter into prayer, we should ask the Spirit, who is the very supplication of the Father and of the Son, to open our eyes that we may see Christ on his knees at our feet in the process of begging for our love. And when we implore him, we are but responding to his prayer of entreaty.

Like the Father, Jesus is someone who is not afraid to plead since he is entirely turned toward the other person and is pure communication: "Do you wish to listen to me, to give me your heart, your freedom?" This is the reason why at Christmas the Church asks us to contemplate God in the form of a child who is "begging". What interests him is not to dominate us, but to be loved. The supplication of Jesus to man is like the triune request. We do not live of love without demanding reciprocal love. Thus, even in God, there is Love and the reciprocal demand of two beings who give birth to a third: to "prayer" itself. This allows us to say that the prayer of entreaty has a triune value. In other words, we shall never transcend the prayer of entreaty: even at the summit of perfection, we will implore God, like Thérèse of Lisieux who promised to spend her time in heaven in pleading and in doing good on earth. God will answer "yes" to our eternal supplication.

We must go to the point of contemplating the triune dialogue to grasp the nature of our dialogue with God. There is, however, a difference, since between the Persons of the Blessed Trinity there is no word or, if there is one, it is the Word who utters himself in an eternal silence and which, at the same time, is a Son for in him the Father spends all his substance. To approach this mystery of the relationship of the Persons among themselves, certain spiritual writers have spoken of the "fire of two gazes who consume each other in love";[11] this image has the advantage of making us understand the nature of the fire of the Holy Spirit which is like the incandescent spark from an electric arc ignited by the meeting of these two gazes. But the word which seems the closest to the mystery of this dialogue is "yes" which unites the intensity of the supplication and the simplicity of the acceptance in the answer. It is with the help of this word that Paul will make us understand the mystery of the person of Christ and also of his prayer. Paul names him the Son of God to stress the fact that his being is

---

11. Translated from Father M.D. Molinié.

received from the Father in a total and absolute "yes":

"For the Son of God, the Christ Jesus that we have proclaimed among you — I mean Sylvanus and Timothy and I — was never Yes and No: but with him it has always been Yes, and all the promises of God have found their Yes in him. That is why it is 'through him' that we answer AMEN to God for his Glory" (2 Co 1:19-20). Thus we enter into this triune dialogue by saying our "Amen" in Jesus. He is the only one to have said a "yes" which committed and consecrated him to the Father in the deepest recesses of his being. And the "yes" which Mary pronounces at the Annunciation was made possible by the unction of God who impressed his seal upon her and placed the pledge of the Spirit in her heart (2 Co 1:21).

It is because of her impregnation by the unction of the Spirit that Mary intercedes with the apostles and the disciples in the Upper Room. As we have suggested, the Spirit is truly the "prayer" of the Father to the Son and of the Son to the Father. This is why a being totally inhabited by the Spirit is transformed into prayer. This is what makes the Fathers of the East say that Mary is the Mother of continual prayer because she is the Mother of the burning Bush. Saint Grignion of Montfort says that "the Holy Spirit has become fecund through Mary whom he has espoused. It is with her and in her and from her that he produced a masterpiece which is a God made man and that he produces, every day until the end of the world, the predestined and the members of the Body of this adorable Head. This is why the more he finds Mary as his dear and indissoluble Spouse in a soul, the more he becomes active and powerful to produce Jesus Christ in this soul and this soul in Jesus Christ".[12] No one in the world has borne a greater resemblance to the Holy Spirit than the Blessed Virgin. The Fathers have compared her to the "Mirror of Justice", a crystal so pure that it reflects the image of the Blessed Trinity

12. Translated from *Traité de la vraie dévotion*, n. 20.

without any flaw. We can truly apply to many what a Syrian monk in the VIIth century said about men transformed by the Spirit: their eyes are lit by the triune light.

"The last sign which shows that the Spirit is at work in you is the clear eye of your spirit which, in the heavens of your heart, appears like a sapphire receiving the light of the Blessed Trinity. This knowledge leads you to a vision of things perceptible to the senses, and from there you gain the knowledge of spiritual realities from which you raise yourself up to the mysteries of the judgment and the Providence of God. This ladder raises you and unites you to the holy light of the vision of Christ our Lord".[13]

This means that the only gift Jesus promises to those who pray in his name is the sending of his Holy Spirit. There is no gift greater or more eminent than the Spirit, since he is God himself surrendering himself to man in the eternal generation of the Son. Thus, when Jesus tells us that prayer obtains everything from God, he is thinking first of the Holy Spirit: "Anything you ask in my name, you shall receive". Nothing procures more joy to God than to see man begging "God himself". When we pray the Spirit to come in our heart, we give God the possibility to "love himself within us". "Not," says Saint Thomas, "that prayer be required for God to know our needs, but that we may see our need of having recourse to God in order to receive the help useful for our salvation and, through that, to recognize him as the only author of all good".[14]

"This is why his power to save is utterly certain, since he is living for ever to intercede for all who come to God through him" (Heb 7:25). When Christ intercedes with

---

13. Translated from Abdicho Sassaja, quoted in Strotman, *Pneumatologie et Liturgie*.

14. Translated from a text quoted by St. Alphonsus of Liguori in *Le grand moyen de la prière*, p. 21.

the Father in our favor, he can but ask for the Holy Spirit, since he has invited us with insistence to desire him in prayer: "If you then, who are evil, know how to give good things to your children, how much more will the heavenly Father give the Holy Spirit to those who ask him" (Lk 11:13). In short, all Christian prayer is summed up in a supplication which should be the "background music" of all life of prayer: "Father, in the name of Jesus, give me your Spirit." All the chords and all the scales are possible when we start from this fundamental groaning: meditation, contemplative prayer, rosary, liturgy, etc... And since the Spirit has made Mary his faithful Bride, we are all invited to call the Spirit in us through her.

5. The Spirit and the Bride say: "Come." (Rv 22:17)

"When the Holy Spirit, the Blessed Virgin's Spouse, has recognized her in a soul, he flies to it, enters it fully; he communicates himself abundantly to this soul as much as it gives room to his Bride. One of the important reasons why the Holy Spirit does not perform spectacular wonders in souls now is that he does not find there a union close enough to his faithful and inseparable Bride. I say: inseparable Bride, for since that substantial Love of the Father and of the Son has espoused Mary to bring forth Jesus Christ, the head of the elect and Jesus Christ in the elect, he has never repudiated her because she has always been faithful and fruitful".[15]

Thus speaks Louis Mary Grignion of Montfort while he lays emphasis on the mysterious bond of fecundity between the Holy Spirit and the Blessed Virgin: "She found herself with child through the Holy Spirit... What she has conceived in her comes from the Holy Spirit" (Mt 1:18 and 21). Because of Matthew's words, Mary

15. Translated from St. Louis Mary Grignion of Montfort, *Traité de la vraie dévotion*, n. 36, Œuvres complètes, p. 507.

is called the spouse of the Holy Spirit, because "the substantial Love of the Father and his Son has espoused her to bring forth Christ." This mystery of the espousals of Mary with the Spirit is well known and real since she carried the fruit of the Spirit nine months in her body.

For Mary, these espousals were not a theoretical consideration but a very concrete experience which she could verify each time she recollected herself and meditated on what was happening in her heart and body. She felt this unceasing life of the Spirit going right through her whenever her child moved within her. She experienced the burden, the joy and the hope in her own body. She recognized the wonder that she was and that she was "moulded" by the Holy Spirit.

We cannot doubt that Mary's prayer was a plunge into the depths of her heart, where living waters are forever springing forth. Indeed, the Book of Revelation asserts "that the Spirit and the Bride say, 'come'... Then let all who are thirsty come: let all who want it receive the water of life and have it free" (Rv 22:17). The Bride is the Church and the Blessed Virgin who unite with the Holy Spirit to ask in all their prayers for the coming of the Lord. All of Mary's prayer was directed towards this return of her Son in glory with whom she had united and identified herself, from the "yes" of the Annunciation to Calvary. She saw him rise in the cloud, not absent henceforth, but hidden in the Glory of God. Daughter of God, she was also hidden with Christ, buried in his death and participating in his resurrection. The Holy Spirit then introduced her to another presence of her Son hidden within herself: "And know that I am with you always; yes, to the end of time" (Mt 28:20).

When we reread with the eyes of the Blessed Virgin the texts where Paul calls to mind the presence and action of the Spirit in our heart and prayer, these appear in a totally different relief, for we then contemplate how a being who has "put on a new self" (Col 3:10) could have allowed the Spirit to move and breathe freely in him.

261

The action of the Spirit in us is so deadened by the oppositions and the burden of our flesh that on certain days we doubt that the Spirit could thus renew us inwardly (Ep 4:23) and make saints of us. As we contemplate Mary, we understand what is a being coming from the hands of the Father in its original purity. She felt through her whole person this breath of life which made her a being living from the very life of the Spirit (Gn 2:7 and 1 Co 15:45).

It is also in the heart of Mary that we must closely examine the mystery of the prayer in the Spirit. We understand that Saint Grignion of Montfort could have said the following: "When the Holy Spirit finds Mary in the heart of a man, he runs and flies to it." Those who practise the Marian prayer, like the rosary or any other prayer, very quickly experience at the beginning of the hour of prayer that the Blessed Virgin sends them back to the Holy Spirit. This is an unexplainable fact that forces itself on the man of prayer. We could almost say that to invoke Mary is to invoke the Holy Spirit present and living in her, so much has she allowed herself to be impregnated by him. We are sent from one to the other like in a game of ball so that we do not know very well anymore where to start.

Let us consider a few texts from Saint Paul on the prayer of the Spirit in us, and let us imagine ourselves in the mind of the Blessed Virgin in order to enter into this prayer or, more simply, let us allow her to pray in us. A first text to begin with is the text in Romans, 8:26-27. It always fascinates those who try to pray and do not manage to do so, but eventually find the wave length which makes them get in touch with the invisible person of the Father who sees in secret. I feel like not transcribing it word for word but transforming it into prayer. This invocation could lead us to contemplative prayer:

"Holy Spirit, come to the aid of our weakness for we do not know how to pray as we should; come to intercede for us in unutterable groanings. And you, Father, who scrutinizes our hearts, you know that the Spirit's prayer is in us and that he intercedes for us according to your plans."

Basically, that is what prayer is. With the use of a formula or without any words, in joy or in grief, through this joy or this grief, we seek for hours to get in touch with the Father... and the contact comes like a thief, the time of a lightning stroke; ultimately, it matters little whether it comes or not, it is the seeking that matters. But to understand that, we must truly have experienced it. I recall what someone told me: this is a young man again of whom prayer has kindly taken hold since the days of his childhood when his grandmother used to teach him the rosary. He has always prayed, or at least what has always struck me in him is prayer. And when I would tell him so, he would reply: "That is exactly what I do not know how to do!" — "Perhaps," I would answer, "but we feel very much that prayer is the only thing that matters to you and about which you are concerned." Once he went through a "desert" during which he knew not only distress and dereliction but the apparent abandonment of God. He would tell me: "Now I know what the prayer of entreaty is and I could speak about it. Not everyone is able to pray (to do contemplative prayer) but everyone can implore if he experiences distress." And he would add: "One really has to go through that to understand it at the bottom of his heart." And truly, in certain moments, when he was crestfallen or in the trough of the wave, I felt prayer rising in him like a pillar of fire. He was not aware of it, but all that made of him a true man of prayer, much more so than the fact of knowing how to pray well.

His prayer was very simple; it amounted to reciting the rosary or the *Memorare* to the Blessed Virgin. Without his knowing it, the Holy Spirit was training him to pray continually and to seek the Father through suffering, temptation and often distress. No prayer is more fruitful even if it is painful. Apparently, he did not seem to experience any great desolations, but everyone knows that appearances are deceiving, for the man who descends into the depths of his being touches heaven but the hell of his passions as well.

It is a great secret and a precious grace to seek contact with God through distress and desolation. God then appears as the refuge, the salvation, the father, the mother wrapping us in his tenderness, understanding and saving us. We can tell God everything, especially our most secret temptations and our laments, for we know that he always listens. I dare say that "it is very clever", not like an acrobatic stunt, but its opposite: a vertiginous fall in a void. How far have we moved from the beautiful definitions of the prayer we were taught: "An elevation of the soul toward God!" Let us rather say that it is a descent into the depths of our own hells, where Jesus was the first to plunge. The only thread that links us to God, while keeping us from falling into despair, is the cry of the prayer of entreaty. The one who climbs down to this depth of distress, sustained by the dynamism of his supplication, can hope to rebound into the heart of the Father, but the rebound is all the more powerful that the descent was vertiginous.

It is obvious that to go down into these mysterious regions, we must have the soul of a speleologist who always digs at the same place and with the same instrument. This means that we must persevere in prayer with one word only, the rosary or the Jesus prayer, which hollows out the soil of our psyche to reach down into the subsoil of our heart, where we are really such as God sees us. Many men avoid prayer because they are afraid of going that far; they are especially afraid of groaning and weeping. We shall see later that Paul uses approximately the same language in his Letter to the Corinthians, when he speaks of the Spirit that probes and scrutinizes the depths of God (1 Co 2:10).

Paul says that "we groan inwardly as we wait for the

filial adoption" (Rm 8:23). Instead of being his sons, we are his slaves torn between a thirst for the Infinite and for human pleasures, between meekness and harshness, humility and pride. We are, therefore, tortured by this struggle and we groan, especially when we realize that we do not have the will to wage this battle. The repeated falls generate a certain despair in us along with the impression of tumbling down to the bottom of an unfathomable abyss: "When shall we see the end of this? Will that never come to an end?" What does he know, the man who has never been tempted to say these words? Blessed are they who do not rebel and who know how to groan inwardly.

The great trial of our life is really the thirst for God, a blessed suffering, but which becomes dangerous if it generates the impression that this thirst will never be quenched. This is where the Blessed Virgin intervenes if we agree to pray her humbly and hand over our struggles to her, our rebellions and sufferings. She is the Mother of Mercy and she can in her motherly heart reach us in the depths of our distress — for she herself has experienced suffering without becoming harsh — and help us "to accept more easily the merciful love of a mother".[16]

Her motherly role has the power of liberating in us another much deeper groaning that we hardly suspect: the unutterable groaning of the Spirit buried in the deepest areas of our heart. In us, the Spirit prays with cries too profound for words; this means that at a level which is not accessible to us, the Holy Spirit joins our own spirit to bear witness and convince us that we are the Father's children (Rm 8:16). The Blessed Virgin and the Spirit join together to reach our spirit and our heart and to make true prayer spring in us. The role of Mary is to teach us to tune in our poor human groans to those

16. Translated from John Paul II, *La miséricorde divine*, n. 9.

265

of the Spirit in us. She purifies the groanings that we utter naturally and transforms them from useless and stifling noises and superficial whims into the true groanings of the Spirit which rise in all honesty before God, this groaning which expresses the most radical wish of our being.

Basically, the role of the Spirit in us always aims at the same attitude which is first an inward movement towards our heart in order to awaken it to the true life of the Spirit. The Spirit is not only the goal to reach, but also the means to deepen and reach that heart. Like Jesus, it could say: "I am the way, the truth and the life" (Jn 14:6). It is always a matter of seeking contact with God, not only external to ourselves but hidden at the bottom of our heart. Most of the time, we do not manage to do so, but the essence of that search does not lie in the goal — we never reach it — but in the motion which makes us come out of ourselves to go towards the other. Ultimately, the fact of not succeeding is a grace, for we are then introduced to a fundamental truth about which no one understands anything except those who experience this painful failure I am speaking about and knock their head against the wall of stone of their heart to seek contact with God. They can then perceive from within what was the Blessed Virgin's original innocence that is that she prayed as she breathed and, at the same time, they are aware that they have lost this innocence. But it is difficult to understand that when we have not experienced failure.

For this reason, we must attempt, try, hollow out... We have used the image of the speleologue. Paul will speak of the Spirit who probes the depths of God — we think of a spatial probe scrutinizing the secrets of the interplanetary world. It is with the prayer of the Spirit that we can penetrate not only the depths of God but also the depths of our own heart:

"The Spirit reaches the depths of everything, even the depths of God. Who among men knows what is in man if not the spirit of man within him? In the same way the depths of God can only be known by the Spirit of God. Now instead of the spirit of the world, we have received the Spirit that comes from God, to teach us to understand the gifts that he has given us" (1 Co 2:10-12).

"To understand the gifts that God has given us", is surely to discover our dearest treasure, the one we carry around with us everywhere but most of the time without knowing it: "God has sent the Spirit of his Son into our hearts, the Spirit that cries: 'Abba! Father!'" (Ga 4:6). In the epistle to the Romans, Paul is even more explicit: the groaning of the Spirit is presented as the first-fruits of the new creation, like a yeast buried in the dough of our heart destined to make it rise, to broaden our prayer, like a seed hidden in our body, making it ripen gradually to bear fruit someday in resurrection. It is the inner groaning of the Spirit in us which turns all our being toward the return of the Lord and the fulfilment we are waiting for: "The Spirit and the Bride say: Come."

At the very bottom of our hearts is hidden the prayer of the Spirit; it is down to this depth that the Word of God must reach to discover it, to free it, to awaken it in us. The groaning of true prayer is there. It comes to us from the Spirit of God; it is strictly the groaning of God himself, a cry of love which unceasingly springs from the Son to the Father in the Spirit. It is a cry of love in a breath which is also a love embrace. The Holy Spirit is the loving embrace of the Father and the Son, with whom Mary was associated in such an intimate way when the Holy Spirit covered her with its shadow. This is the reason why she has a privileged role, if we are willing to go through her to open ourselves to these splendors of prayer hidden in us. That is brought about by the most humble and poor means of the rosary, according to a law very well known by those who have read our work: "The more we are called to the mystical prayer of the Spirit, the more we must limit ourselves to the simple and concrete prayer of the rosary!"

Chapter IX

MARY...
PRAY FOR US, SINNERS

There is a mysterious bond between the Blessed Virgin and sinners. Let us recall what we have said about the prayer of Mary at the foot of the Cross: she shares the sufferings of God in the presence of those who are losing their soul, that is, she has a "weakness" for sinners. I am thinking here of a poem by Dostoïevski: "The Virgin among the damned" which is used as a literary preface for Yvan in his legend of the Great Inquisitor. His insight is surely theologically worthless, but it is very revealing as a spiritual intuition dear to our brothers from the East and which also touches us very much. The Blessed Virgin intercedes with God for the damned themselves (a doctrine stemming from the apocatastasis). So she insists and obtains that between Easter and Pentecost the damned stop suffering and praise the Mother of God:

"The Blessed Virgin is visiting hell, and the arch-angel Saint Michael acts as a guide among the damned. She sees the sinners and their torments. She notes a certain number of damned in a pool of flames: whoever sinks in it cannot come back to the surface: even God forgets him! An extraordinarily strong and profound expression! Keenly impressed, the Blessed Virgin in tears prostrates herself before the Throne of God and begs for mercy for all the sinners she has seen in hell, without any distinction. Her dialogue with God is prodigiously interesting! She implores. She will not let up. When the Lord shows the palms and the feet of his crucified Son and asks: "How could I forgive his executioners?", the Blessed Virgin turns to all the saints, to all the martyrs, to the angels and archangels, so that they may help her obtain mercy for the sinners. God finally allows her to suspend the tortures every year from Good Friday to Pentecost, and the voices of the sinners immediately resound from the pit of hell: "You are right, Lord, and your sentence is just." [1]

1. The Blessed Virgin and sinners

The Church traditionally recognizes that the Blessed Virgin intercedes for sinners. As proof of this, we can look at some liturgical and private prayers. Thus, when the Church invites Christians to sing the Salve Regina, she calls Mary "Mother of Mercy" to whom we are crying and sighing. She is our advocate who turns eyes of tenderness towards us and who shows us Jesus the blessed fruit of her womb. In the Sub Tuum, the most ancient prayer to Mary, found on a papyrus dating from the IIIrd century, [2] she makes us ask to be freed from all dangers and she gives the Blessed Virgin another title, just as traditional: she is the "Refuge of sinners". It is significant that the mediating power of Mary was so

---

1. Translated from *Les Frères Karamazov*, Coll. Marabout géant, 1957, p. 228.

2. The most ancient prayer to the Virgin Mary, quoted by Paul VI in the Apostolic Exhortation *Marialis Cultus*, n. 13, Feb. 2, 1974.

quickly related to the divine motherhood, as this prayer of the *Sub Tuum præsidium* attests:

"Under the shelter of your mercy, we take refuge, O Holy Mother of God. Do not scorn our prayers when we undergo trials, but always deliver us from all dangers, O glorious Virgin, O blessed Virgin."

There is in this prayer the notion of "refuge", that is, of a spiritual "place" where the sinner is sheltered from the attacks of the enemy, in particular of the Evil One who accuses him of sin. We should also mention the *Memorare* of Saint Bernard which is such an effective prayer because it is the expression of a total trust in the power of Mary's prayer and, at the same time, a confession of our helplessness to rid ourselves of our misery. Remember the love Saint Francis de Sales had for this prayer. After vowing chastity, he was to have the worst trial: he had doubts about being in the state of grace and he believed he was damned. "If I must be damned, he said, that I may at least love God with all my soul in this life! If I must go to hell, that I at least may not blaspheme you." In the worst time of his trial, he does not stop praying. One day, when he is afflicted more than ever, he runs to the feet of the one who, in Saint-Étienne-des-Grés, is called "the Virgin of distressed souls" (it is there that the black Virgin of Paris, Our Lady of Good Deliverance was then venerated). He renews his vow of chastity and promises that, if he is freed from his anxieties, he will recite his rosary every day. He recites the *Memorare* of which he sees the text at that moment. Hardly has he come to the end of the prayer that he feels, as it were, "a crust of leprosy" detaching itself from him: his soul is healed! For him as well, the good deliverance has been achieved.

In order to grasp the bond existing between Mary and sinners, we must go back to the rosary, a prayer which is practically the only form of prayer for many Christians, especially among the poor. I am amazed today by the spiritual renewal brought about by the rosary! Many

Christians reach a true prayer of union (the pure prayer of our Eastern brothers) by this most humble means, at any time of the day: in moments of spare time, comings and goings, etc... As soon as their heart is free, they come back to the rosary and thus experience the continual prayer of the heart even if they have the impression of failing lamentably because they recite this prayer so poorly. They repeat untiringly: "Holy Mary, Mother of God, pray for us, poor sinners, now and at the hour of our death." By constantly praying in this way, they are impregnated, as by osmosis, by the prayer of the Blessed Virgin and they bathe themselves in her trust:

"I recommend the Ave Maria to you. Recite it as you come and go, recite it while working: the most Blessed Virgin will watch over you with love... The Ave Maria is the prayer which pleases the divine Mother most, because it recalls the most agreeable memories of her existence".[3]

When Saint Maximilian Kolbe consecrates himself to the Blessed Virgin, he has words that show well how sinners can, with the help of the Blessed Virgin, attract the eyes of Christ, as all the sinners of the gospel have done. In the Act of Consecration composed by himself, Kolbe calls the Blessed Virgin: "Refuge of sinners and most loving Mother to whom God entrusted the whole order of Mercy." We shall have to come back to the bond between Mary and Mercy. Let us simply remember a few expressions which often recur in the Marian vocabulary: salvation of the lame, comforter of the afflicted, help of Christians, refuge of sinners. When John Paul II invites all the bishops to consecrate the world to the Blessed Virgin on March the 25th 1984, he begins his Act of offering with these words: "Under the shelter of your mercy we take refuge, Holy Mother of God".

3. Translated from Blessed Brother Mutien-Marie, of the Institute of the Brothers of the Christian Schools, 1841-1917, General Procuracy, 78 rue de Sèvres 75007 Paris, 1928, pp. 82 and 84.

We may be great sinners, but we can hope to find shelter and refuge near the Blessed Virgin. "Mary plays a great role in our salvation. She will easily obtain forgiveness for our sins. If we have her protection, we shall not fear, not even our Judge".[4] To understand and achieve this movement urging us to take refuge near the Blessed Virgin, we need the light and strength of the Holy Spirit who has a maternal function in the training of our prayer and of our life of communion with God. He does not give us an understanding of the role of Mary at the very beginning of our conversion. It comes at the moment we experience that God is a devouring fire, a burning bush; then we realize that Mary carried within her this fire never consumed. This is why we take refuge near her to be protected by her humility and her meekness, as Moses is placed in the cleft of the rock and protected by the hand of God, for he well knows that we cannot see his Face and remain alive.

But it is precisely at that moment that we discover, like Isaiah, that we are a sinner of unclean lips and that we belong to a people of sinners" (Is 6:6). We then see that to become a sinner agreeable to the heart of God, we must go through the Blessed Virgin. We are confronted there with a paradox. Jesus said: "I have not come to call the virtuous, but sinners to repentance" (Lk 5:32). Elsewhere he says that he did not come to obliterate any letter of the Law. We must, therefore, reconcile obedience to the Law with the experience that we are sinners: there is the paradox.

If we wish to meet Jesus, to be saved by him and become sons of the Father, we must do like sinners who cry to him saying: "Jesus, Son of the saving God, have mercy on me, a sinner." This is the Jesus prayer, familiar to our brothers of the East, which is the surest road towards the continual prayer of the heart. So the only way leading to unceasing prayer is the cry of the pub-

4. Id., p. 84.

lican (Lk 18:13), joined to the supplication of the blind man (Lk 18:39). All the other roads by which we try to climb towards God are dead ends, as Jesus affirms at the end of the parable of the Pharisee and the Publican: "For the man who exalts himself will be humbled, but the man who humbles himself will be exalted" (Lk 18:14).

If sinners are the only ones to be admitted in the kingdom, after the children, the real problem for us will be to become true sinners according to the heart of Jesus, like Zacchaeus, Mary Magdalen, and the repentant thief. From our standpoint, the only way to become a sinner is to sin. That is not God or Christ's view; for them the surest way to become a sinner who draws the Mercy of God is exactly not to sin anymore. This is where we meet the Blessed Virgin who invites all sinners to come to her to place the burden of their sins at her feet. She is, so to speak, the "preserved sinner", the one to whom God forgave the most, since she was exempted from sin; she alone can attract the mercy of God, for sin has never touched her!

In order to understand that, I shall recall the character of Rasputin, this disturbing monk who presented a "sulphurous" mixture of sin and mercy. He belonged to a sect which taught that one had to sin in order to find mercy. This erroneous doctrine is dangerous because it scoffs at mercy in the very name of mercy. But it is almost right, for it is true that to find mercy one must be a sinner. The Blessed Virgin is the one who will set us right, for she is the creature to whom God has forgiven the most by preserving her. To become a sinner agreeable to God, we must go through her so that she may give us the exact tone of the prayers of a sinner. She will teach us the price of sin by making us contemplate her Son on the Cross, dying precisely so that we may be forgiven sinners. In our sin, weakness is mixed with guilt and it is this sulphurous mixture that sometimes lets us have a good conscience. Mary's role is to sort out these roots of self-love lodged in the very heart of our weakness.

2. The heart broken with repentance

At the end of her autobiographical Manuscripts, Saint Thérèse of Lisieux says this: "Yes, I feel that, even though my conscience was burdened by all the sins, I would go with my heart broken with repentance, and throw myself in the arms of Jesus, for I know how much he cherishes the prodigal child who comes back to him. If I raise myself to him through trust and love, it is not because God, in his obliging mercy, has preserved my soul from mortal sin."[5] Thérèse also understood very well what a sinner is; from her modest position she knew that God had forgiven her much by protecting her from sin. A true sinner is the one whose heart is broken with repentance. To become such a man with a heart crushed and broken with sorrow for his sins, we must not have sinned or, at least, we must have the desire to sin no more. The Virgin Mary has a broken heart without having sinned: at the foot of the Cross, she truly has a pierced and melted heart as would say the Curé of Ars about the heart of saints: "When a heart truly prays God, it is like two pieces of wax melted together."

The heart of man is normally hard like stone; it is therefore necessary to subject it to a process of refinement in order to melt it, to make it meek and humble. Only then can he join the triune dance and allow eternal life to move freely within him without being hampered by "stones". The man, meek of heart, who is defenceless before the others can say like Jesus to the Father: "All I have is yours and all you have is mine" (Jn 17:10). In the Blessed Trinity, each of the Persons says to the other what Jesus told his Father during the agony: "Not my will, but yours... not me, but you." The Three repeat that to each other eternally. Each Person stands aside to give his space to the other; and as the other, in his turn,

---

5. Translated from *Manuscrits autobiographiques*, Ms C, f. 36v., p. 313.

also gives his place, there is an immense movement, a circulation of love which Lewis calls the triune dance. In this sense, each of the Persons is on his knees saying to the other: "Will you?" We see that this supplication has a triune value!

To penetrate this mystery, we must have a heart that stands aside for the other. The stages of holiness go therefore from a broken heart reduced to shreds to a melted and dissolved heart. The Blessed Virgin is at the end of the road which for us starts from a heart broken with repentance. We can perform feats of asceticism and yet not allow our heart to be broken because the process is too arduous. One of the first graces the Blessed Virgin will obtain for us is to experience how hard our heart is. Then when we have tried in vain to break it by hammering it away, she will implore the fire of the Spirit to melt it at a high temperature, but always in gentleness.

In spiritual life everything can be an instrument of damnation except having a broken heart. When we realize the width and depth of our sin and also the cruelty we use to ward ourselves off from the Holy Spirit, we see that it is not natural for us to throw ourselves at the feet of the Lord with a heart broken with repentance. The Blessed Virgin is the one who inspires us that trust by suggesting the instinct of refuge, for she knows well the heart of God since she has experienced what the heart of a mother is. We shall never put a stop to her trust.

To present ourselves to God as a sinner because we know the heart of God, is a movement of which the Blessed Virgin has the secret. Think of all the great converts who obtained this grace by the prayer of the Blessed Virgin, in particular Alphonsus Ratisbonne. We are still far from that point, but when we understand the heart of the Blessed Virgin, we shall know at the same time that she feels God and somewhat reads his thoughts. To pray the Blessed Virgin in this way is to step forward in this Marian path which produces a broken heart.

Let us admit that we do not devote much time and strength in engaging ourselves upon this road to holiness. It is very painful to see so many men turn away from the Blessed Virgin by claiming that we speak too much about her and that this turns people off from a conversion to Christ. Basically, we want to keep our heart intact and we do not work in the right direction: the way of the Blessed Virgin. We waste nine tenths of our energy in a sterile struggle, relying uniquely on the help of our will and very little on the help of God. All this nourishes and satisfies our self-love.

It is normal that we would not understand that in the first days of our conversion, but it is unfortunate to see men and women who have reached human maturity and who do not yet see the nature of the true struggle. As Saint Paul says, we cannot teach them yet the true doctrine of the beatitudes and of the Cross for they still need "milk". They are spiritual persons "at a standstill' or "tied up in knots" who have not yet grasped the true way. Only the Blessed Virgin can make them understand that the pure gold of trust must be freed in their heart broken with repentance.

The maternal action of the Blessed Virgin flows from her profound being. Little by little, all her human hopes have been laid bare in order that her trust might rest uniquely on theological hope. Like her Son Jesus upon whom she gazed on the Cross, her only trust rested in the Father. When their eyes met in the fire of Love, Mary truly became the Bride of Christ and of the Spirit: her virginity found all its fecundity there, since at the same moment Jesus made Mary the Mother of all his brothers. This is why she is first the Mother of sinners.

To each one of us she proposes as an ideal to become "sinners", but we must well understand in what sense she means this. She does not tell us to keep on doing the same things, but she proposes as a result of our sin to implore her by saying: "Pray for us, sinners!" and, therefore, to discover that we are sinners unknown to ourselves. We must ask her for the grace of having a broken heart. As Saint Thérese of Lisieux says, we fall because we try to walk on our own and we keep on "raising our little feet" to go up a few steps of the staircase while in fact we cannot go up even one step: the essential is not to succeed but to try.

This is very close to Rasputin, and we must be on guard against this danger. The difference is in the attitude of the heart which admits its harshness and expects conversion from the prayer of Mary. The danger does not come from our weakness, for God can transform it into strength. Pride is the true danger. It makes us think and say that it is too simple to pray the Blessed Virgin, as Naaman found it too simple to bathe in the Jordan and be cured of his leprosy. But Mary's prayer is the great means to arrive at a repentant heart. Saints would weep over this cruelty of the heart of stone and the tears of their repentance would bring about the "thawing of the ice pack".

The Blessed Virgin especially teaches us to become sinners who know how to implore with meekness. She shows us to what extent we are sinners even in our desire for holiness. She is the one who will preserve us from the real dangers of sin, but also from the dangers of virtue which are just as serious. When someone begins to grow in virtue, Mary rushes to show him how much he is a sinner by unveiling his inner depths with her motherly gentleness. At the school of the Blessed Virgin we shall become true sinners on whom God casts an eye of good will and mercy. Thérèse of Lisieux "was of the opinion that all conversions must be obtained by invoking Mary".[6]

6. Translated from *Conseils et souvenirs*, p. 89.

3. Pray for us... sinners

I would like to draw your attention to a little word of the Ave Maria which sums up well what has been said until now and introduces the next part of our subject. This word is found in the second part of the "Hail, Mary" and determines our most concrete attitude towards prayer; it is the word "now". Thus when we ask the Blessed Virgin to "pray for us, poor sinners", we immediately add: "now and at the hour of our death".[7] We do not suspect then what happens in heaven when we utter this apparently innocuous and inoffensive invocation. We must admit that, with repetition, it risks losing its strength and its power of suggestion.

One of the greatest graces which can therefore be granted to us when we say this prayer instinctively is to see the heavens tear open and hear Mary interceding for us, poor sinners. It was given to certain people to "see" and to "hear" Mary's prayer for them, such as Silouane who was praying before the icon of the Mother of God. On this subject, we are not sure whether we should say "see", "hear" or "understand": what matters is the reality behind these words which burns our heart as it burned the heart of the disciples of Emmaus. Let me add immediately that we don't need a perfect understanding of this reality before setting about to it, because this science of prayer often comes to us after we have prayed for a long time.

Thus the first decision to take is to set about to it right away; at the very moment you are reading this, make up your mind to say: "Holy Mary, Mother of God, pray for us, sinners, now and at the hour of our death"... Do not say it only once but repeat this prayer as long as you are not taken up by another occupation. At first, you will

---

7. "How happy we are at the hour of death for having had a great devotion to the most Blessed Virgin" (words of Blessed Brother Mutien-Marie on his deathbed).

simply recite it but, little by little, it will pass from your lips to your heart and light up in you the fire of prayer. When you have other work, simply express to the Blessed Virgin your desire to pray her unceasingly: it takes only a quarter of a second but this desire invades and enlivens all your life. There are men and women who work, talk, eat, and apparently live like everyone else, but they are always in prayer in the upper room of their heart.

What goes on then in the heart of a man who has taken this decision? First, he admits that he is a "sinner" and this is the first condition for his prayer to be agreeable to God since Christ while speaking of the prayer of the publican, asserts that "this man went home again at rights with God, the other did not" (Lk 18:14). Then, he entrusts himself to the prayer of someone else since he asks the Blessed Virgin to pray for him. All the prayers addressed to the Blessed Virgin bear this trait: she is not the object of the prayer, but the intermediary, the one who presents our supplication to Christ and to the Father: "Loosen the bonds of the sinners, restore light to the blind, draw all evil away from us, obtain for us all goods... Show yourself to be our mother and take our prayers to the one who for us wanted to be born of you".[8] She is not the one who gives graces of forgiveness and healing, but she intercedes for us by advising us to do all that her Son will tell us to do.

The first conviction of the one who prays the Blessed Virgin is to believe that Mary immediately hears his prayer, even before he has begun, from the moment the desire appears in his heart. In this sense, he must not rack his brains to pray and still less meditate on how Mary prays. The essential is not to know how to pray Mary well, but to know how never to lose the courage to have recourse to her. This is not difficult: it is enough to say the Ave Maria while setting a limited time for ourselves. The rest does not depend on us but on the Holy

---

8. Ave maris stella.

Spirit alone. As Saint Ignatius often says: the essential is to know "where to start" and "to whom we must recommend ourselves".

The mystery of prayer, which we have called to mind at the beginning of this book while speaking of those who try to do contemplative prayer, begins here. At first, they labor and discover that it is not only difficult to seek a contact with God by catching the eye of the Father, but that it is practically impossible. The first step in the science of prayer is to discover "that we do not know" and that familiarity with Jesus and the Father is not natural for us. In the Garden of Eden, Adam prayed as he breathed. After the fall, he has lost familiarity with God in such a way that he hides and tries to protect himself from the eye of God because he is afraid of him. We are in the same condition, a fact which makes prayer practically impossible without the direct intervention of the Holy Spirit. All those who make the decision to do contemplative prayer must grasp this fact: "Basically, to pray is impossible". I do not say that it is difficult for it comes sometimes, and when prayer comes we understand clearly that it is not difficult at all; but when it does not come, it is not difficult either: it is impossible. When prayer "is given to us", we could pray for hours without being aware of it; but when it is not given to us, we can only lament by saying: "Jesus have pity on me".

The second step in the science of prayer (assuming that we have managed the first) is to stop our useless and disordered efforts to produce prayer, particularly in the realm of the intelligence and the imaginary, and follow a humbler route: the one of entreaty. It does not require any less energy but the effort is really put where it should be, that is in the struggle for perseverance alone. It is then that the supplicant tries humbler means such as the rosary and he holds on to them for some time.

While experiencing that prayer is impossible, he untiringly attempts to seek contact with God as those who delve in amateur radio try to get in touch with an invisible person. We must try every day, every morning and every evening. The day when prayer is given to us we know everything.

It may also happen that we will not reach this point; this may even be better, for we shall then please God and that is the essential of prayer. The effort to pray is discouraging because, apparently, it is sterile. But in itself it is not difficult; indeed, it is a very simple matter. It is not a question of racking our brains but simply of repeating the Ave Maria or the Jesus prayer.

4. When prayer emerges...

The supplicant then discovers that prayer is simple since it is enough for him to keep on using only one sentence: "Holy Mary, Mother of God, pray for us sinners", when prayer depends upon his effort. He does not have to torture his brains nor complicate his life since repetition is the basis of his prayer. As he has set his ambitions much lower, he is not disappointed for he is doing only what is within his means. He does not expect from his dreams anything but what the Holy Spirit will grant him. Such a prayer, so bare and so austere, generates boredom, even a certain distaste.

We react like the Hebrews in the desert who were quickly satiated by the manna. The taste for God is much too bland for our complicated and refined palate. So God has to improve his food a little in order to whet his people's appetite, and he sends them quails. He acts in the same way for us in prayer; he sends us from time to time some little consolations and light to attract us to him. But his most precious and truest countenance is the one which gives us a taste for silence. When we are bored at prayer, we should rejoice and say: "I am bored with God, this is not normal. I should exult in thanksgiving, as the Blessed Virgin did, since he gives me the gift of his presence." Instead of superficially boring ourselves with God, let us learn to be deeply bored because we yearn for a true contact with him. The only consolation the Spirit will be able to give us is the true joy of his presence. Let us not seek solace other than that of the Holy Spirit who rises in us without a moment's warning.

We shall then be introduced to a secret that no one understands nor even suspects except those who receive it through revelation. At a given moment, at the very heart of this austere and boring vocal prayer, the Holy Spirit will appear like the water springing up East of the Temple. He will become a true torrent in our heart: "Mighty rivers of living waters will flow from his breast. Jesus was speaking of the Spirit which those who believed in him were to receive" (Jn 7:38-39). This is the prayer of the Holy Spirit in us. It is the same Spirit who sprang up in the heart of Mary and aroused her prayer. For the Spirit is unique and he always prays the same way with unutterable groanings. He was not able to pray in any other way in Mary, neither in content nor in form. The only difference comes from Mary's greater capacity — deepened by her poverty and her humility — to allow this prayer to rise in her.

If we wish to share Mary's prayer and make it ours, we will have to follow the same road as she did, that of the Holy Spirit. There is no need for us to understand her prayer. The essential thing is that she be present, living and acting in us. Most of the time, her prayer will identify with silence, the highest summit of prayer; at other moments, echoes of this prayer will reverberate under the vault of our heart and, like her, we shall exult with joy.

Such is the unique law of prayer that I would feel like stating as follows, like the apophthegms of the Fathers of the Desert: "The more you are called to enter into the prayer of the Spirit in Mary, the more you feel in yourself the desire for pure prayer, and the more you must limit yourself to the humble invocation of the 'Hail, Mary'

282

without any thoughts or images, simply asking her to implore with you." If I did not fear being offhand, I would say that the more we desire the prayer of the Spirit in us, the more we must stay on "a rather low key". Otherwise, we risk interposing the insulating muff of our intellectual or willful activity between the impalpable prayer of the Spirit and our heart. We always do too much in prayer, and by our exuberant activity we prevent the soft murmur of the Spirit from welling up within us. If we could establish ourselves in the deep silence of all our being, murmuring uniquely the names of Jesus and Mary, we could very quickly feel the prayer of the Spirit rising within us.

At the prayer level, all that we can do is put ourselves at the service of the Holy Spirit in us. What is going on in the depths of our heart, at the geological level, is without any common measure with what we can do in our clear conscience at the geographical level. Thus there are beings who attain a real contemplative prayer without their being conscious of it, only by praying the rosary and staying alert to the words they say. The Blessed Virgin had a mystical prayer without knowing it and she bathed in divine light without needing to give a formulation or a precise content to her prayer. It was up to her to pray as Jesus had taught his disciples to do with the words of the "Our Father" or of the psalms. She especially resembled the obtrusive friend or the insistent widow who pleaded with perseverance.

5. The Rosary and the Jesus Prayer

Those who have read the *Stories of a Russian Pilgrim* or books dealing with the hesychast prayer will have immediately recognized in what has been explained the Jesus prayer which leads to the prayer of the heart since its purpose ("Jesus, Son of the saving God, have mercy on me, a sinner") is to make it come down from the head into the heart by murmuring it on one's lips. This is what the Fathers call the monological prayer (monos = alone): praying with one word alone which must normally awaken the prayer of fire or pure prayer in the heart.

For many people of the West who were trained in the methods of contemplative prayer or in the techniques of prayer, the discovery of the Jesus prayer was a true liberation that led them towards continual prayer or, at least, helped them much to simplify and to "disintellectualize" it. To reach that point, one must truly have experienced the Jesus prayer for a long time for it confides its secret only after years of practice on the condition that exactly what is advised be done without changing any formulas. As we have already seen on the subject of resolutions, this prayer is original only in its exclusivity, i.e. that we must not take any other resolution. As soon as a man has chosen this form of prayer, he must hold on to it for years in order that he may feel its effects. This prayer is not unknown in the West since it is related to ejaculatory prayers. Thérèse of Lisieux was close to the Eastern tradition when she was writing the last page in her own hand:[9] "I repeat, filled with trust, the humble prayer of the publican".[10]

We understand the infatuation of the Catholics for this form of prayer. Our orthodox brothers sometimes chide us for it by explaining that this prayer is tied to a whole system of theology, coming from Gregory Palamas and others, founded on the notions of uncreated light, divine energies and the experience of grace, a theology unknown to the people of the West. They add that we must practise it within the orthodox faith for it to produce effects. Those who use this prayer, it is true, are little conscious of manipulating precise mechanisms which can bring about an explosion of Glory in them. For that reason, we should use them only "under the medical

9. Translated from *Conseils et souvenirs,* pp. 191-192.
10. Translated from *Manuscrit C.,* 36 v.

control" of the Blessed Virgin and of the Church if I may say so! The spiritual masters of the East are very prudent especially when it is a matter of practising this prayer to the rhythm of breathing: we must do it only under the guidance of a spiritual Father.

On the other hand, we are witnessing today a renewal in the recitation of the rosary. Many aspirants to prayer, after having made a detour by the Jesus prayer, which has given them a foretaste of the prayer of the heart (briefly let us say that the prayer of the heart which leads to "pure prayer" finds its equivalent in the prayer of quietude, even of union, in Saint Teresa of Avila), rediscover the prayer of the rosary. In them, prayer has been subjected to a series of treatments which have purified it of all its imaginary or intellectual representations. Ultimately, it has simplified itself and the formula used becomes the bare essential to keep the attention focused on God. The heart inhabited and saturated by prayer uses this very simple means to avoid losing attention but, strictly speaking, he could go without it. In the prayer of silence, says Teresa of Avila, the heart is fixed on God but the imagination and the memory — the mad women of the house — can always be gadding about. So in order to focus the attention we recite the rosary. This vocal prayer functions like a rolling of bearings in a bed of oil: this is the prayer of the heart.

In this area, it is impossible to determine precise rules, for freedom has full play in the prayer of the Spirit. We can even say that the characteristic of this form of prayer is the freedom to choose the means best suited to nourish the prayer of the heart. As much as this freedom could become fantasy for those who did not compel themselves for years to pray with only one word, so is it liberating and a source of joy for a heart truly inhabited by prayer. It is within this freedom that we will have to speak then of the contemplation of mysteries which can be obstacles for some in the measure that the attention is scattered. In this area, we must feel very free and follow the inclinations of the heart: "Go where your heart leads you!"

"The Rosary should be for us the Western people the equivalent of the Jesus prayer in the East, the way of humility needed to reach this engulfment of self in perpetual prayer. The Rosary is one of the quickest means to reach this summit precisely because it is the most "stupid", the one which does not claim to climb to any contemplative summits dangerously seducing for our pride."

"The untiring repetition of the Rosary may seem deplorable if we recite it with the narrow intention of remaining within the rule. But that can also be magnificent if it is a matter of using our eye in constantly scrutinizing the horizon to discover the apparition of the One who is to come. In this perspective, we are not the same anymore at the end of a decade of the rosary as we were at the beginning; we are a little more exhausted, a little poorer and therefore a little nearer to the final capitulation".[11]

The recitation of the rosary is finally the concrete way leading to the bruised and broken heart of which we have spoken earlier. It teaches us little by little through the awkward repetitions of our mumbled prayers the unutterable groanings of the Holy Spirit. The repetition is necesssary in order that this groaning may penetrate our heart of stone as the repeated fall of a drop of water manages to hollow out the hardest rock.

By the repetition of the Our Father, Ave Maria, De Profundis, we can hope to say someday the Our Father and the Ave Maria which will finally spring "de profundis", from the depths of our broken heart and vibrate in perfect harmony with the heart of God. At that moment, a perfect union will bind a totally defenceless prayer and an infinitely helpless love.

---

11. Translated from M.D. Molinié, *Lettre polycopiée*, n. 21, May 1976, pp. 17-18.

God seeks the groaning in us which alone may touch his heart because in reality it comes from his own heart. As long as God has not obtained it, as long as he has not managed to extract it from our soul, he cannot let himself be touched. As in the struggle with Jacob, he cannot be defeated but by the distress of our wounded hip. It's not that he has any resistance but, on the contrary and precisely, his defenceless meekness is allergic to the least resistance. God can only commune with a broken heart, a heart melted by his infinite meekness. In order that the triune current might flow between man and God, we must have like Christ a meek and humble heart which does not offer any resistance to the Father and is entirely poured into him. The purpose of the rosary or of the Jesus prayer is to crush our heart, to reduce it to dust (conterere) by the power of the Holy Spirit and to melt it by the triune meekness.

The rosary is a form of prayer which closely precedes or accompanies the contemplative prayer of the Holy Spirit. Little does it matter whether or not we meditate, or are distracted if we cannot spend a day without reciting the rosary; this is a sign that we are on the way to continual prayer. It is the prayer of children, of simple women or of old men who do not reason about prayer anymore but accept their poverty and their lowliness, surrender themselves in the hands of the Blessed Virgin and put their trust in her final supplication: "Pray for us, sinners".

If we must advise beginners, we must not insist too much that they recite this prayer, especially if they prefer meditation or a more intellectual prayer. The day will come when they will touch the bottom of their distress and reach the point where their strengths will betray them. Then they will discover straightaway the humble recitation of the rosary: "The rosary is a point of arrival, not of departure. For Bernadette, the arrival was almost immediate for she was predestined to see the

Blessed Virgin on this earth. But normally, it is the prayer of spiritual maturity". [12]

I may add that this prayer is suitable for those who have devoted their life to continual prayer. When we pray for an hour or two, we can still fill time with contemplative prayer, meditation or Holy Scripture; but when prayer is prolonged beyond that and the Holy Spirit is calling us to keep on because this is our vocation and our mission in the heart of the Church, then we ponder over the rosary — not to say that we repeat it tediously! — for long hours. I am thinking here of the reflection of a young priest really called to prayer and who was surprised to find one of his friends praying the rosary a great deal. After a few years of commitment in an authentic life of prayer, the priest admitted to him one day that he now understood why we had to use simple means like the rosary to hold on in prayer.

6. The Prayer of the Rosary

We must accept that the practice of the rosary presents problems to the Western people that we are, accustomed to pray with our "grey matter' only, while an Easterner naturally meditates with his lips according to the words of the psalms: "The mouth of the virtuous man murmurs (or meditates on) wisdom, and his tongue speaks what is right" (Ps 37:30). Just going to a Moslem country would make us understand that the repetition of one word is the basic prayer of the believers. For many Christians, the rosary appears as a mechanical repetition of formulas, compared by some to a "prayer mill". Moreover, they tell us, Christ took pains to warn us of the danger of such a prayer: "When you pray do not babble as the pagans do, for they think that by using

12. Translated from Carlo Carretto.

many words they will make themselves better heard"
(Mt 6:7).

We often hear men and women, priests or religious,
true pray-ers, who admit that they are unable to recite
the rosary. Their objection does not bear so much on the
prayer of the Virgin for they well agree on the place Mary
must take in their spiritual life and in their life of prayer.
Therefore, it is not an objection to the content of prayer
but to its practical form which we could word in this
way: "How can you manage at the same time the recitation of the 'Ave Maria's and the contemplation of the
mysteries of the life of Jesus?" True, there may exist a
psychological dualism between these two activities
which make their coordination practically impossible.
We know that anything that distracts the attention in
prayer (circa multa) does not favor the unification of the
heart in the feeling of the presence of the Lord and in
an inner relaxed atmosphere of peace.

Thérèse of Lisieux admitted that she had always
experienced many difficulties in reciting a complete
rosary. Thus, those who labor on the way of the Rosary
are not in too bad company but, like Thérèse, they must
not discredit this form of prayer but remain open to the
Blessed Virgin. The roads that lead to Mary are different
and, someday it may perhaps be theirs to taste the
rosary!

In his Apostolic Exhortation on the Cult of the
Blessed Virgin, Pope Paul VI says that we must remain
very free as regards this prayer: "However, we would
like to recommend that, while spreading a devotion
which is so beneficial, we do not alter its proportions
nor present it with an inopportune exclusivism: the
Rosary is an excellent prayer towards which the faithful
must yet feel serenely free, invited as they are to recite
it in all quietude for its intrinsic beauty".[13]

One of the difficulties of spiritual education is that

---

13. Translated from *Marialis cultus*, n. 55.

we are saturated from the beginning of our Christian life by a number of conferences, sermons and readings on the ways of praying among which there is, surely, the rosary. We are, therefore, used to hear people speak about this form of prayer, its importance, its beauty and often about its irreplaceable role in the act of praying. We do not readily understand well how this prayer fits in the structure of our spiritual life. It is normal that everything is not the same for everyone. But since we are fervent and generous, and that advice emanated from authorized persons, we make a point of saying the rosary each day seriously and with piety until this practice becomes burdensome, sometimes boring and arduous, as we do not see very well its advantage and meaning. It is then that we raise objections, good and true in themselves, but we must not be taken in as to their objectivity.

I would say that this moment of crisis is a necessary phase in understanding the prayer of the rosary. It may be the hour of grace; the work of the Spirit in our heart makes us then able to really understand it because the hour has come to enter into an adult prayer. If this phase of rejection never came about we would risk bypassing true prayer because, precisely, we are too used to it. There is a period in the life of prayer when we must reflect in depth on all the means we use to nourish our relationship with God. It is often a period of disarray which is meant to make us accede to a purer and truer relationship with God. Everytime we go through a crisis, this is a sign that the light of the Spirit will be received.

What we are saying about the rosary also applies to all the other forms of prayer and to all the means used to favor our growth in prayer. There comes a time when prayer simplifies itself so much that it becomes a simple presence to the Father in a movement of pure trust and surrender. We are present to each other and we experience that it is good to be together. It is exactly at this point that the law of freedom mentioned earlier comes fully into play. In our relationship with God, we must not be governed by anyone. The only thing which must impose itself upon us is the soft murmur of the Spirit which groans in our heart. We must authenticate it on the objective level in an exchange with a spiritual father but nothing nor anyone must bend this law of freedom.

The only question to ask ourselves then on the subject of the rosary is: "Where am I in my relationship with the Blessed Virgin as a way to Christ, he who leads us to the Father? What form of prayer is most apt for me to favor this union with Christ? What helps me most in the rosary to reach this goal?" It is often during a retreat that we ask ourselves these questions and that we redis-cover the humble prayer of the rosary as a humble way to give us or to give us again the joy of prayer. In other words, we must not resolve the difficulties in reciting the rosary as they appear to us, but start from the depth of our heart inhabited by the Holy Spirit, source of all true prayer. It is from within that prayer transforms us little by little and not the opposite way around. In doing otherwise, we build ourselves a life of prayer that has nothing to do with our deepest self and, one day or the other, we reject it like a foreign body because it is not well integrated within ourselves.

Then we can discover again all that has been said on the rosary as an interior requirement and we are freed from all exterior influences. We first understand con-cretely that in order to recite the rosary in joy and interior peace we must murmur it slowly and take our time. It is always better to focus on the quality of the prayer rather than on quantity. Otherwise, the Rosary will be a body without a soul: "By its nature, the recitation of the Rosary requires that the rhythm be calm and that we take our time so that the person reciting it may better meditate the mysteries of the life of the Lord as seen through the heart of the one who was closest to him and that in this way unfathomable riches may emerge therefrom".[14]

On the other hand, we must affirm also another law of prayer which seems to contradict — but simply in appearance — what we have just stated. It comes from the Eastern spirituality, especially from the masters who teach the Jesus prayer — and can also be applied to the rosary. A spiritual man, Monsignor Anthony Bloom, often says that "when we cannot make prayer a thing of quality, we must make it a thing of quantity", that is, we must compel ourselves to a certain number of prayers in a limited time. What runs counter to our ideas here is the word "quantity" which seems to go against the words of Jesus about those who babble in prayer (Mt 6:7), but we must enlighten it by studying the meaning of the word "quality". The quality of prayer mentioned here is not the kind we are thinking of, that is, a carefully recited prayer, true and authentic. It must always be so! When he speaks of "quality", Monsignor Bloom is thinking especially of the experience of this prayer in the heart, of its nature, its fervor. In other words, when we cannot manage to obtain pure prayer, the prayer of the heart, when we do not "feel" the prayer within ourselves, we must keep on murmuring it on our lips until the moment the prayer of fire lights up in us.

I would call this the dialectical law of prayer which we cannot reduce to the oversimplification of one sentence. The clash of the opposites is sometimes needed to reach the sought goal: the essential is to come to "feel" what the Spirit wants of us. At one time, he calls us to repeat the rosary tediously and materially while waiting for the true prayer of the heart to rise. At another time, when our heart is saturated with the fire of prayer, he invites us to murmur one only word, as Teresa of Avila says, to throw a few twigs on the fire to nourish it.

---

14. Translated from Paul VI, Apostolic Exhortation *Marialis Cultus*, n. 47.

When we emphasize the true goal of prayer, which is to keep us in the eyes of the Father in union with Jesus during the various phases of his life, we understand better that the essence of the rosary is the contemplation of Christ with the eyes and the heart of the Blessed Virgin. More deeply yet, it is a matter of scrutinizing the mystery of the heart of Christ pierced by the wound of love of his Father's heart. Whether it be in the Incarnation, the Passion or the Resurrection, it is always Jesus dialoguing with the Father reminding him through his wounds of love of his infinite Love for sinners. Little by little, every image, every idea and representation disappears and all becomes unified in the sole gaze on Jesus.

So the essential element of the Rosary is the contemplation of Jesus in his mysteries "interceding with the Father in our favor". In the end, we are not even aware anymore of praying but only of uniting ourselves to the prayer of Jesus in an atmosphere of praise and entreaty. At this moment, vocal prayer can intervene to serve this contemplation of Jesus. Entering into the prayer of Jesus does not depend on us; the Holy Spirit alone can introduce us to it and we use the litany-like repetition of the Ave Maria as the necessary support to sustain our attention and avoid distraction.

There again, we must feel very free concerning which formula, rhythm of prayer or the ejaculatory prayers to be used. On certain days, we would like to recite the first part of the Ave Maria with the Angel and Elizabeth to honor the humility of Mary, to contemplate her Fiat or to examine closely her prayer. At some other times, when we are experiencing the misery of sin or the misery of our brothers, we will repeat indefinitely the second part of the prayer. It is also good sometimes to devote one hour to the recitation of the rosary always aiming, as says Saint Ignatius, not at the abundance of knowledge but at tasting things inwardly.[15] What is important is to

15. Translated from *Exercices*, 2e Annotation.

watch ourselves to see if we keep our heart content, satisfied, in peace, and if the prayer of the heart is establishing itself more and more in our life:

"The Rosary has a clearly christological orientation. As a matter of fact, its most characteristic element — the litany-like repetition of the Ave Maria — becomes an unceasing praise of Christ, the ultimate object of the news of the Angel and of the salutation, of the mother of the Baptist. 'Blessed be the fruit of your womb' (Lk 1:42). We can even say that the repetition of the Ave Maria is the pattern by which the contemplation of the mysteries is developed: the Jesus of each Ave Maria is the very one proposed to us by the mysteries. They propose to us each in turn the Son of God and of the Blessed Virgin born in a grotto in Bethlehem, presented to the Temple by his mother, an adolescent full of zeal for the affairs of his Father, the agonizing Redeemer in the Garden of Olives, scourged and crowned with thorns, carrying the Cross and dying on Calvary, risen from the dead and ascended near to his Father in glory in order that the effusion of the Spirit may become reality".[16]

Praying thus the rosary is a way of contemplating Christ in order to unite ourselves to him in love; it disposes our heart to live the anamnesis of the liturgy where we rediscover these same mysteries of the life of Christ to unite ourselves to him in their sacramental reality. The Rosary can thus be a good preparation to the liturgical celebration and become a prolonged echo of it, says yet the Exhortation of Paul VI. We would willingly add to this a more existential aspect. On certain days, we are given to live painful experiences, to undergo burdensome temptations or, on the contrary, to be inhabited by joy. At other moments, we meet people whose experiences being the same as ours allow us to share their style of life. Why should the rosary not be a

---

16. Translated from Paul VI, Apostolic Exhortation *Marialis Cultus*, n. 46.

way of praying with our cries of pain, anxiety or delight?

Besides, Mary always remains a human being, she accepted in her heart the events her Son's life which resounded in feelings of joy or suffering. This is why, by looking at the depths of Mary's being and our own, we will be able to catch glimmerings of what prayer is. God did great things in Mary. In us as well he does some, not as great as those he did in Mary, undoubtedly, but real just the same. Judging from his action in us, we can have a feeling of his action in her. This manner of praying, so simple, with our feelings, desires, and encounters, has the advantage that it can be used in all circumstances, in the very heart of our activity. Without our being aware of it, we turn over to God "with arms and all", and our existence is the privileged place where the Holy Spirit may act. Little by little, prayer impregnates all our life until there is no distinction between life and prayer. If we have so many difficulties finding the Father's eyes in contemplative prayer and in living of Christ, would it not be because in the remaining part of our existence we have little concern about him and prayer?

If you say "Mary", she says "Jesus"

Here is the reason why the Church proposes the recitation of the Rosary to those who can, magis or shepherds, to introduce them little by little into the prayer of Jesus to his Father. As we have seen, the gates of access to this prayer are numerous: we can start from the mysteries of the life of Jesus, or of the profound life of Mary or the very mystery of our existence, as we said earlier. If we are really at the heart of our life, we shall be, at the same time, in the heart of the life of the Lord. In one way or the other, it is a matter of reaching the ultimate depths of the heart of Christ in order to enter there with our own depths (Ep 3:19). As Mary is all relative to God, so is she all relative to Christ. We can say here the words of Saint Grignion of Montfort by interchanging the name of God for the name of Jesus: "If you say 'Mary', she says 'Jesus'". That is the reason why the Rosary has a christological orientation. Through the events of Christ's life, his words and his preachings, it is the mystery of Christ himself which is at the heart of the Rosary, this mystery contemplated by the Holy Spirit, the Blessed Virgin and the Church.

What Mary contemplates in her child in his lowliness and, when he dies, his distress. It is this poverty and distress which fascinate Mary in Bethlehem and on Calvary. The people, the disciples and the apostles were there when Jesus was successful, his mother watched over him when he was unborn and when he was reduced to nothing. The Holy Spirit invites us to reproduce Mary's feelings toward her son Jesus and foremost to remember his childhood, his death and his glory of which the people of God have an intuitive knowledge in the darkness of faith.

What is fascinating in the Christ seen and contemplated by Mary is that through him we have a feeling of the heart of the Father and his infinite love for us sinners. Just as the Church invites us to follow the stations of the Cross so that the sight of the crucified Jesus might break our heart of stone and bring us to conversion, so she invites us to recite the Rosary in order that through the untiring repetition of the Ave Maria the groaning of the Spirit may deepen our heart hardened by sin. This harshness of heart is what Jesus reproaches the apostles for even after the Resurrection: "He reproached them for their incredulity and obstinacy, because they had refused to believe those who had seen him after he had risen" (Mk 16:14). It is time for us to say as well: "When the Son of Man comes, will he find any faith on earth?" (Lk 18:8).

It is always a question of going through Mary, the Mother of Mercy and of sinners, so that a cry which will touch the Father's heart may finally rise from our own. Saint John of the Cross says that God seeks in the soul an "unknown" that he comes to find by chance, I mean that groaning of the Spirit which alone can touch his heart:

"No, for all the beauty,
No, never will I lose myself
But for a 'I know not what'
Which by chance has just been found."

This is why we contemplate Christ through the mysteries of the Rosary, to reproduce in us his own feelings. Looking over the film of the events of Christ's life is like seeing an X-Ray of the Father's heart projected on the screen of Christ on the Cross. Forgive me for going back again to the mystery of the suffering of God or his mercy but we cannot escape it if we wish to know Christ in all the depth of his mystery.

If we are willing to go beyond the events of Christ's life in order to discover its secret — the mystery the Father unveils to the lowly and humble beyond all vocal prayer and all meditation — we shall quickly discover that Jesus is the revelation of the Father's mercy and we shall witness the battle between light and darkness, what we have called the clash between the infinite meekness of God and the harshness of man's heart. In this sense, the agony of Jesus does not begin at Gethsemane; it begins at Christmas (of which Gethsemane is the paroxysm). It is the introduction of a man, privileged, predestined, unique — the first-born in a multitude of brothers — to this suffering of God, to Mercy.

For this reason, we have established a parallel between the mystery of the Annunciation and that of the Agony of Jesus. For the same reason, we are expected to come back often to this scene of Gethsemane: it is the very mystery of the Cross at its most intimate core and the events of the Passion are its spectacular and acccssible expression for our human eyes. But the true agony goes on in the depths of the heart of Jesus and Mary: there each withdraws before the suffering of God while adhering to his will of love.

The agony of Jesus is in its turn the incarnation of what must be called — for lack of a more suited expression — the Agony of God in the presence of evil, sin, suffering and hell. What the Greek Fathers and the iconographers of the East have sensed about the descent of Christ into hell is revealed through the sweat of blood wiped away by an angel come down from heaven. No human has ever been shaken by suffering in comparison with the shuddering of Mercy experienced by God in his eternal impassibility.

In his Agony, Jesus is introduced to a God torn between sin and holiness, light and darkness, Justice and Mercy. Through his face at Gethsemane, God manifests the Glory of his Mercy which will open out and express itself in the power of the Resurrection. Jesus is the first to have experienced in his flesh the Glory of the Suffering of God when his body through Incarnation entered into an osmotic relationship with the clay of mankind. The Greek Fathers have always seen in the Baptism of Christ the descent of the Word into the stagnant, murky and demonic waters of humanity, first fruits of the second Baptism of Jesus in the Passion and the descent into hell. The Baptism of Jesus is a bath in mire; it sanctifies this clay from which was drawn the first Adam, this clay which he tainted with sin. The Baptism of Christians, on the contrary, immerses them in the pure and luminous waters cleansing them from their mire.

Paul expresses well this descent of Jesus into the mire of sin and the osmosis brought about by the contact of his flesh with ours: "For the one who sanctifies, and the ones who are sanctified, have the same Father; that is why he is not ashamed to call them brothers... Since all the children share the same blood and flesh, he too shared equally the same condition, so that by his death he might destroy the power of the devil, who had power over death, and set free all those who had been held in slavery all their lives by the fear of death" (Heb 2:11 and 14-15).

I would like to quote a testimony showing how the Blessed Virgin is intimately present in this mystery of the mire of sin. It comes from a young man who is going through a great ordeal and who makes the Blessed Virgin speak in this way:

"Mary deserves to be known as the refuge of sinners, not only after sin, but before, during and after. That is what Mary's mystery is: we must go as far as this association, painful but indispensable, to know her well and allow her to do her "Job" as a Mother, as one who accompanies us.

"My children, she says to us, do not leave me in the very heart of your darkness and failures, at the very moments when you fall into temptation; do not leave me for one moment even when you are in mire. The mire of sin does not frighten me. Even if it seemed to you that I was tainted by it, do not grieve, it is my business. Accept to hold my hand in all circumstances, at all times; you will see that the healing of your bodies and your hearts will set you free little by little and make you available at last for the work of my Son. And when it seems to you that the phase of the temptation, even of failure, has come to an end, do not brood over the why and the how, but rise up immediately, purify yourselves, and avail yourselves of the sacraments of reconciliation and the eucharist. Lay your burden at the foot of my Son's cross. I am always there myself, at the foot of that cross which triumphs over the evil in the world. Accept to be consoled by my presence and seek to adjust yourselves to the Love of Mercy of my Son who raises and sets back on his feet every man who turns his eyes to Him."

However, this healing does not go without the pains of childbirth. Christians receive the privilege through these pains they owe their sins of extending in their body what is lacking in plenitude and in fecundity to the Agony of Jesus' body and his pure heart. In other words, they are introduced in their turn and in their own heart to this battle of heaven and hell which opens for them the doors of Mercy. Baptism makes us enter into the mystical Body of Christ and the Eucharist identifies us with Christ in our body and soul with our holiness and our sin; we may then, in this freedom, breathe the triune joy. Through the grace of sacraments we are "carnally" linked to the mystery of Easter and identified with the flesh of Christ crucified and glorified.

This is the reason why the Church suggests that we read the Gospel, follow the stations of the Cross, contemplate the Resurrection or say the Rosary in order to understand a little what is going on in the depths of our heart when we offer all our being to the grace of the mystery of Easter. We contemplate the metamorphosis of the Cross into a throne of Glory and of the crown of thorns into a crown of roses (that is the very meaning of the word Rosary). When Christians have learned to look at the Cross with the eyes of faith, Saint Leo invites them to depart from the suffering and come to the joy experienced in the sweetness of the Holy Spirit.

The recitation of the Rosary introduces us to this sweetness through the joyous mysteries before approaching the sorrowful mysteries and contemplating the wounds of Christ, which initiate us to the great wound of the heart of God, and being at last transfigured by the power of his Glory. The true Transfiguration is the one which transforms the Crucified into the Resurrected in the eyes of faith. Then we can say with Saint Paul: "It is no longer I who lives, but it is Christ who lives in me" (Ga 2:20), with this wound of God stronger than all strength, this meekness that bears no name and goes beyond all feeling, in this still dance where the Three are eternally selfless in order to exist only in the other. In short, the Rosary is an earthly initiation to the life of the three divine Persons in us, a foretaste of what will make our eternal happiness. But it is better not to speak of this on earth...

Postface

A WOMAN CLOTHED WITH THE SUN

After her presence in the Upper Room is mentioned, Mary definitely disappears from the narratives of the New Testament. There are only indirect references to her in the Book of Revelation, in the sign of the Woman and the dragon. She joins her Son again in the desert cloud (Rv 12:14) and she experiences the battle which the dragon wages against the angels and the disciples of her Son. She is not even bespattered by the river of water which he tries to vomit on her. She remains no less attentive to the plight of her children: she has entered into the great silence of the desert and continues her prayer of entreaty which was begun in the Upper Room and which will last until the return of her Son in Glory. She is outwardly clothed with the sun because she radiates the Glory of the burning Bush and, interiorly, her heart burns from a prayer of fire.

She is now the "silent pray-er", as she was during the early childhood of Jesus, and her influence makes itself felt in the Church coming into being. She is always the Mother of Jesus watching over the growth of the Church and surrounding it with motherly care until the end of time, as long as mankind will not have reached its perfection. She joins her prayer to the intercession of her Son on our behalf but in a manner as discreet as it was during the life of Jesus. In the rare "apparitions" which she makes in our history, she always shows herself as the great supplicant calling us to conversion and to unceasing prayer. She also invites us to welcome her in our house just as Jesus, while on the Cross, asked Saint John to do in order that the life of the Spirit may grow in us.

But let us go back a little to the prayerful silence of Mary during her last years on earth. Without any doubt in her heart she goes over the events of the life of Jesus beginning with the radiance of the Resurrection and she journeys towards its fulfilment by immersing herself into a deeper and deeper peace. Like Jesus, she tastes the joy of the victory of Easter and the snake's bite on the heal cannot hurt her anymore. She already knew then an absolutely extraordinary state not exempt from intimate and heartrending suffering but the desire for heaven was undoubtedly the deepest not to speak of the suffering from the persecution plaguing the mystical Body of the Son.

Like the disciples, her heart was wounded because the Spouse had been taken from her, but at the same time she tasted the joy of knowing Jesus to be with his Father: "I am risen and I am always with you".[1] She was then experiencing the "absent presence", the presence in the Spirit..., all this collection of feelings which the Church has been singing for two thousand years, calling the earth "a valley of tears" and weeping with Thomas of Aquinas because, as says Rimbaud, "true life is absent", "media vita in morte sumus". All the saints have experienced this desolation which is an indispensable preparation to what will be not only a consolation anymore but the coming of the Comforter himself.

Jesus dies in the prime of life; Mary will keep on living and she knows that "if the tent that we live in on earth is folded up, we have a house built by God for us

---

1. Introit for Easter.

in the heavens, an everlasting home not made by human hands" (2 Co 5:1). Mary allows herself to be more and more invaded by this treasure of divine life that has become "glory" in her heart and in her body and which she carries in "a vessel of clay". How does the story of Mary end? Many accounts have been elaborated around this event. Was it death, or not? This is a question of no importance, the glorification of Mary being a metamorphosis more fantastic and more awesome than death itself.

1. Borne into heaven

What is certain is that quite soon in Christian milieux there appears a feast of the "Dormition of the Blessed Virgin" celebrating her "death" in peace (not violent like that of her Son), when the time came for her to bring her life on earth to an end. In the traditional language of the Church, Mary was then "borne into heaven" body and soul. Thus she joins her Son again who, the first, had opened the wide gate of the house of his Father. Bossuet says that the Assumption was not a miracle but the end of a miracle which had held back Mary on earth to establish the perpetual Pentecost which is the Church.

What is this miracle? For Mary, her original nature was neither tainted by sin nor deformed by its consequences; she remained totally docile to the Spirit who gave her life in his original breath. Mary's humanity is the expression, "the image and the likeness" (Gn 1:26) as perfect as possible of the divine reality. During her whole life, Mary was obedient to the Holy Spirit in her mind, in her heart and in her very body. Her being was inhabited in such a way that nothing escaped his action. Moreover, a harmony reigned in her heart, her body and her mind, created by the Holy Spirit, which made her perfectly whole. She did not experience this breach of our nature which prevents us from doing the good we wish and avoiding the evil we do not want (Rm 7:19) and obliges us to reweave laboriously the bonds between the mind and the body in the harmony of the Holy Spirit. If she had not been possessed by the Spirit to that extent, she would not have been able to give a body, a heart and a mind to the Word of God.

We must understand what this means. The Son of God did not only become man "in her" but he did so "through her". She participated in the Incarnation with all the functions of her body, all the capacities of her heart and all the faculties of her spirit. This places Mary's humanity in an absolutely particular situation. Moreover, in the glorious Passion of her Son, she went through an extraordinary metamorphosis. At the foot of the Cross and all along the Passion, she was espoused by the death and the glorification of Jesus. In one word, she was "stigmatized" by the suffering and the meekness of God, and she knew martyrdom in her heart and in her soul.

After the victory of Easter, she is totally inhabited by the Glory of the Risen One and she is freed from the grip of hell which makes for all the horror of death. But the nature of this glory is not the killing fire of Sinai (Dt 5) but the merciful Love, that of the wound of the heart of God no less awesome because it is heartrending for those not worthy of it. The miracle for Mary is to live totally invested by this glory of Mercy without dying. We realize that the Assumption was the end of the miracle which held Mary back on earth for she then enters into the true glory, that of the cloud and the pillar of fire. This is the reason why the Assumption is not a favor or reward granted by God to the Mother of his Son; the Assumption is integrated into the very logic of the mystery of Mary.

Let us recall the words of Thérèse of Lisieux when she felt the merciful Love penetrate her at the time she was following the Stations of the Cross: "If that had lasted one second more, I would have died." These words link up with a confidence made by the Curé of Ars: "If we knew what the Mass is, we would die!" Thus the death of Mary (or her departure, it matters little) was of pure glory as should have been that of our first parents if they had not sinned. She died of love, as Thérèse of the Child Jesus is said to have done. Mary did not know the terrible agony which, for Thérèse, was the fulfilment of the Passion in her body. Mary knew only the explosion of glory which, in the case of Thérèse before her death, lasted the time needed to say one Credo. This explosion sometimes sustains the martyrs, whether it be the open heavens contemplated by Stephen at the moment he was to be stoned or the exultation of Saint Andrew before his Cross.

But in Mary, this explosion was preceded by a desire, unthinkable for us, which was her true martyrdom: a martyrdom of pure light, without darkness, of pure love, without sin. It was a martyrdom in the presence of the sufferings of sinners for, the more a being is in the light of love, the more he suffers from the darkness in the heart of his brothers. This is the reason why, when she appears on earth, the Blessed Virgin requests that we pray for the conversion of sinners. Mary experienced the martyrdom of the created being in the distress of not being absorbed by God, dead of not dying, as would say Teresa of Avila, and for whom the Assumption was the blessed fulfilment.

Mary could not live outside the Glory of God for she was inhabited by the Holy Spirit. What separates us from the Spirit is not our body but our sin. In the first plan of God, man animated by the Spirit was to remain always under his power, so that at the time of death the Spirit would regain total control of his being. As we contemplate Mary in glory, we see how the Spirit, who permeated her total being, now makes her live totally and uniquely in divine life, in eternal glory. When we recite the fourth glorious mystery of the Rosary, we contemplate Mary in the glory of her Son, and we understand to what a wealth of glory we also are called If we are willing to have recourse persistently to the power of her intercession. Let her recite again Paul's prayer for us:

"May the God of our Lord Jesus Christ, the Father of glory, give you a spirit of wisdom and a perception of what is revealed, to bring you to full knowledge of him. May he open our heart to his light so that you can know what hope his call holds for you, what rich glories he has promised the saints will inherit and how infinitely great is the power that he has exercised for us believers. He put his strength, his almighty power at work in Christ, when he raised him from the dead and made him sit at his right hand in heaven" (Ep 1:17-20).

2. The incurable wound of love

The last glorious mystery invites us to contemplate Mary in the glory of heaven, absorbed by the vision of the glory of God, and totally transformed by the merciful Love of the Father, who transmits to her at the same time his "passion of love" for the sinners that we are. Like her Son, and as Mother, she is the great initiated to the merciful Love, that is, to the wound of the heart of the Father for us. This is to say that she is eminently active in her entreaty, and always interceding with her Son on our behalf. But her love is of a type altogether different from ours; it invades the totality of her being to such an extent that it brings her to a standstill in pure love. Those who contemplate her and pray her become wounded by the same merciful love.

As a matter of fact, the Mother of Jesus and ours did not shine through brilliant works which would manifest this power of love in her heart as did certain women of our history who have astonished men by their courage or have seduced them by their exceptional beauty. All the beauty of the Blessed Virgin is within. If she is fascinating, it is for having been loved by God more than any other creature. There is one reason alone for this predilection: God had created and chosen her to be the mother of his Son. "God so loved the world that he gave it his only Son" (Jn 3:16). How was he to love the one who was going to conceive his Son? We enter there the great mystery of the very being of God, of whom we perceive only a faint idea and whom John described in three words: "God is Love" (1 Jn 4:8 and 16).

Faith tells us that God wants to have us because he loves us. He loves us, not because we are lovable, but because he is Love and cannot do anything else but love. God is pure Love and his Son is pure Mercy. If we understand this word "to love" in a natural way, as a human thing, it is not sufficient to make us understand the mystery of the Blessed Trinity and the mystery of the Cross. An infinite love must be there, an excessive love, the "too great love of God for us". And if God is able to "suffer", this is not through lack of love, but by an excess of love. Everyone knows by experience that the more we love, the more we suffer. The more love penetrates into the heart of man, the more man suffers because love is cramped in his heart. I would say that the intensity of his suffering is in proportion to the intensity of his love. And this love bears a name in God, it is Mercy: the mystery hidden since centuries (Ep 3:9) and of which Paul received a remarkable intelligence (Ep 3:4).

To understand this merciful love, we must already have received it a little, have received a little drop of this madness which led Jesus to the Cross. Mary surrendered herself totally to this foolish and infinite love of God with all her being as a woman. At the Annunciation, she received a few glimpses of this infinite Love and, by her "Fiat", she allowed it to penetrate within herself. As long as we do not "see" God, we cannot understand this merciful love. Pope John Paul II has said the following on the authentic knowledge of the God of mercy: "Those who manage to know God in this way, those who 'see him' in this way are not able to live in any other way but by converting themselves to him continually".[2] We must, therefore, "see" him to understand him. The only way out is to have with God a certain connaturality, a certain affinity. This is the reason why our "passions", if they play ugly tricks on us, could also play "good ones" if we were willing to use them to understand somewhat the foolish love of God for us. It is not enough to love God only with the "fine edge of our soul", but we must also love him with our heart and our body in order to be totally involved in our relationship with God.

It is in this way that Mary has surrendered herself to love. She lived it, as all women live love, with a totality, a depth and an intensity which find no equal. All her being was involved in the Incarnation, her body, her affectivity, and her mind. This is the reason why her body entered into the glory of the Father without waiting for the end of time and for the second coming of Christ. For her, Christ had already come in totality: he entered first in his glory and he was to make his mother enter also without waiting for the end of time.

Mary thus found again the source of all life, of all light and love. She returned to this divine place from which she had come before all time: the "bosom of the Father". She is at the heart of the Trinity as the one who has been totally invested by the love which binds the Three. We must contemplate the Mother of the Savior in this incandescent fire of the triune love. She is, with and through the Savior, at the core of the relationship of the three divine Persons with mankind and all creation. Thus to glorify Mary is not to accumulate praises, it is to recognize the Glory she has since all time at the heart of the Trinity.

When Saint Grignion of Montfort reminds us of the

---

2. Translated from *Dieu riche en miséricorde*, ch. 7, Cerf, 1983, p. 67.

true reign of Mary, he invites Christians to make a total dedication which he calls a consecration of love. We must likewise understand the consecration of the world and of each of us to the Immaculate Heart of Mary. We are thus consecrated and sanctified by the fire of the merciful love which Jesus has come to cast on earth, since he was himself baptized in this fire by dying on the Cross. Above all, there is a totalitarianism of love without which we would in vain give Mary the title of Queen.

This is the reason why Jesus invites us to pray through her. Indeed, he wants to win our hearts and bodies in what is most intimate to them, our freedom in what is most inalienable to it. In us, all the barriers and all the oppositions must be lifted in order that the fire of love may reach our most remote cell. If we do not let ourselves be won over by the countenance of Mary, we will perhaps agree to the Reign of Jesus, but not to the folly, the folly of the Cross. When we proclaim Mary as Queen, we use the somewhat silly language of lovers: the Father is seeking worshippers, that is, people who are mad with love; the tepid are not agreeable to him and as long as they are tepid, "he vomits them from his mouth".

Saint Grignion of Montfort says again that the apostles of the end of time will be great saints: "The Most High and his holy Mother must train great saints who will surpass as much in holiness most of the other saints as the cedars of Lebanon outgrow the small bushes".[3] When he wonders who these great saints will be, he sees them as Elijah, men of fire whose training and education will be reserved to the Blessed Virgin: "But who will be these servants, slaves and children of God? They shall be a burning fire, ministers of the Lord who will kindle the fire of divine love everywhere..., sharp arrows in the

3. Translated from the *Traité de la vraie dévotion*, n. 47, *Œuvres complètes*, p. 512.

310

hands of the powerful Mary to pierce her enemies".[4]

"They will be purified by the fire of great tribulations and be very close to God; they will bear the fire of love in their heart, the incense of prayer in their spirit and the myrrh of mortification in their body, and they will bear everywhere the sweet fragrance of Jesus Christ for the poor and the lowly... They will be true apostles of the end of time to whom the Lord of virtues will give the word and the power to perform wonders".[5]

Why has Mary received the mission of training these apostles with a heart of fire? Because she was the first to receive at the foot of the Cross the wound of the merciful love, when the eyes of Jesus met hers and melted her heart in the same triune love. Thus when Mary looks in our eyes, she sees in us the wound of sin, but also the countenance of her Son and his wound of love which heals our own wounds by opening them to the Infinite love.

God gave Mary the task of inflicting upon us the folly of Love like a blessed wound — the very wound which made Jesus climb on the Cross, as the poem of the little shepherd boy by Saint John of the Cross sings so well:

"Then much later, slowly he climbed
On a tree where he stretched his beautiful arms
And he died, by them forever bound,
The heart of love all broken."

Away from Mary, we can be all we would want to: passionate, militant, ready to give up our life "so that he may reign" and even yield up our body to fire, but we shall not be wounded by this incurable wound of which she has the secret, a delicious infirmity more desirable than all power and all stability.

---

4. Translated from *ibid.*, n. 56, pp. 520-521.
5. Translated from *ibid.*, n. 56 and 58, p. 521.

Saint Grignion of Montfort yet adds that the saints "will implore the countenance of Mary from age to age and more particularly at the end of the world, that is to say, that the greatest saints, the souls richest in grace and virtue will be the most assiduous in praying the Most Blessed Virgin and in having her always present as their perfect model and their powerful help."[6]

If the world is to be saved today and escape the catastrophes which hang over our heads, the least of which is not the nuclear threat, there remains only one solution: to give ourselves up to the Love of God. God often uses mysterious ways to teach men to throw themselves in his love. He makes them go through trial, misery and distress, hoping that a cry will spring from their heart and bring them to his love.

If we were humble enough, lowly and poor like Mary, we would not need these ordeals to know humility which alone can submerge us in love. This love is the supreme beatitude; it is the invisible unction which transfigures the Cross and whose meekness becomes a torment more burning, ruthless and lethal than all humiliations and all calamities.

The only way to escape these calamities and those humiliations that threaten all of mankind and each of us in our journey towards God is incessant prayer. Why is it that we should know so many painful failures, experience our poverty as much and fall sometimes so low, if not because our Father wants to chastise us and train us in humility and supplication? I am convinced that if we prayed more, God would spare us these burning humiliations. This is what the Blessed Virgin tells us each time she visits us on earth: "Pray, pray, convert yourselves, otherwise great calamities will fall upon you." Her purpose is not to frighten us... She does not preach us catastrophism, but the true security of surrender to God.

6. Translated from *Traité de la vraie dévotion*, n. 46, *Œuvres complètes*, p. 512.

If we want to escape the sufferings and illnesses, whether they be personal or collective, which the Blessed Virgin wishes to spare us, there is but one solution: to emerge from our distress and our fear and immerse ourselves in this "sickness which does not lead to death" and which is love. In our heart, love then ushers us into a battle as unrelenting and as total as death. When we thus throw ourselves in love, we, so to speak, get a headstart on the upheavals and the recasting which, whether we like it or not, death will impose upon us.

"There is therefore one obstacle alone to the fulfilment in our soul of this marvellous battle between life and death which is called the mystery of Easter: it is our obstination in ignoring the simplicity of the opposition between light and darkness... the silent hardening which camouflages itself in the semidarkness of ambiguities to the point of becoming inaccessible to all therapy and finally to the Savior himself.

"The Blessed Virgin is horrified by our tepidity and our half-tones passionately entertained. The Church sees her 'more terrible than an army set for battle' on this point. It would be pointless to turn ourselves towards her in order that she may exempt us from battle or that she respect our compromises. If we are afraid of calamities, let us throw ourselves in Love. If we are afraid of Love, let us throw ourselves to the Blessed Virgin. Her patience is that of a mother; she is willing to weep over our cowardices, she will never bless them".[7]

3. More... and always more prayer

Here we are at the end of this book. Many as they read these pages devoted to the prayer of Mary, will remain

---

7. Translated from Father Molinié, *Lettre polycopiée*, n. 26, Easter 1984.

perplexed and hesitant: are not these lucubrations, perhaps elevated but personal and subjective, even a bit ethereal? Some will say: "Why speak of the prayer of Mary, of whom we know so little? Why speak of the one who said so little? Is it not better to remain quiet about her and let the Spirit murmur in the silence of our heart the prayer he has stirred himself in the heart of Mary?" I have often asked myself the same questions while writing these pages and, more often yet, I had the temptation to stop and destroy what I had written.

For years I have meditated on writing this book on the prayer of Mary, especially after having reflected and written on the mystery of prayer. As I looked at my own experience and as I journeyed with others on the way of prayer, I gradually understood that prayer concealed a true mystery. Whatever we might say about it today, prayer is not natural to man. I shall not say that it is difficult for when it is given to us, it is not difficult at all, it is even very easy! But when it is not given to us, I dare say that it is not difficult, but impossible! It is within our reach to desire prayer, but it is not within our reach to make it a reality.

Why is it so arduous for man to establish a contact with God and, we must acknowledge this as well, to love his brothers? It is worth reflecting on this question which is the most important in life. As a matter of fact, it should be as natural to man to pray as it is to breathe since prayer comes from God and returns to God. There must have been a tragedy at the beginning, a break making man lose his original nature which made him live familiarly with God.

It is while I was meditating on this impossibility for man to pray always that my eyes turned toward the Virgin Mary. All of a sudden there came up in my mind these simple words: "Mary prayed as she breathed for she never left the hands of the God who had fashioned her!" I understood then that she was the "great pray-er" in the Church, the mother of continual prayer, and that we had to contemplate her in order to find the way of the prayer of the heart, the source of continual prayer.

As soon as I received this intuition, the book began to take shape in my mind. To begin with, I wrote the first chapters on the prayer of the heart of Mary and on her prayer at the Annunciation. At the same time, I was working on the last chapter on her prayer for sinners. And I was grasping that there is a mysterious link between Mary coming forth all pure from the hands of God — and who has never left them — and us, sinners, who must convert ourselves every day to find familiarity and friendship with God. Her prayer is indispensable to find the way of continual prayer.

But the final light on this relationship between Mary, the All-Pure, and the sinners that we are was given to me during the Holy week of 1984. I was contemplating Mary at the foot of the Cross when I understood that Mary was prolonging the cry of Jesus on the Cross until the end of time for all the men who are losing their soul. When the cry of Jesus resounded in the heart of Mary, the Son introduced his Mother to the great wound of Mercy in the heart of the Father, this wound which impelled the Son to become flesh and to climb on the Cross. This is what John Paul II expresses admirably in these words: "No one has experienced as much as the mother of the Crucified the mystery of the Cross, the convulsive encounter of the transcendent divine Justice with love: this 'embrace' given by mercy to justice".[8] In this sense Mary is the mother of mercy who does not cease interceding with her Son for us. She is the mother of continual prayer not only because she has never come out from her original nature, but especially because she is the mother of sinners who must experience mercy in order to find the way of continual prayer.

After this understanding of Mary's prayer at the foot

8. Translated from *Dieu riche en miséricorde*, par. 9, Cerf, 1980, p. 49.

of the Cross, I continued to follow her in her prayer in the Upper Room. There, I shared very much with a brother who has been enlightened on this mystery of the Prayer of Mary in the early Church and in the Church of today. We understood better together that Mary did not forget her children on earth and that she was continuing to intercede for them as her Son does with the Father (Heb 7:25). As Jesus pursues today in glory the prayer he inaugurated "in the days of his life on earth, having offered up prayers and entreaty, in loud cries and in silent tears, to the One who could save him from death, and having submitted so humbly that his prayer was heard" (Heb 5:7-8), so does Mary continue in glory the prayer on Calvary and in the Upper Room. Moreover, this prayer today knows an efficacy and a power without proportion compared to her prayer on earth because of the paschal victory of her Son. Mary's prayer in the Upper Room is pursued today wherever some men and women devote their time or even their whole life to supplication for the Church.

I dedicate this book to this brother who, on many occasions, shared the manner in which he sensed the mystery of the prayer of Mary. It is he who incited me to have it published in spite of my reluctance to do so. Obviously, all we are saying here about the prayer of Mary does not claim to describe its objective reality for this escapes us totally. And this is precisely the suffering experienced by the one who is writing on the subject of the Blessed Virgin.

As he prays, he senses he has a few glimpses of the splendors of the dialogue of Mary with Jesus and with the Father and he is dazzled by the depth and, at the same time, the simplicity of this prayer. But when he comes back to the daily reality and to the task of writing something about this mystery, he is very aware that he is crawling and stuttering as he tells these disconcerting commonplaces. He would so wish that his words were burning embers of an experience but they are very often cooled and burnt-out ashes, if not dust carried off by the wind.

And yet, faith and prayer must express themselves. They must not be muted or they cease to be a living reality. The only solution to this difficulty is to be aware that we are not able to say everything about Christ and the Blessed Virgin, but that we are able to say something nevertheless, on the condition that we use an open language and have the clear intention of opening out on this mystery. In other words, we must be convinced that there is a "beyond the Word". This is the reason why the Fathers and the mystics are fascinating. In prayer, they see "things" about God, Christ and the Blessed Virgin, and when they come back to their brothers, they try to express what they have seen by means of poems, hymns and sometimes by simple cries as did Saint Francis of Assisi.

They are well aware of failings in their words; this is the reason why they say "things", extraordinary and interesting, about God, of which they are not aware. They are eager to add: "Especially, do not give too much attention to what I am saying; this is of no importance compared to what I saw!" After having lit in us the fire of the desire of the thirst for living water, they lead us by the hand to the threshold of the mystery while inviting us to pray.

Without claiming to accomplish this, I would like to invite you to follow the same approach to the mystery of Mary. Ultimately, it matters little what is written in this book. It is preferable nevertheless that it be not too poorly done, but what is essential is to give to all those who will read it the desire, the taste and the thirst for prayer. The end result is out of my reach. I entrust it to the Holy Spirit and to the Blessed Virgin, while I pray for those who will read it as I have done for them while writing these pages.

I often say that the test of a true contact with a man of God, whether he be priest, lay, monk or Carmelite, is that these men and these women give me a desire to pray after having met them. If, after having read a few pages of this book, you do not feel like putting it aside, forgetting all about the author and his writings, in order to fulfill an intense desire to pray the Blessed Virgin, I fear very much that this book might not have achieved its goal because it will not have been conceived sufficiently in prayer. After having read these pages, each one should be able to say what the Samaritans were saying to the woman who had just spoken to them about the Messiah: "We believe now not because of what you have told us, but because we have heard him ourselves and we know that he is really the Savior of the world" (Jn 4:41).

All that is said here is but a starting point, an ignition of the rocket which must propel us into prayer. There are many ways of praying Jesus and his mother. We can gaze at the Savior as Mary gazed at him. She is saved as we are and more than we are. But we can also look at the Blessed Virgin as Jesus looked at her: "Behold your mother". No one knows Mary better than her Son Jesus and no one knows Jesus better than his mother.

As soon as contact is made, we must keep watch at the door of the Blessed Virgin and "rub our feet on the doormat" until the moment she chooses to open the door for us and speak to us about herself. It is then that another prayer will take its place in our heart: her prayer within ourselves. As long as we look at the Blessed Virgin or pray by speaking to her, we are still the ones who take the initiative in this prayer; it is our own work, but out of proportion with what Mary can do when she takes over our prayer and when her own prayer flows in us without stopping.

We must pray until the encounter takes place, when the Blessed Virgin manifests herself to us. This is the only "miracle" to ask; the purpose of the miracles in the gospel is always to bring about an encounter with Christ. Christ and Mary are inseparable, but we may be more or less attracted to one or to the other: as we gaze upon Mary, we may sense better the "maternal" spirit of Christ. It matters little whether this prayer includes a formula or not; the essential thing is to see Mary, to be able to speak to her or better yet to listen to her. Blessed Brother Mutien-Marie de Malonne had received this grace to perceive at all times the tangible presence of the Blessed Virgin. He admitted: "I asked her to accompany me everywhere... and she gave me this grace. I speak to her with surrender and an absolute trust".[9] The day when she shows herself to us, we will know everything! In conclusion, I leave you the prayer of the *Memorare*. I learned everything on Mary by saying it; but in order that this may succeed, we must recite it as often as possible. As soon as we have a spare moment, we must persistently throw ourselves in this prayer:

"Remember,
O most gracious Virgin Mary,
that never was it known
that anyone who fled to your protection,
implored your help,
or sought your intercession,
was left unaided.
Inspired with this confidence
I fly to you,
O Virgin of virgins, my Mother
to you I come,
before you I stand,
sinful and sorrowful.
O Mother of the Word Incarnate,
despise not my petitions,
but in your mercy hear and answer them."

Jean Lafrance

Pentecost 1984

---

9. Translated from *Le Frère Mutien-Marie de l'Institut des Frères des Écoles chrétiennes, 1841-1917,* General Procuracy, Paris, 1928, p. 85.

TABLE OF CONTENTS

Imprimerie des Éditions Paulines
250, boul. St-François Nord
Sherbrooke, QC, J1E 2B9

Imprimé au Canada — Printed in Canada